Modern Indian Education

Modern Indian Education

History, Development and Problems

J.C. AGGARWAL

SHIPRA
SHIPRA

(2021PoD, 2018, 2008, 2006 4th Rev Ed., 2004, 2003, 2001)

Rs. 1450; US$ 49.75

ISBN: 978-93-88691-01-7

2025
4th Rev. Ed. Reprint, PoD

Modern Indian Education:

History, Development and Problems

Published by:
SHIPRA PUBLICATIONS
LG 18-19, Pankaj Central Market,
I.P. Ext., Patparganj, Delhi 110092, India
11 47322068; 96500 28065, 9810522367
info@shiprapublication.com
www.shiprapublication.com

Modern Indian Education

History, Development and Problems

J.C. AGGARWAL

SHIPRA

(2021PoD, 2018, 2008, 2006 4th Rev Ed., 2004, 2003, 2001)

Rs. 1450; US$ 49.75

ISBN: 978-93-88691-01-7

2025
4th Rev. Ed. Reprint, PoD

Modern Indian Education:

History, Development and Problems

Published by:
SHIPRA PUBLICATIONS
LG 18-19, Pankaj Central Market,
I.P. Ext., Patparganj, Delhi 110092, India
11 47322068; 96500 28065, 9810522367
info@shiprapublication.com
www.shiprapublication.com

Contents

1

An Overview of Development of Education in India (1800-1947)

(Committees and Commissions and other Documents on Education)

1.1 BRITISH EDUCATION POLICY: POSITIVE AND NEGATIVE EFFECTS ON INDIA: AN OVERVIEW

A. H. Howell in *'Education in British India'* (1872) has described the British policy in these words, "Education in India under the British Government was first ignored, then violently and successfully opposed, and conducted on a system now universally admitted to be erroneous and finally placed in its present setting."

Gandhiji in *'Basic Education'* has observed, "The foundation that Macaulay laid of education has enslaved us."

Prof. Aparna Basu of Delhi University in her publication *'Essays on the History of Indian Education'* (1981) has summed up the positive and negative effects of English education as under:

The introduction of English education was one of a series of acts which collectively opened the doors of the West to the East. In every sphere of modern life, though the influence of tradition persists, the influence of the West can be traced. Much of the organization of the democratic state, its secular character, the nature of its institutions and the political principles underlying them are all largely European in inspiration. Similarly, the social reforms in Hindu society, the movements for the emancipation of women and for the removal of untouchability reflect western influence to a considerable extent.

Negative effects are fairly obvious. The educational system by building up an educated elite and neglecting popular education helped to preserve and strengthen the barrier between the upper classes and the masses. The use of English raised the class barrier even higher. The low rate of literacy, the method of teaching, neglect of training of teachers, contempt for manual work, emphasis on a literary education and neglect of technical education which was inevitable in a colonial context and the creation of a gulf between an elite educated in English and the masses—all these constituted formidable obstacles in the path of development.

1.2 PHASES OF DEVELOPMENT OF EDUCATION IN INDIA DURING THE BRITISH RULE (1800-1947): POLICY DOCUMENTS AND COMMITTEES AND COMMISSIONS

The period was marked by policy decisions. Several Committees and Commissions on education were also appointed to make recommendations on the improvement of Education in India.

Following were the phases of the development of education in India during the British rule.

First Phase—Beginning of State Policy (1813): The Charter Act of 1813: for the first time during the East India Company made an annual provision for a sum of not less than one lakh of rupees for the promotion of learning. Clause 43 of the Act reads, "It shall be lawful for the Governor-General-in- Council to direct that out of any surplus which may remain of the rents, revenues, and profits arising from the said territorial acquisitions, after defraying the expense of the military, civil, and commercial establishment and paying the interest of the debt in manner hereinafter provided, a sum of not less than one lakh of rupees in each year shall be set apart and applied to the revival and improvement of literature and the encouragement of the learned natives of India and for the introduction and promotion of a knowledge of the sciences among the inhabitants of the British territories in India." It was admitted by the British Parliament for the first time that 'education in India had a claim on public revenues'.

Second Phase—Oriental-Occidental Controversy (1823-1835): The parties to the controversies were the 'Orientalists' or 'Classicists' and 'Occidentalists' or 'Anglicists'. The former were in favour of educating the upper classes of the Indian people through the medium of their classical languages and the latter through the medium of English.

Third Phase—Macaulay's Minute: The famous minute of Lord Macaulay, the first Law Member of the Governor-General's Executive Council, submitted in 1835, opened a new chapter in the educational history of India. He advocated the education of the upper classes and through them the education of others—'Theory of Downward Filtration' and made a vigorous plea for spreading western learning through the medium of English. Lord Macaulay thought that it was possible through English Education "to bring about a class of persons Indian in blood and colour but English in tastes, in opinions, in morals and in intellect." (For details *see* 1.3 and 1.4)

Fourth Phase—Bentinck's Proclamation: This was Resolution (order) dated March 7, 1835 of Lord William Bentinck consequent to the acceptance of Macaulay's Minute. It reads: " His Lordship in Council is of the opinion that the greater object of the British Government ought to be the promotion of European literature and sciences among the natives of India, and that all the funds appropriated for the purpose of education would be best employed on English education alone."

This was the first declaration of the British Government in the field of education in India. It eventually determined the aim, content and the medium of instruction in India. Promotion of western sciences and art was acknowledged as the avowed object.

Schools teaching European literature and science became popular because of the great interest shown in English education by some of the educated Indians and more particularly by leaders like Raja Ram Mohan Roy and others.

Fifth Phase—Auckland's Minute (1839): In this minute Lord Auckland, the Governor-General, after studying the causes of the dispute between the 'Orientalists' and the 'Occidentalists' tried to satisfy both the parties and outlined the future policy of the Government : (i) Existing Oriental colleges may continue and receive the same grant as they were receiving previous to Bentinck's Minute; (ii) Existing Oriental colleges may start English classes if they so desired; (iii) One-fourth of the students of these colleges may receive scholarships; (iv) Books of instruction in Oriental languages may be published out of funds sanctioned for Oriental education.

Sixth Phase—Wood's Despatch (1854): The despatch was issued in 1854 by Sir Charles Wood (afterwards Lord Halifax), the President of the Board of Control in India, in which he declared 'the education that we desire to see extended in India is that which has for its object the diffusion of the improved arts, sciences, philosophy and literature of Europe, in short of European knowledge'. The Despatch suggested the creation of the Department of Public Instruction in each province under the charge of an officer designated as the Director of Public Instruction. The Despatch recommended the institution of universities in the Presidency towns (Calcutta, Madras and Bombay). In the words of Lord Dalhousie, Despatch contained "a scheme of education for all India, far wider and more comprehensive than the Local or the Supreme Government could have ever ventured to suggest". (For details see 3.2)

Seventh Phase—Indian Education Commission (1882) or the Hunter Commission: The Commission was appointed in 1882 by Lord Ripon under the Chairmanship of William Hunter to enquire particularly into the manner in which effect had been given to the principles of the Despatch of 1854 and to suggest measures for carrying out the policy as laid down therein. The Commission reiterated the principles which had already been accepted years ago in Wood's Despatch. Among the major recommendations of the Commission were: 1. Strenuous efforts to be made in the sphere of elementary education; 2. Control of primary education to be made over to District and Municipal Boards; 3. Indigenous schools to be encouraged; 4. Local funds to be utilised mainly for primary education; 5. At least one model high school to be established in some districts where people may not be able to establish schools for themselves with grant-in-aid; 6. Missionary enterprise to occupy only a secondary place in Indian education.

The Commission failed to see the financial implications of its recommendations. However, the historical value of this document is incalculable. It is also know as Hunter Commission.

During the period 1882-1902, there was a considerable expansion in the field of secondary education.

Eight Phase—The University Commission of 1902: The Commission was appointed by Lord Curzon in 1902 'to inquire into the conditions and prospects of the universities established in India, to consider and report upon any proposals which have been or may be made for improving their constitution and working; and to recommend to the Governor-General-in-Council such measures as may tend to elevate standard of universities teaching, and to promote the advancement of learning'. Among the important recommendations of the Commission were: (i) New universities should not be established; (ii) Existing universities should be reorganised as teaching bodies; (iii) The Senate and Syndicate should be recognised; (iv) The territorial jurisdiction of each university should be precisely defined; (v) Rules of affiliation should be strict and affiliated colleges should be strictly supervised; (vi) There should be a managing committee for every college; (vii) Hostel should be built for students.

Ninth Phase—Resolution of the Government on Education (1904): The educational policy was declared in the form of a government resolution on 11th March 1904 by Lord Curzon. Regarding recognition of secondary schools it stated, "Whether these schools are managed by public authority or by private persons, and whether they received aid from public funds or not, the Government is bound in the interests of the community to see that the education provided in them is sound. It must, for example, satisfy itself in each case that a secondary school is usually wanted, that its financial stability is assured, that its managing body where there is one, is properly constituted, that it teaches the proper subjects up to a proper standard, that due provision has been made for the instruction, health, recreation, and discipline of the pupils, that the teachers are suitable as regards character, number and qualifications, and that the fees to be paid will not involve such competition with any existing schools as will be unfair and injurious to the interests of education. Such are the conditions upon which alone schools should be eligible to receive grant-in-aid or to send up pupils to compete for, or receive pupils in enjoyment of Government scholarships, and schools complying with them will be ranked as recognised schools. These conditions were soon incorporated in the provincial code of grant-in-aid.

Tenth Phase—Gokhale's Resolution in the Imperial Legislative Council on Primary Education (1911): The Bill was introduced in the Imperial Legislative Council on 16th March 1911 by Gopal Krishna Gokhale, a member of the Council, 'to provide for the gradual introduction of the principle of compulsion into the elementary education of the country'. On March 17, 1912, the Bill was rejected by 38 votes to 13. In 1991 Gokhale had moved a Resolution in the Council 'that a beginning should be made in the direction of making elementary education free and compulsory throughout the country, and that a mixed commission of officials and non-officials be appointed at an early date to frame definite proposals.' Gokhale, however, withdrew the Resolution on receiving an assurance from the Government that the question would be considered. But seeing the indifference of the Government, Gokhale had to introduce this Bill.

Eleventh Phase—Resolution of the Government of India on Education (1913): The Resolution advocated three cardinal principles of educational policy—(1) Instead of increasing the number of existing institutions their standard should be raised; (2) The curricula of primary and secondary schools should be made more practical and useful; (3) Facilities of higher studies and research should be provided in India so that Indian students may not have to go abroad.

Twelfth Phase—Calcutta University Commission (1917-1919): The Commission was appointed by the Government of India in 1917 under the Chairmanship of Dr. Michael Sadler, the Vice-Chancellor of the University of Leeds, 'to enquire into the conditions and prospects of the University of Calcutta and to consider the question of a constructive policy in relation to the question it represents'. Among the Indian Members of the Commission were Sir Asutosh Mukerji and Dr. Zia-Uddin Ahmed. The major recommendations were (i) Introduction of three-year degree course, (ii) Establishment of a Board of Secondary and Intermediate Examination in each province, (iii) Less rigid control over universities, (iv) Appointment of staff by special Selection Committees, (v) Safeguard of interest of Muslim students.

The Report of the Commission became a constant source of suggestion and information. It greatly influenced the subsequent course of secondary and higher education in the country.

Thirteenth Phase—National Movement in Education (1905-1921): The movement demanded national education which became more pressing with the growth of the national movement during the early part of the 20th century. Indian leaders began to condemn the official system in vogue and demanded Indianization of education. In Bengal a Society for the Promotion of National Education was formed under the Chairmanship of Guru Das Banerji. Rabindranath Tagore, Rashbehari Ghosh and Aurobindo Ghosh also took up the cause of national education. Swami Shradhanand established a Gurukul at Haridwar. The main emphasis of the educational movement was on (1) Indian control of education; (2) Indian ideals of education; (3) Reverence for the motherland; (4) Growth of Indian languages; and (5) Development of technical and national education.

Fourteenth Phase—Education under Dyarchy (1921-1937): Education was treated as a transferred subject under a dyarchical system of government in the provinces of India, introduced in 1921 as a result of the Government of India Act, 1919 passed by the British Parliament. Subjects of administration were divided into two categories *i.e.*, Reserved and Transferred Subjects. The reserved subjects were put under the Governor and his executive council and the transferred subjects under the ministers who were responsible to the Provincial Legislature. Education was made transferred subject and the development of education was the responsibility of the Minister for Education. Finance was a reserved subject with the result that the Education Minister had to face many difficulties. Moreover, the Education Minister had no control over the I.C.S. officers whose services were controlled by the Secretary of the State for India.

Hartog Committee (1928): The Committee was appointed by the Simon Commission in 1928 under the Chairmanship of Sir Philip Hartog to review the position of education in India. It regretted the slow progress of literacy and a high percentage of failure at the Matriculation Examination which dominated the secondary education. It recommended that there should be more diversified curricula in the schools.

Fifteenth Phase—Education under Provincial Autonomy and Congress Ministries (1937-39): The Government of India Act 1935, divided all educational activities into two categories Federal: (or Central) and State (or Provincial). (A) Federal Subjects included (i) the Imperial Library, Calcutta; the Indian museum, Calcutta; the Imperial War Museum, the Victoria Memorial, Calcutta; and any similar institution controlled or financed by the Federation; (ii) The Banaras Hindu University and the Aligarh Muslim University; (iii) Preservation of ancient and historical monuments; (iv) Education in the defence forces; (v) Archaeology; and (vi) Education in Centrally Administered Areas. (B) State subjects included all matters regarding education other than those which had been included in the Federal List and were regarded as State or Provincial Subjects.

The Congress Ministries formed in 1937 undertook several steps for the promotion of Basic System of Education propounded by Gandhiji.

Sixteenth Phase (1939-1947): With the resignation of Congress Ministries in 1939 on the eve of the First World War, the new system of education received a set back.

The British rulers made two attempts after 1935 to introduce changes in the system of education. However on account of War, the reports and plans remained on paper. Since these are of some interest, they are given here in the summary form.

1. *Abbot Wood Report (1937)*: The Report was submitted in 1937 by the two expert advisers—A. Abbot, Ex-Chief Inspector of Technical Schools, Board of Education, England and S. H. Wood, Director of Intelligence, Board of Education, England—invited by the Government of India in 1936 on the recommendation of the Central Advisory Board of Education to advise 'whether any vocational or practical training should be imparted in primary, secondary and higher secondary schools, and if so, what should be its nature and extent'. The report consisted of two parts: (i) Report on Vocational Education written by Mr. A. Abbot, and (ii) Report on General Education written by Mr. S. H. Wood. The report stressed that vocational education was as important as general education. "Neither of them can claim to be more useful and necessary. If general education brings about the development of the non-material culture of a country, vocational education does the same thing for material culture. Hence both are necessary for the progress of country."

2. *Report on the Post-War Educational Development in India (1944)*: The report is popularly known as Sargent Report after Sir John Sargent, the then Educational Advisor to the Government of India. The Reconstruction Committee of the Governor-General's Executive Council asked the Central Advisory Board of Education to prepare a plan for the educational development to be taken up after the termination of war. The Board entrusted this work to Sir John Sargent. The memorandum which he submitted to the Board in 1944 is variously known as Scheme of Post-War Educational Development in India, Sargent Report, or Sargent Scheme. The plan aimed at reorganizing the system of education in India. The plan was to be carried out in 8 stages by means of eight five year plans. The plan provided for free, compulsory and universal basic education for all children between the ages of 6 and 14.

1.3 MACAULAY'S MINUTE: MACAULAY AS THE ARCHITECT OF THE BRITISH SYSTEM OF EDUCATION IN INDIA

Lord Macaulay (1800-1859) was an English essayist, historian and politician. He is known for his Minute on Education (1835) which was accepted by Lord William Bentinck, the Governor-General of India (1828-1835). He came to India as a Law Member of the Council of Governor-General on 10th June 1834. He was also appointed the Chairman of the Committee of Public Instructions of Bengal by Lord William Bentinck.

At that time, a major Oriental (classical) and Occidental controversy between the Orientalists (classists) and the Anglicists (Occidentalists) was going on in respect of the following issues:

1. *Aim of Education of the British Policy*: Whether it should be to educate the classes in higher branches of learning or the masses in elementary education.

2. *Type of Knowledge*: Whether to preserve and promote oriental learning (learning of the East) or to introduce Western knowledge, culture and science.

3. *Medium of Instruction*: Whether English or Persian and Sanskrit in Bengal, English or Indian languages in Bombay and Madras should become the medium of instruction. It may be recalled that at that time the Presidencies/Provinces of Bengal, Bombay and Madras contained numerous areas which now form new states like Orissa, Bihar, Bengal, Tamil Nadu etc.

4. *Agency of Education*: Whether the Government should assume direct responsibiiity of educating the Indians or the indigenous system of the country to continue.

5. *Missionaries*: Whether the shores of India to be thrown open to missionaries of all parts of the world to promote education or to a few missionaries or not at all.

There were important English Officers of the East India Company who were the supporters of the Oriental point of view. H. T. Princep, who was the Education Secretary in Bengal was the leader of the Orientalist Group. On the contrary some prominent Indians like Raja Rammohan Roy supported the Anglicists who were in favour of English and Western learning.

Macaulay's Views on Indian and European Literature: Macaulay in his Minute made the following observations.

(i) "A single shelf of a good European literature was worth the whole native literature of India and Arabia."

(ii) Regarding imparting instruction through the media of Arabic, Persian and Sanskrit, he wrote, "We are to teach false history, false astronomy, false medicine, because we find them in the company of false religion."

(iii) About the claim of English language, he stated, "It stands pre-eminent even among the languages of the West..... It is likely to become language of commerce throughout the seas of the East."

Main Aim of Introducing English System of Education in India: Macaulay wrote in his Minute, "We must at present do our best to form a class of persons, Indian in blood and colour, but English in taste, in opinions, in morals and in intellect."

Macaulay's Arguments in Favour of English: Macaulay rejected the claims of Arabic and Sanskrit as against English, because he considered that English was better than either of them. His arguments in favour of English were:

1. It is the key to modern knowledge and is, therefore, more useful than Arabic or Sanskrit.

2. It stands pre-eminent even among the language of the West. In India, English is the language sponsored by the ruling class. It is likely to become the language of commerce throughout the seas of the East.

3. It would bring about renaissance in India, just as Greek or Latin did in England or just as the languages of Western Europe in civilised Russia.

4. The natives are desirous of being taught English and are not eager to learn Sanskrit or Arabic, and that demand of the latter was maintained artificially through, "bounty money".

5. It is possible to make the natives of this country good English scholars, and to that end our efforts ought to be directed.

6. It was impossible to educate the body of people, but it was possible through English education to bring about "a class of persons, Indian in blood and colour, but English in tastes, in opinions, in morals and in intellect" and that education was to filter down from them to the masses.

Acceptance of Minute by Lord William Bentinck: Lord William Bentinck endorsed the Minute by writing one line beneath it, "I give my entire concurrence to the sentiments expressed in the Minute". He passed the Resolution of March, 1835 which determined the aim, content and medium of instruction in India.

Appraisal of Macaulay's Minute: Was He the Torch Bearer? Macaulay's intentions become very clear with his following statements:

In a letter to his father in 1836, Macaulay wrote, "Our English schools are increasing with leaps and bounds and now the condition has reached to a position that it has become difficult to accommodate the students. Hindus are much influenced with education. There is no Hindu who may keep real faith in his religion after studying English. I have full confidence that if our education policy succeeds, then no idolator will be left in Bengal. All this will be done naturally, without any religious preaching and interference."

On July 10, 1837, Macaulay expressed the following views before the House of Commons in England, "It may be that the public mind of India may expand under our system that having instructed in European languages, they may in some future age demand European institutions. Whether such a day will ever come I know not. Whenever it comes it will be the proudest day in English history."

That Macaulay was the torch bearer is an exaggerated claim. Lord Macaulay was not the first person who pleaded the cause of Western Education and inspired the Indian people with ideas. He was also not the founder of Orientalist or Anglicist group as such groups had already been working before his arrival in the country. He, of course, ended the controversy and gave a new direction to the system of education in India. To quote S. N. Mukerji, "Macaulay simply took the tide of popular opinion at its flood that had been running high through the spade work done by Raja Ram Mohan Roy." Again according to him, "Macaulay tried to grow a temperate plant on warm plains of equatorial region, where it was possible for it to survive under artificial circumstance but not to thrive."

Nurrullah and Naik do not call Lord Macaulay as the torch bearer in the path of progress though they admit Macaulay's contribution in this respect.

S. N. Mukerji has given a balanced appraisal of Macaulay's Minutes. "Macaulay's Minutes had all the defects of a preliminary spadework, but it is a very important document, because it influenced Britain's educational policy in this country for more than a century. It should be admitted that Western learning has done good to India, and better results have been achieved through Macaulay's bold policy than it would have been possible through half-hearted attempts of the Orientalists. The new knowledge led to India's unity and her great recovery brought her into contact with scientific research of the West and developed Indian languages to a standard in which a university education became possible. But his Minutes can neither be regarded as the Greater Charter of Indian Education nor it can be condemned as the evil genius of Macaulay.

It should be noted that the movement of Western education had started in the country long before Macaulay's arrival."

1.4 DOWNWARD FILTRATION THEORY OF EDUCATION

Meaning of Filtration Theory: The British rulers in India thought that in order to run the administration peacefully and smoothly it was essential to make the higher classes blind followers of the Britishers. This they wanted to achieve through educating the classes. This theory meant "Education is to be filtered to the common people. Drop by drop, the education would go to the common public so that at due time it may take the form of a vast stream which remained water desert of the society for starved a long time and high class of people would be educated and common people would gain influence from them."

"Education was to permeate from above. Drop by drop from the Himalayas of Indian life useful information was to trickle downwards forming in a time a broad and steady stream to irrigate the thirsty plains."

Reasons for the Adoption of Filtration Theory

1. The British rulers needed various types of employees to run the business and the Government. They wanted educated persons for this. So they started the policy of educating higher classes.
2. The Government did not have sufficient funds for educating the masses.
3. The educated people educated on British lines through English medium would get higher posts in Government services and then naturally they would use their influence in controlling the masses from going against the Government rule.
4. Higher classes educated through the medium of English would adopt English ways and in turn influence the lower classes.
5. After educating some people, the responsibility of educating the masses could be left to them.

Background of the Adoption of Filtration Theory: The Directors of the Company had written in their Despatch, dated 29 September 1830, to Madras Government: "The improvements in education, however, which most effectually contribute to elevate the moral and intellectual condition of a people are those, which concern the education of the higher classes of the persons possessing leisure and natural influence over minds of their countrymen. By raising the standard of education among these classes you would eventually produce a much greater and more beneficial change in the ideas and feelings of the community than you can hope to produce by acting directly on the more numerous class."

Lord Macaulay had ideas similar to those of the Directors of the Company. In his Minute of 1835, he has said, "At present we should create such group of people who may work as a mediator between us and the common people, a class of persons, Indians in blood and colour, but English in tastes, in opinions, in morals and in intellect. It will be their duty to develop the native languages and enable it to convey the knowledge to the common people." Again on 31st July, 1837, he said: "At present we don't aim at educating directly the common people. We aim at creating a class of persons, who among their countrymen distribute some of the knowledge we gave."

The Committee of Public Instruction in Bengal had also approved the same ideal and expressed its ideas in 1839, "Our efforts should be concentrated first on the education of higher and middle class of people". Sir Auckland had also accepted this view and declaring it as Government policy, he said, "The Government should educate the higher class of the people so that the 'Filtered culture' reach to the public." Since then this policy was followed up to 1870 and emphasis was laid on the education of the people of higher classes in the society.

Evaluation of the Filtration Theory: The immediate aim of getting educated people to run the various jobs in the administration was fully achieved. It also helped in creating a faithful class of people. It settled the educational policy of the British rulers and education began to progress rapidly.

The ultimate aim could not be fulfilled as the educated persons were cut off from the common masses. The common masses began to look upon the educated classes as the favoured children of the British Government. The higher and richer classes began to copy British food, taste, behaviour and manners. Their entire daily routine was westernised. They became more and more self-centred and a great cleavage was created between the rich and the poor.

1.5 MERITS AND DEMERITS OF THE EDUCATION SYSTEM DURING THE BRITISH RULE AS INITIATED BY LORD MACAULAY

Merits

1. The system promoted Western knowledge and science among the Indians, which broadened their outlook in life.
2. English education brought about a reawakening and a desire among the people of India to recapture their past glory.
3. Contact with Western thought helped to develop democratic and liberal ideas among the Indians.
4. English education rekindled in the people the spirit of nationalism. By and large, national movement was led by leaders who had received their education through the English medium and were well-versed with Western political thoughts.
5. A uniform system of education through English medium educational institutions brought the people of different provinces together and they waged the freedom struggle.

Demerits of the English Educational System

1. It was an urban system of education in a rural country.
2. English dominated the curriculum and other aspects of education.
3. System was too literary and bookish.
4. Education system was examination-oriented.
5. It stressed knowledge aspects only and ignored other aspects of education.
6. It emphasised rote-memory.
7. It neglected technical and vocational education.
8. It was a single-track system that emphasized humanities.
9. It was unplanned.
10. It was very expensive.

11. It created a gulf between the English educated upper and middle classes and the masses.

12. It neglected democratic values.

In the words of Gandhiji, "The present system of education does not meet the requirements of the country in any shape or form. English has created a permanent bar between the highly educated few and the uneducated many. The excessive importance given to English has cast upon the educated classes a burden which has maimed them mentally for life and made them strangers in their own land. Absence of vocational training has made the educated class almost unfit for productive work and harmed them physically. Money spent on primary education is a waste of expenditure."

1.6 EXPANSION OF EDUCATIONAL FACILITIES (1855-56 to 1946-47)

Table 1: Educational Institutions (1855-56 to 1946-47)

		1855-56	*1901-02*	*1921-22*	*1946-47*
1.	Universities	—	5	14	17
2.	Colleges of General Education	21	145	172	496
3.	Colleges of Professional & Other Education	13	46	74	130
4.	Secondary Schools (General)	281	1,170	1,248	5,297
5.	Secondary Schools (Vocational & Technical)	—	94	292	665
6.	Special and other Schools	7	990	3,729	4,746
7.	Middle Schools		4,323	6,739	11,162
8.	Primary Schools	50,676	97,854	160,070	172,681

Table 2: Enrolment by Stages (1855-56 to 1946-47)

	1855-56	*1901-02*	*1921-22*	*1946-47*
1. University				
(i) Total	4,355	23,007	58,837	237,546
(ii) Girls	N.A.	264	1,529	23,207
2. Secondary Stage:				
(i) Total	33,801	82,312	218,606	370,812
(ii) Girls	N.A.	1,677	5,818	83,270
3. Middle School Stage:				
(i) Total	—	1,080,670	385,372	2,036,109
(ii) Girls	—	8,133	24,655	281,606
4. Primary School Stage:				
(i) Total	885,624	3,564,122	6,404,200	14,105,418
(ii) Girls	—	380,282	1,297,643	3,728,793
5. Total Enrolment of All Stages :				
(i) Total	923,780	3,886,493	7,207,308	17,750,263
(ii) Girls	N.A.	393,161	1,340,842	4,156,742

Sources: (1) Basu, Aparna. '*Essays in the History of Indian Education*' 1981.
(2) Narullah and Naik in '*A Students' History of Education in India*' 1949 gives the number of Universities as 19 with 241,794 students.
(3) '*The Education Commission 1964-66*' puts the number of Universities at 20.

Dr. Veena Bhalla of the Association of Indian Universities, New Delhi, gives the following figures for the year 1947 in '*University News*', 39(2), January 8, 2001.

(i)	Students enrolled in General Higher Education	183238
(ii)	Students enrolled in Professional/Special Higher Education	45643
	Total	228881

Table 3: Sexwise Middle and High Schools 1946-47

Type of Schools	*Number*			*Enrolment*		
	Boys	*Girls*	*Total*	*Boys*	*Girls*	*Total*
1. Middle English Schools	4,169	620	4,789	5,40,441	85,484	6,25,925
2. Middle Vernacular Schools	2,914	567	3,481	4,04,377	92,300	4,96,677
3. High Schools	3,061	576	3,637	13,81,038	1,78,341	15,59,279
Total for 1946-47	10,144	1,763	11,907	23,25,836	3,56,125	26,81,981
Total for 1936-37		13,036				22,87,872

Source: Narullah and Naik (United Punjab).

Table 4: Expansion of Primary Education (1937-47)

Year	*No. of Primary Schools*	*No. of Pupils*
1881-82	82,916	2,061,541
1901-02	93,604	3,076,671
1921-22	1,55,017	6,109,752
1936-37	1,92,244	10,224,288
1946-47	1,34,866	10,525,943

It is difficult to compare the statistics of 1946-47 with those of 1936-37 on account of the establishment of Pakistan.
Source: Nurullah and Naik.

1.7 GENERAL OBSERVATIONS ON THE EXPANSION OF EDUCATIONAL FACILITIES

1. There was a general increase throughout these years though it varied in different periods and regions.
2. It was slow between 1813 and 1854 on account of controversies over goals, methods, contents and organisation of education.
3. Real growth started with the creation of Education Departments in 1855.
4. Establishment of Universities at Calcutta, Bombay and Madras in 1857 promoted higher education.
5. From 1921 to 1947, privately managed schools and colleges with or without government aid played an active role in the expansion of education.
6. Higher education was widely diffused in Bengal.
7. Education had a predominantly literary bias.
8. Primary education lagged education.
9. Agricultural education received little attention.
10. Technological subjects were by and large excluded from the curriculum.
11. Concentration on urbanised upper and middle classes led to the neglect of mass education.
12. Literacy rate remained very low.

2

Pre-Primary/Nursery Education

2.1 MEANING AND NATURE OF PRE-PRIMARY EDUCATION

The education that a child receives before entering school at the age of five or six is known as pre-primary education. Broadly speaking, as Gandhiji has observed, "The real education begins from conception as the mother begins to take up the responsibility of the child." Abhimanyu of the *'Mahabharata'* is said to have learnt the art of entering the *'Chakravyuh'* (A type of very intricate and puzzling military formation) while in the womb of his mother. Pre-primary education, therefore, includes formal as well as non-formal education *i.e.,* education in the school as well as outside. It is not limited to school care or nursery education for fixed hours. Some thinkers refer to this education as early childcare and education (ECCE).

2.2 STAGES OF PRE-PRIMARY EDUCATION

Pre-primary education is not limited to some fixed hours. Pre-primary education in its broader sense may be divided into the following four parts:

1. Pre-primary education from conception to birth.
2. Pre-primary education from birth to two and a half years.
3. From two and a half to four years.
4. From four to five or six years.

The first two stages, *i.e.,* (1) and (2) are the periods of education for the mother and the child together. Stress is laid on the health of the mother and the child. Pre-primary education is informal at this stage.

The task of the pre-primary school at the last two stages is to promote regular habits of personal hygiene, food etc. Efforts are made to enable the child develop habits of self discipline and obedience to others. He is provided with play-activities. Different types of schools for imparting pre-primary education have been started.

Formal and informal education is imparted at the third stage, *i.e.,* during the age two and a half to four.

Pre-primary school as a formal agency of education plays an important role in the education of the child during the last stage, *i.e.,* four to five or six years.

2.3 MULTIPLICITY OF NAMES OF PRE-PRIMARY SCHOOLS

Pre-primary schools have been given numerous names. Some of the popular names are (i) Balwadi, (ii) Balseva Sadan, (iii) Balkan ki Wadi, (iv) Bal Kunj, (v) Bal Leela Mandir, (vi) Bal Udyan, (vii) Children's Garden, (viii) Garden School, (ix) Kindergarden, (x) Kishore Sadan, (xi) Nursery School, (xii) Play-Way,

(xiii) Shishu Kendra, (xiv) Shishu Mandir, (xv) Shishu Niketan, (xvi) Tiny Tot etc.

2.4 IMPORTANCE OF PRE-PRIMARY EDUCATION

Austin A. D'Souza explains the importance of pre-primary education as under:

1. *Physically,* the child benefits greatly from the education and balanced diet. He is trained in hygienic habits and his muscles and limbs are given free expressive play through pleasurable activity, folk-dancing and free-movement.
2. *Intellectually,* he benefits by a stimulating environment and from an education that places emphasis not on sterile instruction but on harmonious creative growth.
3. *Socially and morally,* he benefits for he is weaned from an excessive dependence, and is trained in cooperative living and in the 'give and take' of social life.
4. *Psychologically,* he gets the opportunity for self-assertion and independence. He forms companions and satisfies his social urge. By manipulating objects, he satisfies his creative and destructive urges. He gets opportunities for play, make-believe and phantasy, so natural at this stage. The special environments helps him to make personal adjustments.

The Sargent Report (1944) observed, "An adequate provision of pre-primary, instruction in the form of Nursery School or classes is an essential adjunct to any national system of education."

The Education Commission (1964-66) stressed the importance of pre-primary education in these words, "Pre-primary education is of great significance to the physical, emotional and intellectual development of the children, especially those with unsatisfactory home backgrounds."

2.5 NEED FOR PRE-PRIMARY EDUCATION: PRE-PRIMARY EDUCATION IS A NECESSITY AND NOT LUXURY

As a matter of fact there is no dividing line between the importance and the need for pre-primary education. Both merge into one another. However, the following factors may be mentioned as they are specially relevant to the need for primary education.

1. *Proper Educational Environment:* There is a general feeling that the prevailing educational backwardness of a large section of our children is due to the lack of a proper educational environment in most homes, especially in the villages and that this can be met by providing nursery education.
2. *Provision of Equal Educational Opportunities:* Provision of equal educational opportunities to all is a fundamental principle on which a truly democratic society can be built up. It is an article of faith with us today.
3. *Foundation Stage;* It is well known that the age about 3 to 6 is the most impressionable period of children's growth and that the foundations of future adult personality are laid down in these impressionable years. Future social prejudices and social malajustments are removed by the provision of a properly "controlled environment" for the children when they are at this stage.
4. *Increasing Number of Working Mothers:* The industrial and technological advancement has increased the number of working mothers. Pre-primary institutions are needed to take care of their children.

5. *Filling the Gap Between the Rural and Urban Children:* The widespread provision of facilities for pre-primary education will tend to minimize the gaps that exist between the children in the villages and those in the towns and between the children in poor homes and those who are born in the richer ones.

6. *Pre-Primary Education Essential for Compulsory Primary Education:* Adequate and satisfactory provision of pre-primary education is conducive to the effective enforcement of compulsory education. It contributes to its success. It will minimize the "wastage" in primary education.

7. *Physical Well-Being of Children:* There is another aspect of the question pertaining to the physical health and well being of our children which makes immediate expansion of provision of pre-primary education essential. Most of our children are exposed to the handicaps of unsatisfactory and insufficient nutrition. Physical defects and disabilities become more pronounced at the pre-school stage of growth if not attended to in time. Pre-primary education will have to deal mainly with two aspects which may be broadly called the physical and educational. The first is no less important than the second. The pre-primary school will have to work in close cooperation with other institutions set-up for social welfare, for the purposes of medical relief, health, nutrition, etc.

2.6 AIMS AND OBJECTIVES OF PRE-PRIMARY EDUCATION

The Education Commission 1964-66 explained the aims and objectives of pre-primary education as under:

(i) *Development of Good Habits:* To develop in the child good health habits, and to build up basic skills necessary for personal adjustment such as dressing, toilet habits, eating, washing, cleaning, etc.;

(ii) *Development of Desirable Attitudes:* To develop desirable social attitudes and manners and to encourage health group participation, making the child sensitive to the rights and privileges of others;

(iii) *Development of Emotional Maturity:* To develop emotional maturity by guiding the child to express, understand, accept and control his feelings and emotions;

(iv) *Developing Aesthetic Appreciation:* To encourage aesthetic appreciation;

(v) *Stimulating Curiosity*: To stimulate the beginnings of intellectual curiosity concerning the environment and to help him understand the world in which he lives; and to foster new interest through opportunities to explore, investigate and experiment;

(vi) *Encouraging Self-expression:* To encourage independence and creativity by providing the child with sufficient opportunities for self-expression;

(vii) *Developing Speech Habits:* To develop the child's ability to express his thoughts and feelings in fluent, correct and clear speech; and

(viii) *Developing Physique:* To develop in the child a good physique, adequate muscular co-ordination and basic motor skills.

The primary aim is the creation of a social environment, in which the child may develop his physique and intellect. Co-operation and not competition is emphasised. Spontaneous activities lead to the emotional development. A love for work is developed and the child begins to find work in play and play in work. In short, Nurseries and Nursery Schools are the best places for the would-be citizens of a country where there are provisions for a better social adjustment of the child.

2.7 PROGRESS AND EXPANSION OF PRE-PRIMARY EDUCATION IN INDIA

Pre-Primary Education before Independence: Very little attempt was made to develop pre-primary education in India before independence. The Second Wardha Education Committee of the Central Advisory Board of Education (1939) pointed out the necessity of providing model infant and nursery schools at suitable centres. Thereafter, the Sargent Report or Report of the Central Advisory Board of Education on Post-War Educational Development in India (1944) emphasized the significance of pre-primary education in India and recommended that on the basis of a normal age-range of 3 to 5 years, provision should be made for 10,000 places in nursery schools and classes. However, on account of unstable political conditions and the financial stringency nothing worthwhile could be achieved. With independence, the Government of India started taking some interest in the development of pre-primary education in India.

No systematic survey in respect of progress of pre-primary education in India for this stage has been made. The following table illustrates the position of recognised pre-primary education institutions and enrolment. There is no doubt that at present there would be no village or 'mohalla' or locality in which there is no nursery school or class in one form or the other.

Table 1: Showing Expansion of Pre-Primary Education in India

Year	*No. of Schools*	*No. of Students*
1950-51	303	28,309
1967-68	3,614	2,71,268
1997-98	41,788	28,33,680
1998-99	51,569	29,81,770

2.8 CAUSES OF SLOW GROWTH OF PRE-PRIMARY EDUCATION

1. The schools are a direct transplantation of western system which till recently have not appealed to the people as a whole. The schools do not meet the needs of our children. For instance, foreign language and culture are taught.
2. The nursery schools in general are very expensive. So these are beyond the reach of average class people.
3. There is a great shortage of trained teachers. What we need today is not a few schools for the rich few, but a large number of them so that children from all sections of the community may derive advantage from them.
4. There is an absence of the child laboratories in the country with the result that there is hardly any literature on pre-primary education.
5. There is no clear cut policy of the Government for the expansion of pre-primary education.
6. There is an absence of good training centres for teachers. The Government alone can open model training schools.
7. Suitable methods of instructions need to be evolved. At present, there are hardly any.

8. Many parents have not yet realised the importance of such schools. They feel that this period of the child is not so important and that he should be allowed to have a care-free time. Moreover, some parents feel that it will put strain on young minds.

2.9 RECOMMENDATIONS OF THE EDUCATION COMMISSION FOR THE PROMOTION OF PRE-SCHOOL EDUCATION (1964-66)

The Education Commission felt that for the promotion of pre-primary education, there should be established Pre-Primary Education Development Centres at the District level and State level with the following functions:

(a) to provide supervision and guidance to pre-primary teachers with the cooperation of the Mukhyasevikas;

(b) to hold refresher courses for pre-school teachers and to organize in-service training at block level;

(c) to undertake the preparation of teaching aids out of locally available material and to demonstrate the procedure to the teacher;

(d) to distribute good pictures and posters to the schools; and

(e) to provide education to parents regarding the care and treatment of children.

For performing the above mentioned functions each centre should:

(i) have a pre-primary school to be used for observation and demonstration in refresher courses, in-service programmes and observation-visits by teachers and parents;

(ii) adopt three or four pre-primary centres of the less costly type to work with. These should also be used for the purpose of demonstration since the majority of the trainees will be working in such pre-school centres;

(iii) have a Child Health Clinic;

(iv) have a Library of children's books and books on child development, child health, child education and books useful for the teachers and parents;

(v) have a Library of films with at least two film projectors of 16 mm and 35 mm;

(vi) have Play and Recreation Centres for Children;

(vii) have a Museum;

(viii) have a Workshop.

At the Centre, there would be regular activities of pre-school education, recreation and play for the children of the surrounding area and programme for in-service training courses.

The Centre should have a mobile van, so that it can serve a larger area by sending its workers to the neighbouring villages in the district with books, pictures, films and some useful teaching aids. The mobile van can also be useful in undertaking a parent education programme in the villages visited by the workers.

2.10 SUGGESTIONS FOR THE PROMOTION OF PRE-PRIMARY EDUCATION IN INDIA: INDIANISATION OF PRE-PRIMARY EDUCATION

1. *Clear-cut Government Policy*: The Ministry of Human Resource Development, Government of India should entrust all direction, guidance and monitoring work relating to pre-primary education to the Department of

Education. At present this work is done by several other departments. Like the various other wings, it should have a pre-primary wing also.

2. *Indianisation of Pre-Primary Education:* Most of the pre-primary schools are a direct transplantation of western system which have not appealed to the people as a whole. They do not meet the needs of our children. For instance, foreign language and culture are taught. The kinds of nursery schools that India needs are those which are based on our culture and traditions.

In this regard, following suggestions are offered:

1. Side by side of the teaching of Froebel and Montessori, we should popularise the teachings of Gijubhai Badhaka (1885-1959) and Smt. Tarabai Modak and other Indians in this field. Bal Mandir of Dakshinamurti of Bhavnagar established in 1920 is a great source of inspiration. Gandhiji wrote in 1939 about Gijubhai, "Who am I to write about Gijubhai? His enthusiasm and devotion has baffled me. His work is sure to grow."

2. Efforts need to be made to publish suitable literature in Indian languages. This literature should be in Indian setting and environment. Suitable songs and plays etc. may be prepared which reflect Indian ethos.

3. Inexpensive indigenous pre-primary education material may be prepared. This should be locally made and should be easily available.

Other measures are:

1. Providing appropriate environment *i.e.,* different types of activities.
2. Providing simple but attractive buildings.
3. Establishment of Boards of Pre-primary Education in states.
4. Establishment of model pre-primary schools by the Government and local bodies.
5. Liberal grant-in-aid rules.
6. Suitable training facilities for teachers.
7. Setting up Toy Banks.
8. Preparation of suitable books.
9. Formation of pre-primary teachers' associations.
10. Parental awareness programmes.
11. Encouragement to voluntary organizations.
12. In-service education/training to pre-primary teachers.

A. D. Souza mentions the following conditions which are very helpful for the promotion of pre-basic education. "The open air type of building, the indispensable garden, the inexpensive educative toys and rich play material, the simple balanced diet and healthy food, the ordered routine of nursery school day, the interesting and varied activities and experiences, all these take captive the heart of the young child and, while they give him intense pleasure, also educate him and enable him to make necessary social and personal adjustments."

2.11 PRE-SCHOOL CURRICULUM NOT IN TERMS OF FORMAL SUBJECTS

About pre-school curriculum, the Education Commission 1964-66 observed, "We can hardly talk about a curriculum for pre-primary schools, it is more appropriate to think of it as a programme of activities." According to it, it should consist of:

(a) Play activities.

(i) Free play, including educational and constructional toys, indoor games and outdoor activities in association with children.

(ii) Physical activities involving muscular and limb movement.

(iii) Play involving contact and acquaintance with, imitation and experience of physical, family and social environment.

(iv) Organized play, group activities and directional play.

(v) Playground activities using playground apparatus.

(b) Physical training including simple exercises, dance and rhythmics.

(c) Manual activities and play like gardening, simple chores and participation in simple community efforts.

(d) Sensorial education, using natural objects and specially constructed apparatus.

(e) Handwork and artistic activities involving the use of finger skills and tools; and activities like drawing, painting, singing, music and dancing.

(f) Learning activities, including language; personal hygiene and health rules; elementary nature study involving contact with the physical, plant and animal world; counting etc.

(g) Self-service in school, eliminating as far as possible the use of servants and adult helpers.

2.12 ROLE OF GOVERNMENT AND OTHER AGENCIES IN THE FIELD OF PRE-PRIMARY EDUCATION

The Education Commission considered several aspects of the pre-primary education along with other sectors of education and made the following recommendations in this regard.

1. *Restricted Role of the Government*: While recognising the need to develop pre-primary education as extensively as possible, the Commission felt that our advancement in this sector will be restricted on account of inadequacy of the resources available and especially because primary education must be accorded a higher propriety.

2. *Support to Private Enterprise*: The establishment and conduct of pre-primary schools may be left, as at present, mainly to private enterprises. The State should assist through grants-in-aid on a basis of equalisation. Accordingly, pre-primary schools catering for the need of children from the under-privileged group will have a higher claim on the State funds.

3. *Establishment of Pre-Primary Development Centres and Children's Play Centres*: The role of the State should be to maintain such centres at the State and district levels, train pre-primary teachers, conduct research, assist in the preparation of materials and literature needed for pre-primary education and provide supervision and guidance to pre-primary schools and training institutions. It should assist private institutions at this stage through grants-in-aid; and in exceptional cases, it may also conduct some pre-primary schools to serve the needs of urban slums and rural areas as model institutions.

The National Policy on Education (1986 and as amended in 1992) has not included any chapter/part on pre-primary education. It has, laid stress on Early Childhood Care and Education (ECCE).It is, therefore very clear that for years to come, voluntary organizations would continue to play an important role in the promotion of pre-primary education.

2.13 DIFFERENT TYPES OF PRE-SCHOOL EDUCATIONAL INSTITUTIONS

Report of the Committee on Child Care (1961-62) appointed by the Central Social Welfare Board, India made the following recommendations:

1. *A half-day organization* to be developed as "The minimum standard pre-school."

2. *A pre-school of* minimum standard should provide a playground to look after the health and cleanliness of children, inculcate in them good habits and correct behaviour patterns, and provide opportunities for training in Nature Study, and other subjects which can be easily dealt with by reasonably trained teachers and Bal-sevikas.

3. *Standard pre-schools* following some kind of systems like the Montessori, the pre-basic, and any other system suitable to rural areas and any type of pre-school using programmes, methods and techniques suitable for different types of environments in urban areas. (The true meaning of pre-basic should imply the acceptance of the 'principle of activity'.) The types of activities must be suitable to the needs of the child and the community.

4. *A pre-school project* attached to the village primary school to be located as far as possible in a separate structure or during separate periods, so that classes of pre-school and primary school are not held together.

5. *Infant classes in primary schools and high schools*, with training and programmes modified to conform to principles and programmes of pre-school.

6. *Open air pre-schools with playground* may be created where facilities and resources are inadequate or where there are inadequate number of children to promote a pre-school as a unit.

7. *Other types*

(a) Pre-school attached to institutions where unattached women with children are provided with boarding and lodging facilities.

(b) Special pre-schools in urban areas for sub-normal, feeble-minded and problem children with behaviour disorders.

(c) Special types of pre-schools to help the care, training and rehabilitation of handicapped children.

All the above mentioned types of pre-primary educational institutions exist in India in varying degrees.

2.14 COMPARATIVE DATA ON NURSERY EDUCATION/EARLY CHILDHOOD CARE AND EDUCATION: SELECT COUNTRIES

Country	*Age Range*	*Gross Enrolment Ratios (1990)*	*Gross Enrolment Ratios (1998)*
China	3-6	30% (1991)	49%
Cuba	0-5	29%	98%
Egypt	4-6	N.A.	8%
India	3-6	10.3%	16.9%
Italy	0-5	90%	95%
Japan	3-5	70%	82%

3

Primary/Elementary Education 1800-1947

3.1 DEVELOPMENT OF PRIMARY EDUCATION IN INDIA (1800-1947) AND COMMITTEES AND COMMISSIONS ETC

Primary education in India during the period (1800-1947) developed in the light of the recommendations of the following:

1. Wood's Despatch (1854).
2. Indian Education Commission Report (1882-83).
3. Resolution of Government on Educational Policy (1904).
4. Gokhale's Bill for Compulsory Primary Education (1910-12).
5. Hartog Committee Report (1928-29).
6. Abbot-Wood Report (1936-37).
7. Wardha Scheme of Basic Education (1937).
8. Formation of Congress Ministries (1937-39).
9. Kher Committee Report (1940).

3.2 WOOD'S DESPATCH (1854): BASIS OF THE MODERN SYSTEM OF EDUCATION IN INDIA: BACKGROUND

After Macaulay's Minute (1835), the Court of Directors of the East India Company in England appointed a Select Committee of the House of Commons to hold a thorough enquiry into educational developments in India. On the basis of this enquiry, Wood's Despatch—an important document on education was prepared for the functioning of education system in India. The document written at the instance of Charles Wood, the President of the Board of Control, came to be known as Wood's Despatch. It is a long document of a hundred paragraphs and deals with a number of important questions of educational importance in India.

Major Directions, Observations and Recommendations

1. *Object of Education in India*: The declared object was "not only to produce a higher degree of intellectual fitness but to raise the moral character and to supply with servants."

2. *Spread of European Knowledge*: It was also declared that the function of education was to diffuse European knowledge—arts, science, philosophy and literature.

3. *Languages*: English language and vernacular languages of India would be the media for the diffusion of European Knowledge.

in each of the five provinces under Company's rule—Bengal (Bengal at that time consisted of Bengal, Bihar, Orissa), Madras, Bombay, North-Western Province—NWP and the Punjab.

5. *Establishment of Universities*: The Despatch directed to establish Universities at Calcutta, Bombay and Madras or in any part of India, on the model of the London University, which was then an examining body.

6. *Establishment of a Network of Graded Schools all over India*: The Despatch provided for the establishment of High and Middle Schools and below them the indigenous elementary schools.

7. *Grant-in-aid*: Principles for grant-in-aid were laid down.

8. *Training of Teachers*: The scheme of training of teacher as prevalent in Great Britain was put forward.

9. *Women Education*: Some suggestions for the education of women were offered.

Evaluation of the Report

Some historians and thinkers have described the Wood's Despatch as "The Magna Charta of Indian Education". They argue that Macaulay's Minute was, by and large, translated into action in several matters on the basis of this report. It, once for all, decided that Western Arts, Philosophy and Science were to be the areas of knowledge to be imparted to the people of India. It led to the creation of Departments of Education, establishment of universities, a graded school system, grant-in-aid rules, setting of training colleges and educational institutions—all elements that led to the development of modern system of education in India. The Despatch not only strengthened the foundations lay down by Macaulay but also built up a durable structure of the system of education.

Prof. S. N. Mukerjee observes in his book *'History of Education in India'*, "The Despatch is indeed a very important document and James considers it to be the 'Magna Charta' of English Education in India. It was the first authoritative declaration on the part of the British Parliament about the educational policy to be followed in India. It was admitted that the education of the people is the duty of the State. The Despatch is so comprehensive in its nature that Indian educationists have not yet succeeded in fulfilling the tasks, which it had set. It provided scheme, which tried to touch all aspects of Indian education, right from the primary to the university stage. It partially recognized the value of Indian culture, and at the same time it showed the need for grafting European knowledge on it. The Despatch rightly defined the comparative position of English and Indian languages in a general scheme of education for this country."

Dalhousie declared that Despatch contained "a scheme of education for all India, far wider and more comprehensive than the Local or the Supreme Government could have ever ventured to suggest."

H. R. James observes, "The Despatch of 1854 is thus the climax in the history of Indian education; what goes before leads up to it, what follows from it."

Prof. A. N. Basu has opined "The Despatch is said to be the corner-stone of Indian education. It is said to have laid foundations of our present system of education."

N. R. Paranjee (*'Progress of Education'*, Poona, July 1941), has made these observations regarding the contribution of Despatch to the development of education in India "But in spite of all these features it would be incorrect to describe the Educational Despatch of 1854 as an Educational Charter, *i.e.*, an official paper borrowing or guaranteeing certain rights and privileges. The Despatch does not even refer to the ideal of universal literacy" He has further observed, that the Despatch did not visualize 'education required by the people of a self-government nation". While commending some of the remarkable points of the Despatch, Nurullah and Naik have observed, "The Despatch, no doubt, did a lot towards the evolution of a good system of education in India according to the educational ideas then prevalent. But these ideals have changed so materially since then that it would help India very little to be now guided by the sentiments of the Despatch."

3.3 INDIAN EDUCATION Commission OR HUNTER COMMISSION (1882)

The recommendations of the Hunter Commission (Indian Education Commission) in 1882 were in favour of Primary Education. The Commission made recommendations which were of far reaching consequences as far as primary education was concerned. It suggested:

(a) Primary education should be entrusted to the newly created Municipal and District Boards.

(b) Definite funds for primary education should be set aside by the local bodies.

(c) Primary education should be through vernaculars.

Despite these important suggestions, very little could be done in the field of primary education. The recommendations, however, awakened people to the need for primary education.

3.4 GOVERNMENT RESOLUTION (1904)

In the year 1904, there was Government of India Resolution on Education in India and Lord Curzon was the prime mover of the resolution. Lord Curzon was keen that something solid was done in the direction of primary education. He allocated Rs. 35 lakhs for the spread of primary education. State Governments also sanctioned money for this purpose.

3.5 BEGINNING OF COMPULSORY EDUCATION IN INDIA AND GOPAL KRISHNA GOKHALE'S EFFORT (1906-12)

The first successful experiment of compulsory education in India was conducted in the State of Baroda. In 1893, Maharaja Sayajiro Gaikwad, the ruler of Baroda, introduced compulsory education as an experiment in the Amreli Taluk of his State. The success of the experiment made him to extend it to all parts of the State in 1906.

Gopal Krishna Gokhale made emotional as well rational speeches in the Imperial Legislative Council in 1906, 1907 and 1908 suggesting that primary education be free all over India and compulsory at some selected places. In 1910 he moved a resolution recommending "that a beginning be made in the direction of compulsory primary education throughout the country and a mixed commission of officials and non-officials be appointed at an early date to frame definite proposals". The House was sharply divided over the issue. Gokhale, therefore, withdrew the resolution on an assurance from the Government that his proposals would be examined carefully. But no action was taken.

On March 16, 1911, Gokhale brought in a bill to make better provision for the extension of elementary education. On March 18, 1912, he moved a resolution that his bill be examined by a Select Committee of 15 members of the Viceroy's Council. The Bill had four features. Firstly, it left it to the option of the local bodies to introduce compulsory education in any selected area. Secondly, it left the initiative for introducing compulsory education to local bodies. Thirdly, it visualized a compulsory period of four years only, *i.e.*, for boys from the age of six to ten. Fourthly, it did not directly place any financial obligation on Government. The bill, however, was rejected by 38 votes to 13. Gokhale's statement deserves careful attention, "My Lord, I know that my bill will be thrown out before the day closes. I make no complaint. I shall not even feel depressed...But my Lord. . .one thing is clear. We shall be entitled to feel that we have done our duty, and where the call of duty is clear it is better to labour and fail than not to labour at all."

Compulsory Education Acts and Vithalbhai Patel's Efforts: Gokhale's work was taken up by Shri Vithalbhai Patel. In 1917, he moved in the Bombay Legislative Council, a bill for the introduction of compulsory primary education in the Municipal limits of the Province. The bill was passed with some modifications and became the first law on compulsory education in India. It is known as the Patel Act of 1918.

System of Dyarchy and Primary Education: Indian Ministers took charge of primary education in 1921. The year 1921 may be considered as a landmark in the history of elementary education in India. Compulsory Education Acts were passed in most of the provinces of British India.

3.6 HARTOG COMMITTEE REPORT (1929) AND OTHER EVENTS

The Hartog Committee (1929), reviewed the position of education in India at the school level and made specific recommendations on primary education and on the quality and status of teachers. Sir Philip Hartog who had been a Vice-Chancellor of the Dacca University was the Chairman of the Committee.

Observations of the Committee on Primary Education: Throughout the whole educational system there is waste and ineffectiveness. In the primary system, which from our point of view should be designed to produce literacy and the capacity to exercise an intelligent vote, the waste is appalling. So far as we can judge, the vast increase in number in the primary schools produces no commensurate increase in literacy, for only a small proportion of those who are at the primary stage reach Class IV, in which the attainment of literacy may be expected. The wastage in the case of girls is even more serious than in the case of boys......"

Wastage and Stagnation in Primary Education: According to the Committee, "Wastage meant the pre-mature withdrawals of children from schools at any stage before the completion of the primary course."

Stagnation means detention in lower classes of a child for a period more than what was needed for that class.

Major recommendations:

1. Primary education should be made compulsory but there should be no hurry about it.

2. Instead of increasing the number of primary schools, qualitative development should be made.
3. A policy of consolidation of primary education should be taken up.
4. At least four years should be devoted to primary education.
5. The programme of schools should be drawn up in accordance with the environment and circumstances of the schools.
6. Curriculum of primary schools should be made more liberal and scientific.
7. Due attention should be paid to include subjects of practical utility to the students in life.
8. Primary schools should serve as centres for rural uplift, medical relief, adult education, mass literacy, sanitation, recreation etc.
9. Standard of teachers of primary schools should be improved.
10. Salary and conditions of service of teachers of primary schools should be improved.
11. Inspecting Staff should be increased so as to exercise adequate control over these schools.

Evaluation of the Report: The main observations on stagnation and wastage are still quite valid. It is very unfortunate that even after seven decades, we are facing the same problem in education at the primary stage. Its recommendations on the quality and status of teachers have gone a long way in bringing about substantial improvements but still a lot remains to be done.

Basic System of Education (Discounted Separately): The year 1937 was an epoch-making year in the history of elementary education in India as it saw the emergence of the scheme of Basic Education enunciated by Gandhiji. The Congress Ministries were also formed in many provinces, which paid more attention to elementary education. In 1939, the Second World War broke out and the Congress Ministers resigned. Education became the first casualty.

The Plan of Post-War Educational Development prepared by the Central Advisory Board of Education, popularly known as the Sargent Plan (1944) adopted the Scheme of Basic Education with some modifications.

3.7 GENERAL OBSERVATIONS ON PRIMARY EDUCATION DURING THE PERIOD 1800-1947

Primary Education (1854-1904): The progress was slow on account of the non-introduction of compulsory education. However there was some improvement in the quality. Girls education got some attention. Likewise was the case of Harijan pupils. There was improvement in the quality and qualification of teachers.

Primary Education (1904-1921): Compulsory primary education received encouragement.

Primary Education (1921 to 1937): Primary Education Acts were passed in most of the provinces of India. The recommendation of the Hartog Committee (1929), though very valuable, failed to make much headway on account of the 'Great Worldwide Economic Depression.'

Primary Education (1937-47): The Congress Ministries during 1937-39 did useful work in promoting Basic Education at the primary stage. However, after their resignation in 1939 and during War (1939-1944), state of primary education and in fact, education at all stages, declined (*For Statistical Data, see Chapter 1*).

4

Universalisation of Elementary Education (UEE)

4.1 MEANING OF UEE

Universalisation of education in India implies "Elementary Education for All" (classes I to VIII) and not for a selected few. This concept accepts that education is the birth right of every child. This means that all children belonging to the rich and the poor, living in towns as well as rural areas and in places which are accessible with difficulty have to be provided with facilities for elementary education. It is accepted in UN's Declaration of Human Rights and 'Children's Rights'. It is universally accepted that the universalisation of the elementary education is the true index of the general, economic, political and social development of a country.

Universalisation of elementary education also means free education. In some of the advanced countries free education means no fees, free books and stationery, free mid-day means and free school transport. But in developing countries like India, it has not been possible to provide all these facilities free of cost. Of course, education at this stage is free of tuition fee. Other facilities on a selective basis are also provided.

Universalisation of primary or elementary education involves the following three stages or steps:

(a) Universalisation of Provision.

(b) Universalisation of Enrolment.

(c) Universalisation of Retention.

(a) *Universalisation of Provision*: It means that school facilities should be provided to all the children between the age group 6 to 14 years in the country. The schools be easily accessible—within the walking distance of a child. We have fairly succeeded as far as this provision is concerned.

(b) *Universalisation of Enrolment*: All children between the age group 6 to 14 years must be enrolled. For this, compulsory legislation must be passed. Under legislation, parents can be fined for not sending their children to schools. However this provision has remained on paper only.

(c) *Universalisation of Retention*: By this we mean that once a child joins a primary school, he should remain there till he completes all 8 classes. If the child leaves the school in between, the idea of universalisation stands defeated. Unfortunately, 70% of all the first admissions leave the primary school before completing it. It gives birth to problem of wastage. Mere enlistment of children is not enough. They have to be retained.

4.2 CONSTITUTIONAL COMMITMENT ON UNIVERSAL ELEMENTARY EDUCATION

The universalisation of elementary education has been one of the most important goals of educational development in India since Independence. It found expression in Article 45 of the Indian Constitution as a Directive Principle of State Policy. It reads under the caption *Provision for Free and Compulsory Education for Children:* "The State shall endeavour to provide, within a period of ten years from the commencement of the Constitution, for free and compulsory education for all children until they complete the age of fourteen years." In other words this task should have been completed by 1960. However, this resolve could not be accomplished on account of several problems such as the rehabilitation of displaced persons after partition and lack of resources. As a result the target date had to be revised first to 1970, then to 1976 and later on to 1990. The target date, according to the National Policy on Education, 1986 was 1995. The Resolve contained in the policy reads as: "The new Education Policy will give the highest priority to solving the problem of children dropping out of school and will adopt an array of meticulously formulated strategies based on micro-planning, and applied at the grass-roots level all over the country, to ensure children's retention at school. The effort will be fully coordinated with the network of non-formal education. It shall be ensured that all children who attain the age of about 11 years by 1990 will have had five years of schooling, or its equivalent through the non-formal stream. Likewise, by 1995 all children will be provided free and compulsory education upto 14 years of age." The modified NPE 1992, further revised the date. It states, "It shall be ensured that free and compulsory education of satisfactory quality is provided to all children up to 14 years of age before we enter the twenty first century. A National Mission will be launched for the achievement of this goal." Alas ! This goal is also elusive. The following table illustrates the progress:

Table 1: Sexwise Enrolment at Primary Stage (1950-51 to 1998-99)

(In Millions)

	Classes I to V			*Classes VI to VIII*		
Year	*Boys*	*Girls*	*Total*	*Boys*	*Girls*	*Total*
1951-51	13.8	5.4	19.2	2.6.	0.5	3.1
1955-56	17.1	7.5	24.6	3.8	1.0	4.8
1960-61	23.6	11.4	35.0	5.1	1.6	6.7
1965-66	32.2	18.3	50.5	7.7	2.8	10.5
1970-71	35.7	21.3	57.0	9.4	3.9	13.3
1975-76	40.6	25.0	65.6	11.0	5.0	16.0
1980-81	45.3	28.5	73.8	13.9	6.8	20.7
1985-86	52.2	35.2	87.4	17.7	9.6	27.1
1990-91	57.0	40.4	97.4	21.5	12.5	34.0
1995-96	62.4	47.4	109.8	25.0	16.0	41.0
2000-01	64.0	49.8	113.8	25.3	17.5	42.8
2002-03*	64.9	57.2	122.1	26.3	20.6	46.9
2003-04	–	–	122.4	–	–	46

* Provisional.

The total enrolment at the primary stage (Classes I to V) during the period 1950-51 to 1998-99 increased by 5.77 times while for the girls, the increase was 9 times. At the upper primary stage (Classes VI to VIII) the increase during this period was more than 13 times while that of girls, the increase was more than 32 times, which is quite appreciable.

Table 2: Gross Enrolment Ratios (1950-51 to 2003-2004)

Year	*I-V Primary*	*VI-VIII Upper Primary*	*I-VIII Total*
1950-51	42.6	12.7	32.1
1960-61	62.4	22.5	48.7
1970-71	78.6	33.4	61.9
1980-81	80.5	41.9	67.5
1990-91	100.1	62.1	86.0
1995-96	104.0	67.6	90.7
2001-02	96.3	60.2	82.4
2003-04	98.31	62.49	84.91

Note: Gross Enrolment Ratio (GER) is defined as the percentage of the enrolment in classes I-V and VI-VIII and/or I-VIII to the estimated child population in the age groups 6 to 11 years and 11 to 14 and or 6 to 14 years respectively.

Source: Economic Survey 2005-2006, Government of India.

Table 3: No. of Recognised Primary Schools Since 1950-51

Year	*Primary*	*Middle*
1950-51	2,09,671	13,596
1955-56	2,78,135	21,730
1960-61	3,30,399	49,663
1965-66	3,91,064	75,798
1970-71	4,08,378	90,621
1980-81	4,94,503	1,18,555
1990-91	5,60,935	1,51,456
2001-02	6,54,041	2,19,626
2003-04	7,10,471	2,62,649

Note: Use of the terms 'Primary' and 'Elementary' has not been uniform. Sometimes they are used interchangeably. Middle Schools sometimes include classes I to VIII and mostly classes VI to VIII.

4.4 CAUSES AND PROBLEMS FOR NON-FULFILMENT OF CONSTITUTIONAL PROVISIONS REGARDING UEE

Following are the important causes and problems of slow progress:

1. Problems of priority to Elementary Education.
2. Problems of Finance.
3. Problem of Population Explosion.
4. Problem of Reconstruction of the Education System.
5. Problem Resulting from Poverty of Parents.
6. Problem of Illiterate Parents.
7. Problem of Wastage and Stagnation.
8. Problem of Girls Education.
9. Problem of States with Low Enrolment.
10. Problem of Education of Backward Sections and Classes.
11. Problem of Unattractive Schools.

12. Problem of Small Habitations.
13. Problem of the Education of the Handicapped.
14. Problem of Enforcing Compulsory Primary Education Acts.

4.5 MEASURES FOR THE ACHIEVEMENT OF THE GOAL OF UEE

1. *Priority to Primary Education*: Primary education should be developed on priority basis and percentage of budget under this sector should be suitably raised. There has been a decline in expenditure in this sector. From 55 per cent of the total educational budget spent on primary education during the First Plan, it came down to 36 per cent in the Sixth Plan, 34 per cent in the Seventh Plan and 47 per cent in the Eighth Plan.

2. *Rational Use of Finance*: Cost on primary education may be rationalized by:

(a) Introducing double shift wherever possible.

(b) Harnessing community resources in men, material and monetary terms.

(c) Evolving a system of voluntary service in the form of teaching by young persons who have completed secondary school or college.

3. *Population Education*: The problem of population explosion has upset all our planning including education. Family planning must be adopted as a way of life. Population education should be promoted in educational institutions.

4. *Restructuring Education*: The single point entry system must be replaced by multiple entry system under which it will be open for older children of 9, 11 or 14 to join primary schools in separate classes organized for their needs. Facilities for part time education even at primary stage should be introduced. It should also be made possible for older children to join the prescribed courses at any time and also complete them in much shorter period.

5. *Provision of Facilities to Poor Students*: Facilities such as free supply of books and stationery, free uniforms and school meals can be helpful in retaining children in schools. But more than that is the need for providing part-time education facilities to the children from the poor families.

6. *Adult Literacy*: Nearly 50 per cent of the people in India are illiterate and as such they do not fully realise the importance of education for their children. They are indifferent to education. The prevalence of illiteracy is one of the factors that has stood in the way of universalization of primary education. A massive programme for removing adult illiteracy should be taken up.

7. *Attractive School Environment*: Education should be suited to the environment and lives of children so that they do not regard it as a waste of time. Audio-visual aids should be made available in schools. Methods of teaching should arouse the curiosity and interest of children.

8. *Checking Wastage and Stagnation*: Nearly 60 per cent of the students enrolled in class I reach class V and only 45 per cent reach class VIII. To reduce wastage and stagnation a number of steps need to be taken. The holding power of schools should be increased through the provision of better teachers and equipment. (For details *see* 4.8).

9. *Promoting Girls' Education*: Although girls education has made much headway since independence, yet there is still a wide gap between the education of boys and girls. Adequate attention should be given to education of girls at all stages. Special schemes should be prepared for this purpose and the funds required for them should be provided on a priority basis.

10. *Special Attention to States with Low Enrolment*: Special attention to universal enrolment has to be paid in these States. Provision for part-time education should be made and more schools should be set-up at suitable places.

11. *Education of Backward Classes*: The Backward classes include the Scheduled Castes, the Scheduled Tribes, Denotified Communities and few nomadic and semi-nomadic groups.

The Scheduled Castes and Scheduled Tribes constitute respectively 15 per cent and 7 per cent of the total population of the country. Special efforts should be made to enroll girls, children of Scheduled Castes and Scheduled Tribes and children of other weaker sections like landless agricultural labourers.

12. *Providing Education in Small Habitations:* The number of small habitations with a population of less than 200 is nearly four lakhs and a half. The population of these habitations is nearly 15 per cent of total rural population. Suitable measures need to be devised to tackle this problem.

13. *Education of the Handicapped:* According to the Programme of Action 1986, the population of handicapped children of the school going age is about 43 lakhs. This also requires special attention.

14. *Enforcing Compulsory Primary Education Act:* Although the Compulsory Primary Education Act have been passed, yet this has not been properly enforced. Parents who wilfully do not sent their children to school should be fined as provided in the Act.

4.6 KOTHARI COMMISSION (1964-66) ON UNIVERSALISATION OF PRIMARY EDUCATION

Important recommendations for universalisation were as under:

1. Abolition of tuition fee at the primary stage.
2. Providing facilities for part-time education at the primary stage.
3. Provision of free textbooks and writing material.
4. Liberal provision of scholarships.
5. Establishment of Ashram Schools in the sparsely populated and tribal areas.
6. Ensuring 80% of children reaching class VII by checking stagnation and wastage.
7. Undertaking special measures for qualitative improvement.
8. Giving special attention to girls' education.

4.7 MAIN RECOMMENDATIONS OF THE REVIEW COMMITTEE—RAMAMURTI REPORT (1990) REGARDING UEE

The Committee appointed to review the implementation of National Policy on Education (1986) made the following recommendation:

1. The Right to Education should be examined for inclusion among the Fundamental Rights guaranteed under the Constitution.
2. Non-detention policy should be followed at the primary stage.
3. Corporal punishment should be firmly excluded.
4. Community should be involved in the improvement of quality of education.
5. The curriculum at the +2 stage should not be allowed to determine the content and process of education at the primary stage.
6. School hours may be shifted according to community needs.
7. Child-centred approach should be adopted.

8. School hours should be reduced but learning hours increased.
9. Non-formal education should be provided on a wider scale.
10. 'Para-teachers' (*Shiksha Karmis*) should be appointed by the school heads. Para-teachers were helpers for the morning and evening classes. Remuneration proposed was one-third of the regular teacher.
11. Adequate attention should be given to make the enrolment data more reliable.

4.8 STRATEGIES PLANNED BY THE GOVERNMENT TOWARDS UEE AND CHECKING DROP-OUTS, STAGNATION AND WASTAGE

Following are the salient features of the strategies:

1. Laying emphasis on retention rather than on merely enrolment.
2. Strengthening the alternatives of schooling, particularly, the Non-Formal Education System for working children, girls and children from other disadvantaged or marginalized sections of the society.
3. Shifting focus from educationally backward states to educationally backward districts.
4. Preparing and implementing district specific and population-specific plans.
5. Providing more facilities to girls.
6. Introducing Minimum Levels of Learning for the enhancement of learner's achievement.
7. Improving teacher competence, training and motivation.
8. Decentralising planning and management through Panchayati Raj Institutions/Village Education Committees.
9. Coordinating all early childhood care and education and school health and nutrition programmes, etc.

(*For details see Chapter 5*)

Passing of Constitutional (86th Amendment) Act by the Parliament

The Government is fully committed to the goal of Universalisation of Elementary Education (UEE). For promotion of UEE and Social Justice, the Parliament of India has passed the Constitutional (86th Amendment) Act, notified on 13 December 2002, making free and compulsory elementary education a Fundamental Right, for all the children in the age group of 6-14 years.

The Constitutional Amendment provides for the following:

- Insertion of Article 21A in the Part III dealing with Fundamental Rights as follows:
  'The State shall provide free and compulsory education to all children of the age of six to fourteen years in such manner as the State may, by law, determine.'
- Rewording of Article 45 in Part IV dealing with Directive Principles as follows:
  'The State shall endeavour to provide early childhood care and education for all children until they complete the age of six years.'
- Introduction of a new Fundamental Duty Article 51A(k) in Part IVA as follows:
  'who is a parent or guardian to provide opportunities for educaiton to his child, or as case may be, ward between the age of six and fourteen years.'

5

New Initiatives in Univeralisation of Elementary Education

Since the formulation of the National Policy on Education—NPE, (1986) and the Programme of Action—POA (1986), several new schemes for the qualitative as well as quantitative improvement of primary education and reaching the goal of UEE, have been initiated by the Government of India, Ministry of Human Resource Development (MHRD). Department of Education. Some of the old schemes have also been revised and strengthened. In this regard, a brief review of the following scheme is provided in this chapter:

1. District Primary Education Programme (DPEP).
2. Elementary Education as a Fundamental Right.
3. Lok Jumbish (LJ).
4. Minimum Levels of Learning (MLLs).
5. National Elementary Education Mission (NEEM).
6. National Programme of Media Publicity and Advocacy of UEE.
7. Non-Formal Education (NFE).
8. National Programme of Nutritional Support to primary Education (NP-NSPE).
9. Operation Blackboard(OBB).
10. Shiksha Karmi Project (SKP).
11. Teacher Education: Restructuring and Reorganization.

5.1 DISTRICT PRIMARY EDUCATION PROGRAMME (DPEP)

DPEP launched in 1993 is a national initiative to achieve Universalisation of Elementary Education (UEE) through district level intervention. The overall goal of the programme is the reconstruction of primary education system to operationalize the strategy of UEE as envisaged in NPC 1986 (as updated in 1992) and its Programme of Action—POA (1992) through decentralised planning and management, disaggregated target setting, community mobilization and population specific planning. The fundamental principle of DPEP is to evolve strategy at state and district level. It goes beyond the conventional packages such as opening of new schools and appointing new teachers and addresses the issues of content, process, quality and equity in education.

The objectives of DPEP are:

(i) to reduce difference in enrolment, drop-out and learning achievement among gender and social groups to less than 5 per cent.

(ii) to reduce overall primary drop-out rates for all students to less than 10 per cent.

(iii) to raise average achievement levels of at least 25 per cent over measured baseline levels and ensuring achievement of basic literacy and numeracy competencies and a minimum of 40 per cent achievement levels in other competencies, by all primary school children.

(iv) to provide, according to national norms, access for all children to primary education (classes I-V), *i.e.*, primary schooling wherever possible, or its equivalent non-formal education.

Coverage: The programme initially launched in 42 districts of 7 States has since then been extended to 219 districts of 15 States.

Funding: DPEP is a centrally sponsored scheme. Funds have also been provided by the World Bank, European Community (EC), International Development Agency (IDA), Overseas Development Agency (ODA) of U.K., UNICEF and the Government of Netherlands.

Impact: Analysis of achievements in 42 districts in 1998 showed the following trend:

(i) The average Gross Enrolment Ratio (GER) went up to 94%.

(ii) Girls participation increased considerably.

(iii) The repetition rate of children showed a decline.

The DPEP has opened 11,000 new formal schools, over 41,000 alternative schools and 10,000 child care centres.

5.2 ELEMENTARY EDUCATION AS A FUNDAMENTAL RIGHT

The Cabinet of the Government of India, in its meeting held on May 16, 1997, approved the proposal of making right to free and compulsory elementary education as a fundamental right. This step was taken on the recommendations of the Committee of State Ministers of Education. It involves amending the Constitution of India. At present there is no such provision in the Constitution. With this amendment, it would be possible to achieve the target of providing UEE. The Government will be required to take vigorous steps including compulsory enforcement of Compulsory Education Acts. The parents would be required to ensure that their children of primary school age attend school. However it is not clear how vast funds required for this would be forthcoming.

5.3 LOK JUMBISH (LJ)

An innovative project called "Lok Jumbish"—People's movement for Education of All—with assistance from Swedish International Development Authority (SIDA) has been undertaken in Rajasthan. The basic objective of the project is to achieve education for all by the year 2000 through people's mobilization and their participation. Government of India approved the first phase of the project for a period of two years, 1992-94 to cover 25 blocks spread over several districts with an estimated cost of Rs. 18 crores to be shared by SIDA, Government of India and Government of Rajasthan in the ratio 3 : 2 : 1. The Phase-I concluded on 30th June, 1994. The Second Phase of the project was taken up for implementation during 1994-98. The project covered 75 blocks.

The LJ, has undertaken environment building activities in 5,683 villages. 383 new schools have been opened while 227 primary schools have been upgraded.

An innovative and successful NFE programme launched by LJ has spread to more than 3,000 centres. The programme has close linkage with the community. The NFE centres are called "Sahaj Shiksha Centres".

5.4 MINIMUM LEVELS OF LEARNING (MLLs)

Meaning: In accordance with the direction of NPE, the initiative was taken in India in 1991 to lay down MLLs to be achieved at the primary stage. The concept of MLLS implies well-defined standards of learning by children. This was done on the basis of the recommendations of the Committee on Minimum Levels of Learning (1990). All children irrespective of their background are expected to reach a minimum level of learning before they finish primary education. Subjects covered are languages, mathematics and environmental studies.

Integration of Components: This new approach integrates various components of curriculum, classroom work, evaluation and teacher education.

Coverage: Most of the State Governments have introduced MLLs in most of their primary schools including local body/private schools.

The first phase of the programme was implemented through 18 voluntary agencies, research institutions and State Councils of Educational Research and Training (SCERT)

The NCERT, the RIEs, SCERTs and DIETs are providing necessary academic and other guidance.

5.5 NATIONAL ELEMENTARY EDUCATION MISSION (NEEM)

The objective of NEEM is to mobilize all the resources—human, financial and institutional—necessary for achieving the goal of UEE. It is expected to boost the efforts being made by the Government and Non-Governmental Organizations (NGOs) to achieve UEE.

5.6 NATIONAL PROGRAMME OF MEDIA PUBLICITY AND ADVOCACY OF UEE

For building up public opinion and mobilizing social support, a national programme of media publicity and advocacy for UEE is proposed to be launched. The programme has four focal points:

(i) Teachers and all those involved in education of children.

(ii) Students and parents of students, particularly non-literate parents.

(iii) Community opinion builders.

(iv) Policy makers and public representatives.

5.7 NON-FORMAL EDUCATION (NFE)

Objective: The NPE envisages a large systematic programme of NFE for those who cannot attend the full day school. It aims at providing education comparable in quality with formal schooling.

Coverage: The focus is on educationally backward states with special attention to urban slum areas, hilly tribal and desert areas and education of working children.

Strategy: (i) Condensed course of about two years' duration.

(ii) Part-time instruction at a place and time convenient to learners in small groups.

(iii) Part-time honorary instructor/supervisor locally recruited and trained.

(iv) Teaching learning material relevant to local environment and learners' needs.

Involvement of NGOs: At present 740 NGOs are implementing NFE programmes in 25 states/ UTs. Hundred per cent central assistance is provided to NGOs for the programme.

5.8 NATIONAL PROGRAMME OF NUTRITIONAL SUPPORT TO PRIMARY EDUCATION (NP-NSPE)

Objective: A nation-wide programme of NP-NSPE launched on August 15, 1995 is intended to give a boost to universalisation of primary education by increasing enrolment, retention and attendance and simultaneously to make an impact on nutritional levels of students in primary classes.

The ultimate aim under the programme is the provision of wholesome cooked/processed food having a calorific value equivalent to 100 gms. of wheat/rice per student per school day.

Implementing Agency: The implementing agencies of the programme, namely, local bodies/authorities, such as, Panchayats and Nagarpalikas are expected to develop institutional arrangements for providing cooked/processed food within a period of two years from the date of commencement of the programme in the local areas. In the interim period, foodgrains (wheat or rice) at the rate of 3 kgs. per student per month subject to a minimum attendance of 80 per cent were being distributed.

Central Support: The central support under this programme is on the following lines:

(i) Provision of foodgrains free of cost to the implementing agencies.

(ii) Reimbursement of transportation cost to district authorities for moving of foodgrains from Food Corporation of India godowns to schools/villages at the rate of Rs. 25/- per quintal as applicable under RPDS.

(iii) Besides, labour charges for conversion of foodgrains into cooked food as well as expenditure on construction of kitchen sheds, will be eligible for coverage under the Poverty Alleviation Schemes being administered by the Ministry of Rural Development.

Coverage: The coverage of children during 1995-96, 1996-97, 1997-98 and 1998-99 was 3.34 crore, 5.57 crore, 9.10 crore and 9.75 crore respectively.

5.9 OPERATION BLACKBOARD (OBB)

Objective: The scheme of Operation Blackboard is a Centrally Sponsored Scheme for bringing about improvement in primary education by providing additional facilities to the schools already established.

Use of the word 'Operation' indicates that there is an urgency in this programme. Its goals are clear and well-defined and the government is determined to achieve these goals with the cooperation of the people within a pre-determined time frame.

Components of the Scheme: There are three components of Operation Blackboard:

1. Provision of at least two reasonably large rooms that are usable in all weathers, with a deep veranda along with separate toilet facilities for boys and girls.

2. Provision of at least two teachers, as far as possible, one of them a woman, in every primary school.

3. Provision of essential teaching and learning materials.

Responsibility: For the operation of the Scheme, responsibility is shared by the Central Government, State Government and the local community.

Role of the community in OBB scheme is as under:

(i) Necessary land for the construction of school building including land for games and sports has to be provided by the local community.

(b) The local community, preferably Village Education Committees, have to give a formal undertaking that they will accept responsibility for repair and maintenance of the building.

(c) The local community has also to accept responsibility for an appropriate fencing around the school compound.

Hundred percent central assistance is provided for appointment of an additional teacher in the single teacher schools.

Operation Blackboard Achievements (up to March 1998)

1. More than 5 lakh primary schools had been provided with teaching-learning equipment.
2. About 1.50 lakh additional teachers had been sanctioned.
3. 1.82 lakh classrooms had been constructed .

Every possible effort is made to utilise locally available material.

In the Eighth Plan, nearly 30% schools were provided the third teacher with enrolment exceeding 100. Likewise 30% upper primary schools were covered under the scheme of supplying teaching-learning material.

Problems: Financial sanctions for the programme reach towards the fag end of the year resulting in purchase of material which sometimes is sub-standard. Sometimes locally made material is not included in the list of approved articles.

Suggestions: 1. Demands for the required material must come from the grass-roots level.

2. Necessary timely sanctions for the equipment needed for storage of material should also be made.

3. It must be ensured that the teachers selected join the institutions immediately after their selection. At the same time, sanctioned posts of teachers may not exist on paper only.

5.10 SHIKSHA KARMI PROJECT (SKP)

Shiksha Karmi Project started in Rajasthan in 1987 remained in operation up to June 1998. It was a scheme jointly sponsored by Swedish International Development Agency (SIDA), Government of India and the State of Rajasthan.

Aims of the Project: 1. Universalisation of education.

2. Checking drop-out.

3. Qualitative improvement of primary education.

Target Area: Socio-economically backward villages in Rajasthan.

Target Group: Specially girls.

Teachers: Replacement of regular teachers by local teachers who were less qualified but specially trained. A *'Shiksha Karmi'* (SK) was a local person with minimum educational qualifications of class VIII for men and class V for women. To overcome the basic lack of qualifications, special training was given to these teachers.

Role of the Community: Active involvement of the Non-Government Organizations (NGOs) and the Village Education Committees (VECs).

Prehar Pathshalas (PPs): (School of Convenient Timings) providing educational programmes for out of school children who cannot attend regular day schools. About 22,000 girls who constituted 71% of learners in PPs have been benefited.

Coverage: About 2 lakh children (1.18 lakh boys and 0.82 lakh girls) in 32 districts, 146 blocks attending 2,697 day schools and 4,335 Prehar Pathshalas. Number of Shiksha Karmis: 6,285.

Evaluation: A unique successful experiment. Positive results with minimum costs.

5.11 TEACHER EDUCATION RESTRUCTURING AND REORGANISATION

Objectives: As envisaged in the NPE and Programme of Action (POA), 1996, a Centrally Scheme of Restructuring and Reorganisation of Teachers Education was taken up in 1987 for the following purposes:

(i) Creating a viable institutional infrastructure of teacher education.

(ii) Building up an academic and technical base for orientation, training and continuous upgrading of knowledge, competence and pedagogical skills of elementary school teachers in the country.

Components of the Scheme: (i) Setting up District Institute of Education and Training (DIETs) in each district to provide academic and resource support to elementary education teachers, and non-formal and adult education instructors.

(ii) Establishment of Colleges of Teacher Education (CTEs) and Institutions of Advanced Study in Education (IASEs) to organise pre-service and in-service training for secondary teachers.

About 450 DIETs have been set up. It has been envisaged to cover all districts in the country *i.e.,* DIET in each district during the Tenth Plan.

DIETs have been playing an important role in the new educational initiatives like DPEP.

5.12 SARVA SHIKSHA ABHIYAN—SSA (EDUCATION FOR ALL MISSION)

Today nearly four out of five children in the age group 6-14 years are in the school. Two out of three persons are functionally literate. Progress achieved is by no means small. But it falls short of meeting the goal of Education for All.

The World Declaration, 'on Education for All—EFA' (1990) adopted in Jomtien gave fillip to national commitment for reaching basic education for all children.

Following are the targets of Education for All:

A. *Primary Education*

1. Providing access to all children in the age group 6-14 through formal primary schools or through other equivalent alternative delivery means by 2003.
2. Completion of five years of primary education by all children by 2007.
3. Completion of eight years of elementary education by all children by 2010.
4. Provision of elementary education of satisfactory quality for all by 2010.

5. One teacher for every 40 children in elementary school. At least two teachers in a primary school.

6. School or alternative school within one kilometre of school-less habitations.

7. New school buildings, classrooms and resource centres, and one classroom for every teacher.

8. Free textbooks to girls and SC/ST children up to Rs. 150 per child.

9. Annual School grant of Rs. 2000 per school and Teacher Grant of Rs. 500 per teacher.

10. Teaching-learning equipment of Rs. 50,000 for uncovered schools.

B. *Adult Education*

(i) Attainment of full literacy in 15-35 age group by 2005.

(ii) Special focus on promotion of literacy among women, scheduled castes/tribes and backward classes.

With a strong resolve to address the issue of Education for All, the Prime Minister in his Independence Day Speech on August 15, 2000 announced the launching of SSA.

The SSA envisages a close partnership of the Government of India, State Governments, Local Bodies and Non-Government Organizations (NGOs).

6

Wastage and Stagnation, Neighbourhood School, Recent Developments and Administration of Primary Education

6.1 WASTAGE AND STAGNATION: DROP-OUTS AND RETENTION IN PRIMARY EDUCATION

Meaning of Wastage and Drop-outs: Wastage implies dropping out of pupils *i.e.,* leaving school before completing a primary stage.

Meaning of Stagnation: The Hartog Committee (1929) defined stagnation as "the retention of a child in a class for a period of more than one year." Normally every student should be promoted at the primary school but this has not happened.

Gravity and Seriousness of Stagnation and Drop-outs: The Education Commission (1964-66) observed, "Wastage and stagnation like headache and fever are not diseases in themselves, they are really symptoms of other diseases in the educational system, the chief among which are the lack of a proper articulation between education and life and the poor capacity of the schools to attract and hold students. To these may be added a third ailment poverty, which falls outside the system."

School Education After Independence, (1988), a publication of NCERT points out the seriousness of the problem of drop-out in these words, "While the increase in enrolment at the elementary stage recorded since 1950 has been satisfactory the problem of drop-outs has been more or less negating the progress achieved. Of every 100 children enrolled in class I, only about 40 reach class V and only about 25 reach class VIII." Since then there has been appreciable improvement.

6.2 DROP-OUT RATES (1960-61 TO 2001-2002)

Table 1: Drop-out Rates at Primary Stage

		1960-61	*1970-71*	*1980-81*	*1990-91*	*1999-00*	*2000-01*	*2001-02*
Class I-V	Boys	61.7	64.5	56.2	40.1	38.7	39.7	38.4
	Girls	70.9	70.9	62.5	46.0	42.3	41.9	39.9
	Total	64.9	70.0	58.7	42.6	40.3	40.7	39.0
Class V-VIII	Boys	75.0	74.6	68.0	59.1	52.0	50.3	52.9
	Girls	85.0	83.4	79.4	65.1	58.0	57.7	56.9
	Total	78.3	77.9	72.7	60.9	54.5	53.7	54.6
Class I-X	Boys	NA	NA	79.8	67.5	66.6	66.4	64.2
	Girls	NA	NA	86.6	76.9	70.6	71.5	68.6
	Total	NA	NA	82.5	71.3	68.3	68.58	66.0

As observed in *Education for All by 2000; Indian Perspective* (1990), "The efficiency of an education system is determined not only by enrolling more and more children but also by ensuring their retention in the system...It may be observed that retention is a very serious problem at the primary stage."

Rate of drop-outs is defined as percentage of the number of children to total enrolment dropping out of the school system. Although there is some improvement yet much more remains to be done.

6.3 CAUSES OF STAGNATION, DROP-OUTS AND WASTAGE

Important causes are as under:

1. Irregular attendance of the pupils.
2. Book-centred, unrelated to life and dull environment.
3. Uninspiring and ineffective methods of teaching.
4. Faulty system of examination and evaluation.
5. Unattractive school environment.
6. Lack of good health, underfed and undernourished children.
7. Rigid school timings.
8. Poverty of the parents.
9. Lack of adequate awareness regarding education among parents.

6.4 SUGGESTED MEASURES FOR CHECKING WASTAGE AND STAGNATION AND DROP-OUTS.

1. *Making School Environment Attractive:* A primary school should have a playground attached to it. There should be no over-crowding in classes so that the teacher can give individual attention. There should be audio-visual aids to excite the curiosity of the young learners. The methods of teaching should be inspiring. Play-way techniques should be adopted in class I to introduce the child pleasantly to school life.

2. *Reforming Curriculum:* The curriculum should be made meaningful and relevant to the environment and life of the children. Work experience should form an integral part of the curriculum.

3. *Adjusting School Timings and Vacation:* There is need for adjusting the school vacations suitably so as to make them synchronize with the sowing and harvesting of crops.

4. *Providing Facilities to Needy Students:* Students whose parents are poor should be provided certain facilities such as free supply of books and stationery, free uniforms and even stipends. Provision of subsidized mid-day meals should be made by enlisting the co-operation of the local community.

5. *Providing Part-time Education:* Facilities for part-time education need to be greatly expanded. The cost of part-time education can be reduced by arranging classes in the regular school building in the evening and employing the same staff by giving them some extra allowance.

6. *Educating Parents:* The parents need to be educated about the importance of education in individual and social development. A massive programme for removing adult illiteracy should be taken up. An educated parent is the best guarantee to ensure that his children also get education. A climate for education should be created by pressing the mass media such as the radio and television into service.

7. *Changing Admission Policy:* All the children to class I should be admitted at the beginning of the session. In no case child should be admitted to school after two months of the beginning of the session.

8. *Provision of Non-Formal Education:* Non-formal education may be defined as an educational activity carried on outside the framework of the established formal system. (*see* 4.7).

9. *Establishing Ungraded School:* As suggested by the Kothari Education Commission, lower primary schools should be ungraded. To begin with, the first two classes should be treated as one unit, later on the 3rd and 4th classes may be considered as another unit. The idea behind ungraded schools is to enable each child to progress at his own pace.

10. *Reconstructing Examination and Evaluation System:* There should be no examination at the middle stage and all children should be automatically promoted to the next class.

11. *Removing Social Evils:* Steps should be taken to remove social evils such as early betrothal or marriage. Social taboos against the education of girls in mixed schools even in the age group 6-11 should be removed. These can be done through persuasion and propaganda.

6.5 NEIGHBOURHOOD SCHOOL

Meaning of Neighbourhood School: The Education Commission (1964-66) explained the concept of neighbourhood school in these words, "The neighbourhood school concept implies, that each school should be attended by 'all' children in the neighbourhood irrespective of caste, creed, community, religion, economic conditions and social status so that there should be no segregation in schools."

The Commission recommended the neighbourhood school first at the lower primary stages and then at the higher primary.

Why Neighbourhood School: The Education Commission put forward the following arguments or advantages of the neighbourhood school:

1. *Social Integration:* The Commission drew attention to the social segregation that now takes place in our primary and secondary schools and pointed out that such segregation should be eliminated if education is to be made a powerful instrument of national development in general, and social and national integration in particular.

2. *Provision of Good Education:* A neighbourhood school will provide 'good' education to children because sharing life with the common people is, in our opinion, an essential ingredient of good education.

3. *More Interest in School:* The establishment of such schools will compel the rich, privileged and powerful classes to take an interest in the system of public education and thereby bring about its early improvement.

4. *Elimination of Strain on Children:* Thousands of students spend two to three hours in reaching schools in large towns and cities when they do not attend the nearby school on account of its poor teaching and infrastructure. Usually they go by school buses and sometimes by private buses or other mode of transport. This puts a heavy physical strain as well as lot of extra financial burden.

5. *Long School Hours:* Long travel results in long school hours indirectly.

6. *Saving of Oil:* Neighbourhood school will eliminate travel by buses. Hence saving of oil.

Following are other considerations that matter in the light of several new factors emerging in big towns and cities.

A Phased Programme: We are of the view that the neighbourhood school concept should be adopted as a long-term goal, to be reached in a well-planned programme spread over the next 20 years. The strategy for its adoption should be as follows:

1. During the next ten years, two programmes should be pursued side by side. The first to improve all primary schools to a minimum level prescribed and to raise about ten per cent of them to a higher standard of quality.

2. Simultaneously, the neighbourhood school system should be introduced at the lower primary stage, as a pilot project, in a few areas where public opinion is favourable to the acceptance of the proposal.

Working of Neighbourhood School: Several attempts have been made by many Departments of Education in the states to implement this concept. The success ratio is not encouraging. Influential parents and all those who can afford expensive education make all efforts to send their children to the schools of their own choice. This results in the non-implementation of the neighbourhood school concept. It is also observed that the standard of State-run schools (Government Schools) and Local Bodies schools, in general, is considered very low. Therefore, people try to send their children to Public Schools which have their own admission criteria.

For the successful functioning of the neighbourhood school, it is very necessary that the standard of teaching of the schools run by the government and local bodies is raised.

6.6 PRIMARY SCHOOL CURRICULUM AND RELATIONSHIP WITH THE NEEDS OF THE COMMUNITY

Interrelationship between the School and the Community: Before describing community need based curriculum, it is very important that the inter-relatedness of the school and the community must be adequately understood. The school should not be treated as an institution outside the community around it. There should be a friendly-oriented partnership between the school and the community. No education programme will be acceptable to the community if the school does not give due consideration to the culture and values of the community. Similarly a school will be able to discharge its functions effectively only when the community appreciates the work of the school and provides full cooperation to it. Both exist for each other.

Meaning of Curriculum: Curriculum does not consist of various subjects like History, Languages, Mathematics, Craft etc. It is the sum total of all school programmes undertaken in the classroom, school playground, school farm, school library, school workshop etc. Farm visits, visits to places of geographical and historical importance etc. also come under the concept of curriculum.

Curriculum related to Real Life: The studies within the school must be related to the life outside. The subject matter of the various subjects of the curriculum should be carefully planned and brought into relation with the problems of society. The curriculum should reflect all that is significant and characteristic in the life of the community in its natural setting. "In the rural areas, the school" according to K. G. Saiyidain "should help the children to realize sympathetically the problems of rural life and train them to take part in it effectively when they have finished schooling..... Similarly in an industrial area the school should gradually make the child familiar with the industrial tools and processes and the conditions of life in the factories so that he may appreciate both the technical and the human elements of the situation."

Likewise a school situated in coastal areas should include activities and programmes related to coastal areas. Apart from content matter of various subjects, following programmes should also be taken up to serve the needs of the community.

(i) *Social Clubs:* Social survey clubs should be organized in schools which should undertake to investigate some of the pressing needs and problems of the surrounding areas, *e.g.*, the survey of the condition of roads, the percentage of literacy, the drainage of the street etc.

(ii) *Social Service Leagues:* As a corollary of the above, social service leagues may be organized. Cleaning the lanes and streets, organizing first-aid centres for the public, constructing some drains etc., are some of the activities to be undertaken by these leagues.

(iii) *Adult Education Centre:* In the evening or in the morning, literacy classes for the adults should be started in the school building. Elder students can do a lot of work.

(iv) *The School as a Recreational Centre:* Recreational programmes like games, dramas, bhajans etc., for children and adults of the community may be undertaken. Radio listening, film shows and exhibitions may be organised.

(v) *Celebration of national days and festivals:* Important community festivals should be organized in the school premises at which the residents of the locality are cordially invited to attend and participate.

(vi) *School Library and Reading Room:* Books catering to the needs of the adults should be provided in the school. The adults may be encouraged to make use of the school library and reading room after regular school hours.

Gandhiji advocated the community-need-based curriculum through the Basic Curriculum but unfortunately the scheme was not given a fair trial (*see* Basic System of Education in the next chapter)

Observations: Theoretically and ideally speaking, the curriculum of a school should be community-need-centred. But the important issue is: What is a community? The term community has several connotations—Village community (agricultural community, labour community, landless agricultural labour community etc.); Muslim community, Hindu community etc, Vaish community, Jat community etc; Urban community, tribal community etc. Then there is the international community.

Every community as stated above cannot have a separate curriculum. Textbooks cannot be written for the needs of a specific community.

Subject matter cannot be designed exclusively in accordance with the needs of a specific community. Of course, various programmes and activities as stated at (i) to (vi) above can be organized very conveniently to serve the needs of the specific community.

6.7 ADMINISTRATION OF PRIMARY EDUCATION

Historical Background

Decentralization Commission (1908): For the first time in the history of modern education in India, recommendation regarding the management of primary education in the village schools was made by the Decentralization Commission, 1908. However, this recommendation remained on paper.

Committee on the Administration of Primary Education (1951-54): The Committee appointed under the Chairmanship of B.G. Kher, Chief Minister, Bombay, considered in detail various aspects of administration of primary education and made important recommendations in this regard.

1. It would be an advantage to associate local bodies with the administration of primary education in some form and for this, it recommended the creation of educational bodies in village panchayats and smaller municipalities.
2. In district local boards and in bigger municipalities, it suggested the constitution of school board for primary education.
3. Inspection should be regarded as the duty of the State Government.
4. The service conditions of primary teachers should be determined by the local bodies concerned with the sanction of the State Government.
5. The Municipal Acts should be amended so as to make the levy of an education less obligatory.
6. In village panchayats, a portion of the total revenue should be earmarked for primary education.

CENTRAL ADVISORY BOARD OF EDUCATION (CABE). COMMITTEE ON DECENTRALIZED MANAGEMENT OF EDUCATION (1993)

Introduction: The Ministry of Human Resource Development, Government of India, appointed a Committee in February 1993 under the Chairmanship of Shri M. Veerappa Moily, Chief Minister of Karnataka to formulate guidelines on decentralized management in the context of 73rd and 74th Constitutional Amendments which provide for a framework of decentralization of powers and authorities to the Panchayati Raj and Municipal bodies at different levels.

The Committee took note of the NPE and Programme of Action, 1986 and made the following important recommendations on the role of the Panchayati Raj Institutions in the field of primary education.

Major Recommendations Relating to Primary Education Administration

1. It recommended the Constitution of Panchayat Standing Committee on Education, Village Education Committee as Subcommittee of Panchayat and Panchayat Samiti Standing Committee on Education and laid down their functions.
2. It recommended the setting up of Zila Parishad Standing Committee on Education and defined its role.
3. It also suggested the formation of Education Committee in Municipal areas and laid down its functions and structure.
4. The Panchayat Standing Committee on Education should perform these functions (i) It should be the endeavour of this committee that every child in every family participates in primary education. It should also exercise supervision over composite upper primary schools.
5. The Committee should receive adequate funds from Zila Parishads and Panchayat Samities. It should also raise funds locally.
6. All existing government schools up to upper primary level with their staff should come under the control of Panchayat Samities. It should appoint staff to

schools under its control. Funds should be made available from the Zila Parishads and other agencies.

7. The Zila Parishads should establish and maintain schools up to secondary levels. It would give grant-in-aid to aided secondary schools and exercise academic supervision.

8. The State Government would lay down academic standards and norms, formulate curricula, prescribe text books, arrange teacher training, determine scales of fee and conduct public examination etc.

Decentralization of Educational Administration

Before discussing the administration of primary education, it would be important to say a few words on decentralization of administration as such as it is the basis of local administration of primary education. The basic function of democratic decentralization is to ensure that the development planning and implementation is more responsive and adaptable to regional and local needs. It ensures people's participation. Part IX of the Constitution of India deals with the functions of the Panchayats and Part IXA with that of Municipalities. Thus it is very clear that local bodies have an important role to play in the administration of primary education.

Role of the Central Government in Primary Education

Free and Compulsory Primary Education: Article 45 under Directive Principles of State Policy, lays down:

"The State shall endeavour to provide within a period of ten years from the commencement of this constitution, for free and compulsory education for all children until they complete the age of fourteen years."

The expression 'State' occurring in this article is defined in Article 12 to include "the Government and Parliament of India and all local or other authorities within the territory of India or under the control of the Government of India."

Thus the task of universal elementary education is the joint responsibility of the Central Government, the State Governments, and the local bodies, as well as the voluntary organizations.

In respect of primary education, the Union Government has some important functions;

(i) acting as co-ordinating agency;

(ii) developing research in elementary education;

(iii) starting pilot projects;

(iv) levelling out the differences between the different States and ensuring equality of opportunity; and

(v) providing financial assistance to the less advanced States.

Role of State Government. The State Government has to shoulder the major responsibility in respect of passing laws. Compulsory Education Acts have been passed and enforced in the States, with the result, that there has been a phenomenal increase in the enrolment of both boys and girls. The programme received considerable attention in the Five Year Plans. It also exercises control on several matters relating to primary education under local bodies.

Primary Education and Local Bodies

Except Assam and Jammu and Kashmir, the major responsibility of primary education rests with the local bodies.

In most of the States, municipalities have the legal authority to administer primary education in their areas. In some States (Gujarat and Maharashtra) only the bigger municipalities are authorised to administer primary education and the smaller ones have to contribute their financial share without having any voice in the management. In some States (Uttar Pradesh) municipalities run secondary schools and colleges also.

In rural areas, District Boards (now called Zila Parishads) are made responsible for administering primary education. Some of them run secondary schools also. In some States (Andhra Pradesh and Rajasthan) Panchayat Samities in Block areas and Zila Parishads in non-Samiti areas administer primary education.

With the introduction of Panchayati Raj, and the policy of democratic decentralization, the Local Bodies have been playing an important part in the maintenance and improvement of primary education. They now have a three tier system (two tier in some States) of organization—(1) the village panchayat at the village level, (2) Panchayat Samities at the Block level, and (3) Zila Parishads at the district level.

Recruitment of staff is generally done through a selection Committee on which the District Education Officer also serves. The State Government is exclusively responsible for training of teachers, prescribing syllabi and preparing textbooks and the local Bodies have to follow them. The State Government gives grants-in-aid to Local Bodies. The district boards receive more generous grants than municipalities.

Merits of Administration of Primary Education at Local Level

Following are the major advantages:

1. We have accepted democracy as a way of life and form of government : Educational administration, therefore, should be decentralized.
2. Administration of primary education at the local level will stimulate local initiative.
3. Administration of primary education at the local level leads to sharing of financial burden of the Central and State Governments.
4. There is a strong tradition of local participation in education in our country.
5. The administration at the local level is very helpful in solving local educational problems.
6. The concentration of authority in a few hands kills the initiative of the local people and undermines authority. Local administration is conducive to creativity in education.
7. The experience of foreign countries also supports the scheme of educational administration at the local level.

Drawbacks/Limitations of Administration of Primary Education at Local Level

1. There is the element of undue interference of political leaders and state administration in the day to day functioning of schools.

2. Community, religious or political bias is likely to vitiate the environment of the primary school.

3. In view of limited funds at the disposal of local bodies, primary education is likely to suffer.

4. The local bodies in general, do not have competent and efficient staff as they are low paid and only join this service when no other avenue or government service is available.

5. It is observed that mostly being illiterate, the members of Education Committee are not able to understand educational issues in their proper perspective.

6. The Education Commission 1964-66 has very significantly observed, "Their main weaknesses, however, are the harassment caused to teachers through frequent transfers and postings and through involvement in local functions and policies."

7. The instructional standards at the educational institutions managed by local bodies do not compare favourably with the educational institutions managed by other bodies.

Summing up: A good deal of criticism is unfounded. Perhaps there is no area of life which has remained unaffected by party politics.

The real problems are primarily two—(i) The bureaucracy at the higher level is reluctant to part with power, (ii) Financial resources at the disposal of local bodies for primary education are very meager. They should share some sources with the State Government.

7

Basic Education

Wardha Scheme of Education

7.1 BRIEF HISTORY OF BASIC EDUCATION

1. *Gandhiji's Educational Experiments*: It was in July, 1937 that M. K. Gandhi (Mahatma Gandhi) wrote in the *'Harijan'*, "By education I mean an all-round drawing out of the best in child and man—body, mind and spirit. Literacy itself is no education. I would, therefore, begin the child's education by teaching it a useful handicraft and enabling it to produce from the moment it begins its training. Thus every school can be made self-supporting, the condition being that the state takes over the manufacture of these schools." Earlier, Gandhiji had conducted educational experiments at Phoenix Settlement in 1904 and Transval Ashram (Tolstoy Farm) in 1911 in South Africa. On his return to India, Gandhi set up the Sabarmati Ashram at Ahmedabad in May 1915 and started a school attached to the Ashram. In this school, literary training was imparted through the crafts of carpentry and spinning.

2. *Wardha Education Conference (1937)*: In October 1937, a Conference of National Workers was held at Wardha under the presidentship of Gandhiji and after considering his ideas, the Conference passed the following resolutions:

(i) That in the opinion of the Conference, free and compulsory education be provided for seven years on a nation-wide scale.

(ii) That the medium of instruction be the mother tongue.

(iii) That the Conference endorses the proposal made by Mahatma Gandhi, that the process of education throughout this period should centre round some productive form of manual work, and that all other abilities to be developed or training to be given should, as far as possible, be integrally related to the central handicraft chosen with due regard to the environment of the child.

(iv) That the Conference expects that the system of education will be gradually able to cover the remuneration of teachers.

3. Zakir Hussain Committee (1938): The Wardha Conference appointed a Committee of distinguished educationists under the Chairmanship of Dr. Zakir Hussain to present a detailed curriculum and syllabi. Among others who served on the Committee, Prof. K. G. Saiyidians's name is prominent. The report of the Committee, published in 1938, came to be known as the Wardha Scheme of Education.

The main outlines of the seven years course of Basic Education was as under:

1. *The Basic Craft:* Selection to be made by schools, out of the following:
   (a) Spinning and Weaving.
   (b) Carpentry.
   (c) Agriculture.
   (d) Fruit and Vegetable Gardening.
   (e) Leather Works.
   (f) Any other craft for which local and geographical conditions favour.
2. Mother Tongue.
3. Mathematics.
4. Social Studies.
5. General Science.
6. Drawing.
7. Music.
8. Hindustani.

4. *Congress Session (1938)*: The Scheme was approved by Gandhiji and was placed before The Indian National Congress at its Haripura Session held in March 1938. The Congress accepted the Scheme.

5. *Congress Ministries (1937-39)*: After the introduction of the Government of India Act (1935), elections were held in the country. The Congress Ministries formed in 9 provinces took several steps for the promotion of Basic Education. However, after their resignation in 1939 before the Second World War, the progress of Basic Education declined.

6. *Sargent Report or the Report of the Post-War Educational Development in India (1944)*: The Report endorsed the Basic System of Education as contained in the Wardha Scheme.

7. *Concept of Basic Education (1956)*: With a view to removing misunderstanding on the concept of Basic Education, the Basic Standing Committee of the Central Advisory Board of Education, classified, the concept of Basic Education in a publication '*Concept of Basic Education*' (1956)

8. *Assessment Committee on Basic Education (1955-56)*: The Ministry of Education, Government of India appointed the Assessment Committees with G. Ramachandran as its convene. The Committee gave its recommendations on the role of the Central Government, State Governments, Universities, Administration, Basic Teachers Training Colleges, Basic Schools and the Public.

9. *Five Year Plans and Basic Education*: Since the Government of India had accepted the system of Basic Education as the national system of education, sincere efforts were made in all directions to popularize it.

The progress of basic education in the four plans is set out below:

Schools	*1st Plan*	*2nd Plan*	*3rd Plan*	*4th Plan*
Junior basic schools	33,379	42,971	1,00,000	1,53,000
As percentage of total primary schools	15.9	15.4	29.2	30.9
Senior basic schools	318	4,842	11,940	16,700
As percentage of total middle schools	1.9	22.3	30.2	28.9
Basic training schools	114	520	715	1,424
As percentage of total number of training schools	15	56	70	100

(*See* 7.6 also)

7.2 REASONS FOR THE FORMULATION OF THE SCHEME OF BASIC EDUCATION BY GANDHIJI

Gandhiji realized fully that the system of education introduced by the British rulers was unreal and artificial. He said, "I am convinced that the present system of education is not only wasteful but positively harmful. Most of the boys are lost to the parents and to the occupations to which they were born. They pick up evil habits, effect urban ways and get a smattering of something which may be anything but education." Gandhiji also felt, "The present system of education does not meet the requirements of the country in any shape or form. English has been made medium of education in all the highest branches of learning. It has created a permanent bar between the highly educated few and the uneducated many." He further added, " We have up to now concentrated on stuffing children's minds with all kinds of information without even thinking or stimulating or developing them. Let us now cry a halt and concentrate on educating the child properly through manual work not as a side activity but as a prime means of intellectual activity."

7.3 FUNDAMENTAL FEATURES OF BASIC EDUCATION

The fundamental features of the scheme having undergone lot of changes are as follows:

1. A school of say 5½ hours could roughly be divided on the following basis:

Physical activities	20 minutes
Mother Tongue	40 minutes
Social Studies and General Science	60 minutes
Art	40 minutes
Arithmetic	20 minutes
Craft work including study of correlated subjects	2½ hours

Thus the craft work will have 2½ hours instead of 3 hours and 20 minutes as originally proposed.

2. Free and compulsory education to be given in 8 years (from 6 to 14 years) in two stages, instead of 7 to 14. The junior stage will cover five years and the senior 3 years.
3. The medium of instruction is to be the mother-tongue.
4. Education is to centre round some form of productive work. The social and physical environment should be used for correlation in addition to craft.
5. The self-supporting aspect is not to be over-emphasized. The sale proceeds of the finished goods should be able to help the school to cover some part of its expenditure.
6. External examinations are to be abolished. The day-to-day work of the students is to be the determining factor.
7. Textbooks to be avoided as far as possible.
8. Cleanliness and health, citizenship, play and recreation are to be given sufficient importance.

7.4 DISTINCTIVE MERITS OF THE SCHEME OF BASIC EDUCATION

Craft work in Schools: Modern educational thought is practically unanimous in commending the idea of educating children through some suitable form of productive work. This method is considered to be the most effective approach to the problem of providing an integral all-sided education.

Psychologically, it is desirable, because it relieves the child from the tyranny of a purely academic and theoretical instruction against which its active nature is always making a healthy protest. It balances the intellectual and practical elements of experience, and may be made an instrument of educating the body and the mind in co-ordination. The child acquires not the superficial literacy which implies, often without warrant, a capacity to read the printed page, but the far more important capacity of using hand and intelligence for some constructive purpose. This, if we may be permitted to use the expression, is "the literacy of the whole personality."

Socially considered, the introduction of such practical productive work in education, to be participated in by all the children of the nation, will tend to break down the existing barriers of prejudice between manual and intellectual workers, harmful alike for both. It will also cultivate in the only possible way a true sense of the dignity of labour and of human solidarity—an ethical and moral gain of incalculable significance.

Economically considered, carried out intelligently and efficiently, the scheme will increase the productive capacity of our workers and will also enable them to utilize their leisure advantageously.

From the strictly educational point of view, greater concreteness and reality can be given to the knowledge acquired by children by making some significant craft the basis of education. Knowledge will thus become related to life, and its various aspects will be correlated with one another.

Educative Aspect of the Craft Extracts from Zakir Hussain Committee Report: First, the craft or productive work chosen should be rich in educative possibilities. It should find natural points of correlation with important human activities and interests, and should extend into the whole content of the school curriculum. Later in the report, in making our recommendations on the choice of basic crafts, we have given special attention to this point, and we would urge all who are in any way concerned with this scheme to bear this important consideration in mind. The object of this new educational scheme is not primarily the production of craftsmen able to practice some craft mechanically, but rather the exploitation for educative purposes of the resources implicit in craft work. This demands that productive work should not only form a part of the school curriculum—its craft side—but should also inspire the method of teaching all other subjects. Stress should be laid on the principles of co-operative activity, planning, accuracy, initiative and individual responsibility in learning...By merely adding to the curriculum one other subject—weaving, spinning, or carpentry—while all other subjects are still taught in the traditional way we shall, we are convinced, encourage passive assimilation and the division of knowledge into unintelligible water-tight compartments, and thus defeat the real purpose and spirit of this scheme.

Ideal of Citizenship Implicit in the Scheme: This scheme is designed to produce workers, who will look upon all kinds of useful work—including, manual labour, even scavenging—as honourable, and who will be both able and willing to stand on their own feet.

Such a close relationship of the work done at school to the work of the community will also enable the children to carry the outlook and attitudes acquired in the school environment into the wider world outside. Thus the new scheme which we are advocating will aim at giving the citizens of the future a keen sense of personal worth, dignity and efficiency, and will strengthen in them the desire for self-improvement and social service in a co-operative community.

Self-supporting Aspect of the Scheme: It seems necessary to make a few remarks about the "self-supporting" aspect of the scheme, as this has occasioned considerable misunderstanding. We wish to make it quite clear that we consider the scheme of basic education outlined by the Wardha Conference and here elaborated to be sound in itself. Even if it is not "self-supporting" in any sense, it should be accepted as a matter of sound educational policy and as an urgent measure of national reconstruction. It is fortunate, however, that this good education will also incidentally cover the major portion of its running expenses...

Apart from its financial implications, we are of opinion that a measurable check will be useful in ensuring thoroughness and efficiency in teaching and in the work of the students. Without some such check, there is great danger of work becoming slack and losing all educative value. This is only too obvious from the experience of educationists who from time to time have introduced "manual training" or other "practical activities" in their schools.

But here we must sound a necessary note of warning. There is an obvious danger that in the working of this scheme the economic aspect may be stressed at the sacrifice of the cultural and educational objectives. Teachers may devote most of their attention and energy to extracting the maximum amount of labour from children, while neglecting the intellectual, social and moral implications and possibilities of craft training. This point must be constantly kept in mind in the training of teachers as well as in the direction of the work of the supervisory staff and must colour all educational activity.

Following merits may be summed up:

1. Basic system of education is craft-centred.
2. It is related to community life and needs.
3. It is based on the concept 'learning while earning'.
4. It is work centred.
5. It stresses dignity of labour.
6. It advocates mother-tongue as the medium of instruction.
7. It imparts education through correlation.
8. In it, learning is by doing.
9. It is based on democratic values.
10. It provides greater freedom to the teacher and the taught.
11. It is not a class education.
12. It attempts to create a social order in which there is no unnatural division between 'haves' and 'have nots'.
13. It is for rural as well as urban areas.

Significance of the Word 'Basic' in Basic Education: The word 'Basic' is derived from the word 'Base' which means the bottom or the foundation of a thing upon which the whole thing rests or is made.

1. It is basic because it is closely related to the basic needs and interests of the child.
2. It is basic because it comes first in the primary period of our education.
3. It is basic because it makes use of the native potentialities of the child.

4. It is basic because it is intimately related to the basic occupations of the community.

5. It is basic because it is for the common man of the country who is the foundation and backbone of our nation's life.

6. It is considered basic because it is based on ancient Indian culture.

7. It is basic because it lays down the minimum educational standards which every Indian child is entitled to receive without any distinction of caste or creed.

7.5 DEMERITS, LIMITATIONS AND CAUSES OF FAILURE OF BASIC SYSTEM OF EDUCATION

There is no denying the fact that Basic Education has not been a success. Even Dr. Zakir Hussain was constrained to remark "Basic Education as practised is a fraud." Some of the causes for the failure of Basic Education are discussed here.

1. *Misunderstanding About Concept:* There had always been confusion about understanding the concept of Basic Education. In the words of Professor Saiyidain, "The Basic Education Movement is in some ways, a radical departure both in theory and practice and it requires a careful reorientation of ideas, attitudes and techniques. It is therefore, a matter of no great surprise—though it is certainly one of disappointment—that the full implication of basic approach has not yet been realized by many teachers and educational administrators."

2. *Economic Aspect Over-emphasised:* Too much emphasis was laid on economic aspect or the productivity aspect and this fact was responsible for the unpopularity of Basic Education. Teachers remained busy either in the garden or in the workshop and they lost sight of educational objectives of the craft.

3. *Lack of Competent Teachers:* Most of the teachers who taught in basic schools were not trained for this type of education.

4. *Dearth of Textbooks:* Suitable books to teach in accordance with the requirements of Basic Education were not made available.

5. *High Cost of Basic Education:* A good Basic school can only be established with a good deal of initial cost on the purchase of equipment for different crafts. In addition to this cost, there is always a recurring expenditure on the successful running of a good craft. The income from the products is not commensurate with the financial outlay.

6. *Lack of Provision for Individual Differences:* It failed to provide for the individual differences of the pupils and, therefore, the drawbacks of traditional system of education continued to harm the individuality of the child.

7. *Artistic and Aesthetic Aspects Neglected*: In some of the Basic schools, these aspects were not attended to. Children did very little art work which was generally confined to the drawing of charts depicting the techniques of correlation. The appreciation of art or beauty was altogether neglected.

8. *Rigidity:* The scheme was rigid in several aspects and did not accept even sound and practical suggestions. Any such technique for primary school children must be flexible and must accept suggestions with the change of time and objectives of education.

9. *Apathy of Administration:* In the words of Assessment Committee on Basic Education (1956), "It is at the administrative level today, more than any other, that serious difficulties arise in the development of Basic Education. Departments are concerned with innumerable problems. Basic Education is a

small and side item in their programmes of work. In none of the States did we find a Director of Public Instruction, to whom Basic Education was an issue of utmost importance nor did we find any of them fully conversant with the problems of Basic Education in their respective States."

In view of above, it is sometimes said by critics that Basic Education is a Fad, A Fallacy, A Farce and A Fraud.

Some Critics of Basic System of Education

A. N. Basu. In a hurry to pay more attention to craft, it has neglected the child.

P. S. Naidu. (i) Child is considered as a means—the end being earning capacity.

(ii) In the training for teachers, child psychology is conspicuous by its absence.

(iii) It ignores 'effective' aspects of human nature.

(iv) The Scheme will hit the professional artisans hard by creating ruinous competition.

(v) It is absurd to hang all knowledge from the peg of a single craft.

(vi) It has no religious element.

J. Lahri: There is lack of sufficient intensive and repetitive drill.

R. K. Singh: (a) Craft is only a slogan, a fiction, which is practised on ceremonial occasions for the benefit of visitors.

(b) Literacy and knowledge of subject matter are considered to be of secondary importance.

S. Natarajan: The emphasis on craft is out of place in a community which has its face turned towards developing its economy to the full.

'Educational Review' (i) Everything cannot be taught through craft or practical activities.

(ii) Teaching in basic schools has lost emphasis on the quantum of knowledge stipulated to be conveyed to the children during particular periods.

7.6 EDUCATION COMMISSION (1964-66) AND WITHERING AWAY OF THE BASIC SYSTEM OF EDUCATION: RELEVANCE OF BASIC EDUCATION TODAY

The Commission believed that the essential elements of basic education were fundamentally sound, but some modifications were needed. It observed, "The movement of basic education launched by Mahatma Gandhi more than 25 years ago, proposing a new type of elementary education for the nation which would centre round some form of manual and productive work and have intimate links with the life of the community, was a landmark in the history of education in India. It was a revolt against the sterile, book-centred, examination-oriented system of education that had developed along traditional lines during several decades of British rule. It created a national ferment, which may not have transformed the quality of education at the primary stage, but which has certainly left its impact on educational thought and practice on a much wider sphere. We believe that the essential elements of the system are fundamentally sound, and that with necessary modification these can form part of education, not only at the primary stage but at all stages in our national system. These elements are: (1) productive activity in education; (2) correlation of the curriculum with the productive activity and the physical and social environment; and (3) intimate contact between the school and the local community."

The Commission popularized the concept of 'work experience' and saw that two ideas—work experience and basic education—were essentially similar. It stated, "In the curricula of most contemporary school systems, particularly in the socialist countries of Europe, a place is found for what is variously called 'manual work' or 'work-experience'. In our country, a revolutionary experiment was launched by Mahatma Gandhi in the form of basic education. The concept of work experience is essentially similar. It may be described as a redefinition of his educational thinking in terms of a society launched on the road to industrialization."

The Commission gave a call for the reorientation of the basic education programme in view of the changed character and need of the new society.

After the *Report of the Education Commission* (1946-66) the phrase 'work-experience' came in more frequent use than that of 'basic education'. The Government of India's Resolution on National Policy on Education (1968) has not made any mention of 'basic education'. It, however, declares that work-experience should become an integral part of education.

The Ishwar Bhai Patel Committee (1977) and the Adiseshiah Committee (1978) used the term 'Socially Useful Productive Work'—SUPW

The National Institute of Basic Education set up by the Government of India, which functioned as an important department of NCERT for the purpose of research, extension and training in basic education, has been wound up.

Some educators consider that recommendations of the Kothari Commission came as 'Death Certificate' of Basic Education. If the recommendations of the Kothari Commission are any indication, Basic education will remain 'a matter of history of education'.

Again in the National Policy on Education 1986, there is no mention of Basic system of education at the school stage.

It must, however, be admitted that the Basic System of Education was the forerunner of the concept of 'Vocationalization of Education'. The concepts of 'Work Experience' and SUPW derive their inspiration from Basic Education.

8

Secondary Education

8.1 OBJECTIVES OF SECONDARY EDUCATION

The formulation of educational objectives in general and of each stage in particular is very crucial in the entire educational enterprise as the objectives determine the contents, methods, discipline and all other aspects of education. Another point of great importance is that the objectives of education are determined in accordance with the needs and requirements of a country. Here an attempt is made to discuss the objectives of secondary education in the light of the recommendations of committees and commissions on education.

Secondary Education Commission (1952-53)

The Secondary Education Commission, appointed by the Government of India, under the Chairmanship of Dr. A. Lakshmanaswami Mudaliar, Vice-Chancellor, Madras University, went into all aspects of secondary education in the light of the changed needs of India and made recommendations on all aspects of secondary education. While formulating the aims of secondary education, the Commission observed, "As political, social and economic conditions change and new problems arise, it becomes necessary to re-examine carefully and restate clearly the objectives which education at each stage, should keep in view. Moreover, this statement must take into account not only the facts of the existing situation but also the direction of its development and the nature and type of the social order that we envisage for the future to which education has to be geared."

The Secondary Education Commission pointed out the following needs of India:

(a) Transformation of India into a secular democratic republic.
(b) Improvement of productive efficiency.
(c) Stimulation of a cultural renaissance.

In the light of the above mentioned needs the Secondary Education Commission stated the following aims of secondary education:

1. Developing democratic Citizenship.
2. Improvement of vocational efficiency.
3. Development of personality.
4. Development of qualities of leadership.

1. **Developing Democratic Citizenship.** Citizenship is a very exacting and challenging responsibility for which every citizen has to be carefully trained. For democratic citizenship, education should develop then the following five qualities:

(i) *Capacity for clear thinking*: The first requisite in this connection is to develop capacity for clear thinking and receptivity to new ideas. This is the hall-mark of educated mind. A democratic citizen should be able to sift fact from fiction and reject what is bad.

(ii) *Clearness in speech and writing*; It is an essential pre-requisite for successful living in a democracy which is based not on force but on free discussion, persuasion and peaceful exchange of ideas.

(iii) *Education for living*: Education should initiate the students into the many-sided art of living in a community graciously. This art should be imbibed. Amongst the qualities which should be cultivated for this purpose are: (a) discipline, (b) co-operation, (c) social sensitiveness, and (d) tolerance.

(iv) *Sense of true patriotism*: The concept of patriotism is three fold: (a) a sincere appreciation of the social and cultural achievements of one's country, (b) a readiness to recognise its weaknesses frankly and work for its eradication, and (c) an earnest resolve to serve it to the best of one's ability. Education should develop these.

(v) *Sense of world citizenship*: Lastly, education must instill in an individual sense of one world and we must discharge our duties accordingly. 'My country—right or wrong' is a dangerous slogan these days. These are the days of internationalism.

2. **Improvement of Vocational Efficiency.** We must concentrate on increasing the productive efficiency of students. New attitude towards work has to be created. No work is lowly. Secondly, education is to lay stress on technical skill and efficiency.

3. **Development of Personality.** The third aim of education includes:

(i) to release the sources of creative energy in the students so that they may be able to appreciate their cultural heritage;

(ii) to cultivate rich interests.

4. **Development of Qualities of Leadership.** The special function of the secondary school in this context, is to train persons who will be able to assume the responsibility of leadership—in the social, political, industrial or cultural fields—in their own groups of community or locality.

Aims of Secondary Education and the Education Commission (1964-66)

The Education Commission stated the overall objectives of education and not of a particular stage. It set forth the following objectives which are applicable to the secondary education as well.

1. Relating education to productivity.
2. Strengthening social and national integration.
3. Consolidating democracy as a form of government and helping the country to adopt it as a way of life.
4. Hastening the process of modernization.
5. Striving to build character by cultivating social, moral and spiritual values.

Ishwarbhai Patel Committee (1977)

Ishwarbhai Patel Committee (1977) on the Review of Curriculum lists the following objectives of secondary education (VIII/IX-X):

1. Acquisition of the skills and habits of self-learning.

2. Acquisition of a broad-based general education consisting of science, mathematics, social sciences, languages and socially useful productive labour.

3. Acquisition of habits of helpful living and participation in games, sports and athletics for the maintenance of physical fitness.

4. Development of aesthetic appreciation and creativity through participation in artistic activities.

5. Exploring the world of work and understanding the realities of life in order to prepare for a confident entry into the world outside the school.

6. Participation in and promotion of social activities in the school and the community in such a way as to imbibe democratic values and to work towards the achievement of equality through service to weak and the deprived.

National Policy on Education and Objectives of Secondary Education

Though the NPE has not listed the separate aims of secondary education, yet from Part 5-B of the Policy, following specific aims emerge:

(i) To expose the students to the differentiated roles of science, the humanities and social sciences.

(ii) To provide children with a sense of history and national perspective.

(iii) To give children opportunities to understand their constitutional duties and rights as citizens.

8.2 STRUCTURE OR PATTERN OF SECONDARY EDUCATION: 4 YEARS OF SECONDARY EDUCATION IN 10+2

Present Position of the Structure of Secondary Education: The term secondary education has different meanings in India as well as in different countries. Even in the year 2000, no clear-cut concept of secondary education had emerged. The NCERT *'National Curriculum Framework for School Education'* (2000) used the two terms: Secondary Stage (Class IX and X) and Higher Secondary Stage (Class XI and XII). The Central Board of Secondary Education, lists Secondary Stage (Class IX and X) and the Senior Secondary Stage (Class XI and XII).

The National Policy on Education 1986 and as modified in 1992 has explained in Part III, the structure of the National System of Education as, "The National System of Education envisages a common education structure. The 10+2+3 structure has now been accepted in all parts of the country. Regarding the further break-up of the first 10 years efforts will be made to move towards an elementary system comprising 5 years of primary education and 3 years of upper primary, followed by 2 years of High School. Efforts will also be made to have the +2 stage accepted as part of school education throughout the country." In Part V, the NPE has used the term secondary education which indicates that it includes classes IX to XII.

Brief History of Structure of Secondary Education

(i) *The Wood's Despatch:* (a) Indigenous Elementary Schools, (b) Middle Schools, (c) High Schools, (d) University.

(ii) *Indian Education Commission or Hunter Commission (1882-83):* (a) Primary, (b) Middle, (c) High, (d) Secondary (Middle and High)

(iii) *Calcutta University Commission or Sadler Commission:* High School and intermediate to constitute secondary education (12 years of schooling).

(iv) *Secondary Education (1952-53):* Secondary education after 4 or 5 years of Primary or Junior Basic as under: (a) A Middle or Junior Secondary or Senior Basic which should cover a period of 3 years. (b) A Higher Secondary stage which should cover a period of 4 years.

(v) *Committee on Emotional Integration (1962):* (a) High School Stage (Standard IX-X), (b) Higher Secondary Stage (Standard XI- XII).

(vi) *Education Commission (1964-66):* After 7 or 8 years of primary and higher primary stage. (a) A lower secondary or high school stage or three or two years of general education or one to three years in vocational education. (b) A higher secondary stage of two years of general education or one to three years of vocational education.

(vii) *National Committee on +2+3 Educational Structure (1973):* (a) Secondary Stage (IX and X), (b) Higher Secondary Stage (XI and XII)

(viii) *Review Committee or Ishwarbhai Patel Committee (1977):* Lower Secondary Stage (Classes VIII/IX-X)

(ix) *National Review Committee on Higher Secondary Education (1978):* Higher Secondary Education (Class XI-XII)

8.3 WHY 15 YEARS OF SCHOOLING INCLUDING 4 YEARS OF SECONDARY EDUCATION OR UPGRADING OF SECONDARY EDUCATION OR 10+2 NEW STRUCTURE/PATTERN OF EDUCATION?

The duration of secondary education was increased by one year with the introduction of the New Pattern of Education, popularly called 10+2 in 1975 by the Central Board of Secondary Education in its affiliated schools. Since then it has been adopted almost by all States and Union Territories. Under this pattern, there is 12 years of schooling (8 years of elementary and 4 years of secondary) and three years of the first degree. Previously, secondary education structure consisted of 3 years.

Now, why 15 years! Besides other things, it was felt the standard of education must be raised if India has to take her rightful place among other nations. No advanced country in the world honours a young man with the award of a first degree in less than 15 years of preparation and hard work. In the U.S.A., the high school is up to 12th grade which is followed by a 4-year course in a college or university leading to a bachelor's degree. In the erstwhile U.S.S.R., the complete secondary education ended with grade 10 and then began 5 years of higher education in a university. In England, after 13 years of schooling, three years are needed in a college or university to obtain the first degree. Thus it will take total 16 years in U.S.A., 15 years in U.S.S.R. and 16 years in England to be awarded the first degree. Which is why a graduate from India was not considered equivalent to a graduate in U.K. and therefore a graduate needed to graduate again in U.K. before pursuing higher education for which B.A. is the minimum qualification. The 10+2+3 pattern or extension of one year in secondary education provides the answer.

The new structure of secondary education does not envisage mere addition of one year to the total period of secondary education. It envisages raising the standard of education.

8.4 EVALUATION OF THE 'NEW STRUCTURE' OR PATTERN OF SECONDARY EDUCATION IN PARTICULAR AND EDUCATIONAL STRUCTURE IN GENERAL (10+2+3)

Historical Educational Background and Introduction of the Structure: (At that time it was called 'New' and now it is the 'Present pattern'). Towards the end of Third Five Year Plan, a need was felt to have a comprehensive review of the educational system of the country with a view to initiating a fresh and more determined effort at educational reconstruction. Accordingly, the Kothari Commission (1964-66) was appointed to advise Government on the national pattern of education and on the general principles and policies for the development of education at all stages and in all aspects. One of the most important recommendations of the Education Commission headed by Dr. Kothari was to have a uniform pattern in the country. This recommendation was discussed and debated at various educational forums and was made as the focus of the recommendations of the Resolution of National Policy on Education (1968). The Resolution stated, "It will be advantageous to have a broadly uniform educational structure in all parts of the country. The ultimate objective should be to adopt the 10+2+3 pattern, the higher stage of 2 years being located in schools, colleges or both according to local conditions."

The Government of India, Ministry of Education, appointed a National Committee in 1973 to formulate practical measures for introducing the new pattern of 10+2+3.

The New Structure/Pattern was first introduced is Delhi in 1975 and in all secondary schools affiliated to the Central Board of Secondary Education. Now almost all the States and Union Territories have adopted the pattern.

Main Characteristics of the New Structure/Pattern

1. *Duration:* (a) The first degree course is of three years duration after 12 years of schooling. (b) It provides for 12 years of schooling in place of 11. (c) The first university degree is obtained after 15 years of study. (d) It provides for adopting selective approach in upgrading the existing higher secondary schools. (e) There is a common 10-year schooling.

2. *Curriculum:* (a) It provides for the compulsory teaching of two languages, Mathematics, Science, Social Studies. Work-experience, Moral Education and Physical Education in classes IX and X. (b) It provides for two levels of courses in various subjects—advanced level and ordinary. (c) It takes care of individual differences of students by providing for grouping of students based on their attainment in different subjects. It will be possible to have a student doing advanced level work in one subject and ordinary level work in another.

3. *Vocational Courses and Socially Useful Productive Work:* (a) It aims at establishing a close link between the school and the environment by modifying the present emphasis on theoretical aspects of education. (b) It provides for appropriate opportunity to students to take up vocational courses.

4. *Diversification after Class X:* It provides for diversification after 10 years of schooling in Class XI and XII.

Merits of the New Structure

1. *Mature Students:* With a 2-year preparation, instead of one-year after class X, students will become more mature and will be able to do more advanced work than is possible now.

2. *Specialization at the Appropriate Time:* The New Pattern provides reasonable opportunities at the appropriate time to the students to take decisions about the particular stream to be studied by them after a terminal point. Thus it does away with the criticism that is usually leveled against the higher secondary system that the students are required to take a decision at too early an age. Modern research has pointed out that streaming of pupils into specialized groups from class IX is undesirable. The world trends in secondary education are in the direction of lengthening the period of general education and postponing diversification and specialization to the higher stage of secondary education.

3. *Raising Standard of Education:* The indiscriminate rush to universities may be stemmed and more places in colleges may be released for those best fitted for higher education. This would tend to raise the standard of higher education.

4. *Vocationalization of Education:* Vocationalization of education at the higher secondary stage is another limiting factor in higher education. Vocationalization is an essential and urgent reform intertwined with the New Pattern and the programme for this purpose will have to be based upon detailed man-power estimates formulated on the basis of district surveys. It must ensure that the school leaver is ready to enter the world of work either as an employee or as a self-employed person.

5. *Education for Employment:* The New Pattern envisages great help in providing employment after completing secondary education. Many people can now enter public services after class XII. The position is comparatively less advantageous after class XI when one is below the prescribed minimum age (generally 18) or does not warrant enough maturity for employment.

6. *Implementation of National Programmes of School Improvement:* A broadly uniform pattern in all parts of the country is intended to facilitate the implementation of educational programmes, production of books and teaching material, reforms in evaluation and training of teachers. Centre can play a stimulating, innovative, consultative and promotional role in educational development and can make larger grants available for the Central as well as Centrally sponsored sectors.

7. *Strengthening National Unity:* A broad uniform structure is conducive to the strengthening of national unity and emotional integration. Uniformity and unity have both literal and psychological proximity. Both words have the prefix 'uni' meaning 'one'. Both the words connote 'oneness'. India very much needs this sense of 'oneness' belonging the awareness of parts that constitute a whole. The uniformity of educational structure in all parts of the country brings up a visual image of belonging to the same country, doing the same thing, intellectually maturing the same way, maintaining the same standards, achieving the common objectives and nearing the common goals.

8. *Inter-State Adjustments:* Uniformity of structure facilitates education of the mobile population which is continuously increasing in the country.

Differences in structures and standards cause considerable inconvenience to students migrating from State to State. The opening of Central Schools by the Central School Organization may be one small answer to a part of the problem, but it does not solve the whole problem.

Limitations of the Structure

1. *Heavy Curriculum:* The curriculum laid down for students is very heavy.

2. *Ill-equipped Schools:* The scheme of vocationalization could not be successful as necessary facilities were not provided.

3. *Non-availability of Teachers:* Suitable teachers for work-experience not available. Likewise, there is dearth of trained teachers for teaching vocational subjects.

4. *Non-Recognition of Vocational Qualifications:* Students who pursue vocational courses find it difficult to pursue higher education and at the same time they are not adequately equipped to take up a vocation.

5. *Costly Scheme:* Adding one more class to school involves a lot of expenditure on the part of Central Government, the State Governments and private bodies.

6. *Loss to Parents and Children:* The parents have to support their children for 12 years instead of 11 under the old system. Thus the parents spend more money in educating their children in school. The students themselves spend 12 years in schools and 15 years in getting the first degree. Earlier they spent 14 years.

The critics of the pattern do not consider it revolutionary in any way. They call it a fraud, a fad and a fallacy.

New Pattern is a Fraud: They argue that the implementation has been a fraud as we have miserably failed to provide necessary teachers, buildings and equipment, etc.

New Pattern is a Fad: It is fad because it envisages that the compulsory introduction of science and mathematics will lead to the development of scientific temper of mind of the students. On the other hand it has disregarded the aptitude and ability of the students.

New Pattern is a Fallacy: It is a fallacy to assume that by adding one year at the school stage, we would be turning out more mature students.

The introduction of the new pattern has not decreased pressure for admission on colleges and universities.

Similarly vocationalization of education has not made any significant progress. Students still prefer academic courses.

Concluding Observations: Most of the criticism of the new structure was valid when it was introduced in a hurried manner. Although the Commission had recommended the structure in 1966, for about 7 years the educators and thinkers remained silent on this issue. There was practically no debate on this issue. The pros and cons of the structure never came under discussion before the introduction of the structure. The new scheme was criticized after its introduction. It is of interest to note that the scheme was announced abruptly with the result that necessary preparation could not be made and the scheme came under heavy criticism. Moreover, whenever any new scheme, however good, is introduced, it is criticized by some thinkers who want 'status quo'. One advantage regarding vocationalization of secondary education which was loudly claimed has not accrued. Nevertheless the structure has proved to be advantageous on the whole.

8.5 DIVERSIFICATION OF COURSES

Meaning of Diversification of Courses: Diversification of courses according to Secondary Education Commission implies the provision of courses to students "to meet their varying aptitudes, interests and talents which come into prominence towards the end of the period of compulsory education". This postulates that our secondary schools should no longer be 'single track' institutions. Before the introduction of 10+2 pattern, streaming or diversification was done in class IX and after that it began to take place in class XI.

Reasons for the Streaming at the Higher Secondary Stage

1. *Psychological:* Education system must keep in view the individual differences of children. At the higher secondary stage there emerge marked individual differences which must be catered to.
2. *Varied Needs of the Country:* Country needs craftsmen, engineers, doctors, etc., for different fields and industries. Resources of the country are to be utilised to the maximum. Same set of people, trained in the same occupations or trained for the same services can hardly meet the growing demands of trade, industry, commerce and agriculture etc.
3. *Age of Specialization:* Modern age is the age of specialisation. Plus 2 stage seems to be the most suitable occasion for the diversification of courses as the interests and abilities of students are adequately developed and they are in a better position to take decisions about their future career. At the age of 13, under the old pattern, students were required to take decision regarding their future career at an early date. The recent world trend in secondary education is providing for diversification and specialization at the age of about 15 years or senior stage of secondary stage.
4. *Education According to 3A's:* The fundamental principle of education is that it should be according to the age, ability and aptitude so that the learners may derive the best benefit and lead a fuller and richer life.

Comparative Study of the Diversified Scheme Suggested by the Secondary Education Commission and the Education Commission (Kothari Commission)

The Secondary Education Commission suggested seven groups of subjects out of which a student in Class IX was expected to select one group or stream. On the other hand the Education Commission suggested to broad types *i.e.,* General Stream and the Vocational Stream. There was no grouping in the General Stream. A student could select any three subjects from a number of subjects, for instance he could select History, Chemistry and Home Science. Likewise there were several choices in the Vocational Stream.

The Central Board of Secondary Education permits a wide range of choices.

8.6 THREE LANGUAGE FORMULA

Complexity of the Language Issue: On account of the multiplicity of languages in India, the language problem has posed several serious problems. At even one stage, it posed a great threat to the National unity and integrity of India. Language controversies have resulted in violence and bloody riots also. States have been bifurcated on the basis of languages. It is, therefore, natural that its impact should be felt in the formulation of the language policy in the curriculum at various stages of education.

Origin of the Three Language Formula: The Central Advisory Board of Education—the Chief Advisory Body at the Central Level on Educational affairs, suggested in 1956 a language formula known as the Three Language Formula. This formula envisaged the study of three languages at the secondary stage. These languages were (1) The Regional language, (2) English, and (3) Hindi in non-Hindi areas and a modern India language for Hindi speaking areas. Several difficulties cropped up in its implementation and no uniform policy could be implemented. In general, there was unanimity on two languages, *i.e.*, Mother Tongue/Hindi and English.

The non-Hindi areas introduced Hindi although reluctantly but the Hindi speaking areas did not introduce any language of the South. They were in favour of Sanskrit as the third language.

Three Language Formula and the Education Commission: After tracing the origin of the three-language formula and the difficulties experienced, the Commission suggested that the following guiding principles would help in evolving a *workable* three-language formula in schools:

1. Hindi is the official language of the Union and is expected in due course of time to become the *lingua franca* of the country. Its ultimate importance in the language curriculum will be second only to that of the mother tongue.

2. English will continue to enjoy a high status so long as it remains the principal medium of education at the university stage, and the language of administration at the Centre and in many of the States. Even after the regional languages become media in higher education in the universities, a working knowledge of English will be a valuable asset for all students and a reasonable proficiency in the language will be necessary for those who proceed to the university.

3. The degree of proficiency that can be acquired in learning a language at school depends not only on the number of years during which it is learnt but also on the motivation of the students, the stage at which it is studied, the types of teachers and equipments provided and the methods of teaching adopted. A short period under favourable conditions might achieve better results than a longer period without proper facilities.

4. The most suitable stage for making the learning of three languages compulsory appears to be the lower secondary stage (Class VII-IX) where smaller numbers of pupils are involved and better facilities and teaching personnel can be provided.

5. The stage at which Hindi or English should be introduced on a compulsory basis as a second language and the period for which it should be taught will depend on local motivation and need, and should be left to the discretion of each State.

6. At no stage should the learning of four languages be made compulsory, but provision should the available for the study of four or even more languages on a voluntary basis.

The Three-Language Formula—How it will Operate in Different Classes. The following is the summary of the recommendations of the Education Commission on the Three-Language Formula.

Classes I-IV	The study of only one language should be compulsory. It will naturally be the mother-tongue.
Classes V-VIII	The study of two languages should be compulsory at this stage. First language should be the mother-tongue. The second language may be either the official language of the Union (Hindi) or the associate official language of the Union (English), so long as it is thus recognized.
Classes IX-X	The study of three languages should be obligatory at this stage and one of these three languages should be the official language of the Union or the associate official language whichever was not taken up in classes V-VIII.
Classes XI-XII	The study of two languages should be compulsory. The student should be given the option to select any two languages.

General Observations: The approach of the Commission was very pragmatic. It should serve as a practical basis of compromise on various schools of thought on this vexed question.

National Policy on Education and the Three Language Formula: The National Policy on Education, 1968 and the National Policy on Education, 1986 have upheld the views of the Education Commission. The 1968 observed, "At the secondary stage, the State Governments should adopt and vigorously implement the three-language formula." The National Policy on Education 1986 made these observations on this issue. "The Education Policy of 1968 had examined the question of the development of languages in great detail; its essential provisions can hardly be improved upon and are as relevant today as before. The implementation of this part of the 1968 Policy has, however, been uneven. The Policy will be implemented more energetically and purposefully."

Difficulties in the Implementation of Three Language Formula: Difficulties are given below:

1. The study of three languages puts heavy load on the students.
2. Since the time to be devoted to the study of language/languages is limited, students do not acquire proficiency in any of the three languages.
3. A school is expected to engage a large number of teachers with the result that there is a heavy financial burden on the institution.
4. A compulsory study of three languages is not in conformity with the concept of 'child-centred' education. A student is compelled to study three languages, irrespective of any utility to him.
5. There is little motivation among the students to learn three languages.
6. On the one hand there is resistance to Hindi in the non-Hindi speaking areas and on the other hand, Hindi speaking areas pay little attention to the learning of a language of the South.
7. There are political pulls and pressures in the proper implementation of the Three-Language Formula.

Concluding Remarks: Under the existing linguist, political and social scenario in the country, it would be appropriate not to interfere in the existing scheme of languages, notwithstanding its limitations. 'Let sleeping dogs lie' seems to be the best policy.

8.7 SOCIALLY USEFUL PRODUCTIVE WORK (SUPW)

Meaning of Socially Useful Productive Work: The Review Committee or the Ishwarbhai Patel Committee (1977) which popularised the concept of SUPW has described it "as purposive, meaningful manual work resulting in either goods or services which are useful to the community. Purposive, productive work and services related to the needs of the child and the community will prove meaningful to the learner." The committee has further observed, "The purpose of demarcating a distinct curricular area as 'Socially Useful Productive Work' is to emphasize the principle that education should be work-centred, as the concept of Socially Useful Productive Work is to be developed in the light of the Gandhian philosophy of Basic Education, in and through work."

Objectives of Providing Socially Useful Productive Work Experience: The objectives of Providing Socially Useful Productive Work Experience may be stated as follows:

(i) Acquainting students with the world of work and services of the community and developing in them a sense of respect for manual workers.

(ii) Developing a desire to be useful members of the society and contributing their best to the common goods.

(iii) Inculcating/positive attitude of team work and socially desirable values like self-reliance, dignity of labour, tolerance, co-operation, sympathy and helpfulness.

(iv) Helping in understanding the principles involved in the various forms of work.

(v) Leading children to participate increasingly in productive work, as they go from one stage of education to another, and thereby enabling them to earn while they learn.

(vi) Providing opportunities for creative self-expression and for the development of problem solving abilities.

Contents: The contents of Socially Useful Productive Work should be need-based and depending upon the problems of the child, the school and the community. Therefore, it will be very flexible in nature and no fixed programme can be prescribed in all the schools at a time. Even the details of the programme may vary from year to year in the same school according to the changing needs.

Merits of the Programme: (1) The gap between the work and education will be reduced.

(2) The school will not remain isolated from the community.

(3) The gulf that divides the affluent from the weaker and poorer sections of the community will be bridged.

(4) Such a scheme will provide equality of opportunity for working and learning to all children irrespective of caste, creed, sex and economic status.

(5) Those children who receive education under the new scheme will not migrate from the villages to the towns, deserting the community which had nurtured them and spent money on their education.

(6) The new pattern will assist in checking the cleavage that has been created between the so-called educated and the rural masses and which has resulted in lack of harmony.

(7) The introduction of 'Socially Useful Productive Work' will avert the paradoxial situation in which national resources are spent on the education of the villagers only to help them join the ranks of the unemployed.

(8) The reaffirmation of the Gandhian concept of work-education is the very first step in giving the right direction to our present system of education. Therefore work-education must find a central place in the school curriculum. The Committee made it clear, "We are not advocating education plus work but education in and through work as this is the basis of the Gandhian philosophy of Basic Education."

(9) The merit of education through work is that it follows the natural instinct of man to translate into activity and activity into thought.

The close co-ordination of the senses and thought and also the reciprocal influence between brain activity and material creative activity will be secured.

Difference Between Social Useful Productive Work and Other Similar Activities

1. The programme of Socially Useful Productive Work is different from crafts in this respect that whereas the crafts aim at developing manipulative skills only, the former aims at harmonious development of the whole man, *i.e.,* his body, mind, heart and spirit.
2. The programmes of work-experience lacks the components of social usefulness and in practice are not even casually correlated to other subjects. The remunerative aspect of this programme is also given high priority at the cost of creativity and scientific planning and intelligence performance.
3. Originating from the Gandhian concept of education, Socially Useful Productive Work is a tool for inculcating Gandhian values, *viz.,* truth, non-violence, self-reliance, dignity of labour, co-operation, classless society etc.

Present Status of SUPW in School Curriculum

The CBSE has included Work Experience or Pre-vocational Education in its scheme of studies for class IX and X. However, some work is to be done out of school hours and assessment is internal.

The National Curriculum Framework for School Education (2000) prepared by the NCERT has used the concept Work Education at the primary stage (Classes I to VIII); Work Experience/Pre-Vocational Skills (Classes IX and X) and Work Education at the +2 stage.

8.8 COMMON SCHOOL SYSTEM

Concept of Common School System and Its Chief Characteristics: The Kothari Commission has explained the concept of common school system by listing its following characteristics:

(i) It will be open to all children, irrespective of caste, creed, community, religion, economic conditions and social status.

(ii) There will be access to good education which depends not on wealth or class but on talent.

(iii) It will maintain adequate standards in all schools and provide at least a reasonable proportion of quality institutions.

(iv) There will be no tuition fee.

(vi) It would meet the needs of the average parent so that he does not feel the need to send his children to expensive schools outside the system.

Main Benefits Claimed: The Kothari Commission felt that the common school system would bring the different social classes and groups together and thus promote the emergence of an egalitarian and integrated society. It would narrow down the gulf between the classes and masses.

Reasons for the Unsatisfactory Working of the Common School System: Following are the important causes for the almost failure of the scheme:

(i) Lack of political will.

(ii) Poor standard of education of government and local bodies schools.

(iii) Lack of adequate amenities in government and local bodies school.

(iv) Constitutional guarantee to minorities to establish and administer their own schools. Thus it goes against the concept of common school system.

(v) Growth of institutions like Sainik Schools, Kendriya Vidyalayas and Navodya Vidyalaya in the government sector.

(vi) Profileration of rich classes resulting in the profileration of expensive public schools.

(vii) Neglect of English in government and local bodies schools.

Measures for the Promotion of Public School System

1. *No Discrimination in Teachers Service Conditions:* The first is to ensure that the undesirable discrimination that now exists between teachers working under different managements—government, local authority and private organizations—should be done away with. In this regard following steps to be taken:

- all teachers should have equality of privileges irrespective of the different managements under whom they serve;
- teachers with similar qualifications and responsibilities should have a similar system of remuneration;
- there should be a uniform system of retirement benefits for all teachers;
- the conditions of work and service under the different types of managements should be similar; and
- the methods of recruitment of teachers in institutions of different categories should also be essentially similar.

2. *Tuition-Free System in a Phased Manner:* The ultimate goal should be to provide tuition-free education at the school stage. From this point of view, tuition fees will have to be abolished in a phased programme.

3. *Provision of Adequate Facilities in State Managed Schools and Raise in their Educational Standards:* The roles of local bodies and private organizations in school education should be properly integrated with those of the State Governments to ensure that the minimum conditions necessary for the successful working of educational institutions are provided in *every* institution within the common system of public education, irrespective of its management. For instance, every such institution should be intimately involved with its local community. Each should be regarded as an individuality and given adequate freedom. A continuous attempt should be made to develop each school to the best extent possible in accordance with a plan to be prepared and implemented jointly by the management, parents, teachers and students and the Department;

and every institution should be assured of adequate financial support to discharge its responsibilities to its student body.

4. *Adoption of the Neighbourhood School Plan:* The neighbourhood school plan should be adopted as a step towards eliminating the segregation that now takes place between the schools for the poor and the underprivileged classes and those for the rich and the privileged ones.

5. *Liberal Scholarship:* On grounds of social and national integration, all the children of the country should study in the common school system of public education, because this experience is extremely significant for their development as citizens. To encourage this trend in the national interest, it is recommended that the public scholarships at the school stage, *i.e.,* those given by government and local authorities, should be tenable only in a school functioning within the common school system of public education, which will ultimately charge no fees and to which every child shall have access. This will not cause any hardship, because it is mostly the children of the rich persons who will be attending the independent schools and they will not be in need of any such scholarships.

6. *Admission Policy at the University Stage:* At the university stage also, it is essential to see that children coming up from the common school system of public education are not at a disadvantage in comparison with those appearing from the independent schools. It is, therefore, suggested that ninety per cent of the scholarships awarded from public funds at the university stage should be open only to those students who have received their secondary education in schools functioning within the common school system of public education.

Conclusion: If the proposals made above are implemented, we will have created a common school system of public education embracing three categories of educational institutions—government, local authority and private-aided—which form the vast bulk of all the educational institutions at this stage. The residual responsibility for the financial support of this system will be borne entirely by the State, although the local authorities and private management will be raising some resources of their own to supplement State effort. Within this organization, the existing 'caste' system on the basis of management will largely disappear and a number of common features will be maintained for all schools, such as parity with regard to teachers; common admission policies which will prevent segregation of classes and ensure admissions to all quality institutions on the basis of merit; involvement with local communities; and freedom for experimentation and creativity.

8.9 KENDRIYA VIDYALAYAS

Origin of the Scheme of Central Schools now known as Kendriya Vidyalayas: The scheme of Kendriya Vidyalayas was approved by the Government of India in 1962 on the recommendation of the Second Pay Commission for catering to the educational needs of the children of transferable Central Government Employees including defence personnel who are liable to frequent transfer. The scheme came into operation in 1963.

Objectives of the Scheme: These are as under:

(i) To check the disruption of studies of the children of Central Government employee on account of transfers.

(ii) To facilitate the admission of the children on the transfer of their parents.

(iii) To provide education of a reasonable quality.

(iv) To provide inexpensive education.

(v) To promote national integration. This objective is being achieved by having the same syllabus, textbooks, medium of instruction, colour of the uniform of children and flag of the organization also.

Main Features: (i) These schools are co-educational.

(ii) These are composite schools.

(iii) There are common textbooks and common curriculum.

(iv) They are bilingual *i.e.*, medium of instruction is English and Hindi.

(v) Teaching of Sanskrit from Class V to IX is compulsory.

(vi) The wards of staff of KVS, SC/ST students, children of officers and men of the Armed Forces killed or disabled during hostilities are exempted from paying tuition fees.

(vii) Attempts are made to maintain a proper teacher-pupil ratio.

Management: Kendriya Vidyalayas are managed by Kendriya Vidyalaya Sangathan. The Minister of Human Resource Development is ex-officio Chairman of the Sangathan. The Commissioner is the executive head of KVS and is guided by its Board of Governors.

Achievements: The Scheme has served its purpose to a great extent.

Number of Kendriya Vidyalayas: The number of Kendriya Vidyalayas is nearly 900. All these schools are affiliated to the Central Board of Secondary Education (CBSE), Delhi.

8.10 PUBLIC SCHOOLS

Public Schools—A Misnomer Concept: Technically speaking, the concept of a public school is misnomer in the Indian context. We have public sector undertakings and public system of transport etc. This connotes state run, controlled and managed to a great extent. Unlike this system, public schools are not run by the government. They are independent of government finance and management. In general they are managed by trusts as well as individuals.

Origin of Public Schools: They are of British origin. The year 1440 A.D. saw the birth of the first public school at Eton and it became the model for many others that followed.

Chief Features of a Public School: According to the Indian Public Schools Conference 1939, a public school should satisfy the following conditions:

(i) It is intended mainly for Indian boys.

(ii) It accepts the general principle that a boy otherwise suitable shall not be excluded from admission on the ground that he does or does not belong to any particular class or creed.

(iii) It accepts the general principle that all boys admitted shall be treated alike and to this end will arrange that all boys shall join a common mess and will not allow any boarder to have a private guardian, tutor or servant, or to live anywhere else except in one of the school boarding houses.

(iv) It has an effective governing body, the meeting of which the Headmaster has the right to attend.

(v) It is financially stable and agrees to send annually a copy of its audited balance sheet and statement of accounts to the Honorary Secretary of the Conference.

(vi) It provides adequate salaries and satisfactory conditions of service for members of its staff.

(vii) It possesses adequate buildings, equipment and playing fields.

(viii) It provides a course of study extending over at least five academic years beyond the age of 11.

(ix) It regularly prepares and enters a reasonable number of candidates for a public examination of the standard of the Cambridge School Certificate and provides facilities for education beyond this stage.

(x) It gives boys opportunities for social service and training in leadership and responsibility.

(xi) It provides regular organized games and physical training for all boys.

(xii) It provides for adequate medical inspection and remedial treatment.

In actual practice, very few schools conform to these conditions.

Types of Public Schools. Public schools are of six categories: (a) Schools which were once meant for the princely families. Under this head we may mention the names of Mayo College at Ajmer and Raipur. These schools and colleges are now attracting students from the general public; (b) Schools which were once intended for European and Anglo-Indian children. These schools were established at Shimla and Darjeeling; (c) Schools which formerly catered to the needs of the children of military personnel. These schools have now thrown open their doors to the general public. Lawrence School at Sanawar and Lovedale and also the King George V Schools come under this category; (d) Schools which have been opened as public schools for Indian children. The Delhi Public School, the Delhi Modern School, etc., may be placed in this category; (e) Under the National Policy on Education 1986, Navodaya Vidyalayas may also be placed in the category of public schools. Lastly, schools which, by and large, have been opened allegedly for earning profits. These are managed by individuals.

Merits of Public Schools: Following advantages are generally claimed:

Sir John Sargent Educational Commissioner of the Government of India has observed, "Democracy stands in even greater need of leaders than any other form of government and there is nothing in the pursuit of the ideal of equality of opportunity which conflicts with or in any way reduces the importance of selecting and training those who display a potential capacity for leadership. After all, as an eminent educationist said not many years ago, the main purpose of higher education is to form an elite not for its own sake but for the sake of society."

About the English Public School, Kurt Hahn states: "They instill fairness in anger, coolness in danger, grace in defeat, readiness for service at all times. They best emerge from our traditional institutions, knowing how to argue without quarrelling, how to quarrel without suspecting, how to suspect without slandering."

Prof. Humayun Kabir felt that these public schools have an important place in the educational ladder of the country provided: (1) They conform to the pattern of Indian life and considerably simplify the customs of the school life. They steadily draw closer to the general educational system of the country without losing their special merit. (3) They take steps to bring down the cost of education while maintaining their special features of quality. (4) They become the visible symbols of the principle that the role of education is the equalization of opportunity within the community.

In general, following merits of public schools may be listed:

1. Development of qualities of leadership.
2. High standard of education.
3. Better teaching facilities.
4. Conducive physical environment.
5. Discipline of high quality.
6. Favourable service conditions of teachers.
7. Relatively free from political interference.

Criticism of Public School and the Education Commission

High Fees. The Commission has spoken of these institutions in scathing terms. The system of schools largely reserved for those who have the capacity to pay high fees, "was transplanted in India by British administrators and we have clung to it so long because it happened to be in tune with the traditional hierarchal structure of our society".

Wide Gulf between the Classes and Masses: The Commission has regretfully noted that "what is worse, this segregation is increasing and tending to widen the gulf between the classes and the masses".

Undemocratic: This undemocratic feature of the Indian school system has been described by the Commission as one of the major weaknesses of the present educational structure. The children of the masses are compelled to receive sub-standard education and, as the programme of scholarships is not very large, sometimes even the ablest among them are unable to find access to such good schools as exist, while the economically privileged parents are able to "buy good education for their children".

The Commission has stated that whatever the past history of the so called public schools they have no valid place in the new democratic society we desire to create.

Common School System

The Kothari Commission urged that the present segregation in primary and secondary schools must be eliminated and schools must be attended by all children in the neighbourhood without exception.

Concluding observations: In spite of the fact that most of the public schools charge high fees and huge donations, they have come to stay. They cannot be ended but some administrative check can be exercised over them. The craze for public schools is so much that the parents leave no stone unturned to get their wards admitted in these schools. However, while giving recognition to these schools, the government must ensure that they fulfill the required conditions.

8.11 NAVODAYA/JAWAHAR VIDYALAYAS (PACE-SETTING SCHOOLS)

Origin of the Navodaya Schools: The National Policy on Education, 1986, pointed out the need for setting up pace-setting schools which came to be known as Navodaya Vidyalayas or Jawahar Navodaya Vidyalayas. At present about 400 such Vidyalayas are functioning in different parts of the country. Eventually the Central Government plans to open one such school in every district.

Need for the Pace-Setting Schools: The NPE observed, "It is universally accepted that children with special talent or aptitude should be provided opportunity to proceed at a faster pace through quality education, irrespective of their capacity to pay for it."

Main Features of Navodaya Schools

1. They cater to the talented students.
2. They are residential.
3. They provide free education.
4. They cater primarily to rural areas. 75 per cent seats are reserved for rural areas.
5. They have reserved seats for SC and ST as per their actual population in the district subject to a minimum of nationally prescribed figure of 15 per cent and 7.5 per cent for SC and ST respectively.
6. They are expected to foster national integration by providing opportunities of living and learning together.
7. A certain proportion of students comes from other States.
8. Special emphasis is laid on diagnostic and remedial teaching.
9. They are expected to provide full scope for innovation and experimentation.
10. They are expected to become catalysts of nation-wide programme of school improvement.
11. Selection for admission is based on different types of scholastic aptitude tests which aim at eliminating the element of subjectivity.
12. It is envisaged that in these schools three-language formula will be implemented in its true spirit.

Organisation of Navodaya Vidyalayas: A Navodaya Vidyalaya Samiti, an autonomous organization in the Ministry of Human Resource Development has been set up to manage these schools. These schools are affiliated to the Central Board of Secondary Education, Delhi. The Central Government bears 100 per cent expenditure for running these institutions and it is the responsibility of the State Governments to provide a plot of land, about 30 acres in area, free of cost.

The Navodaya Vidyalayas (NVs) have started functioning in almost all the States with some glaring exceptions—Tamil Nadu and West Bengal, for instance, have not yet agreed to the scheme for certain reasons which include opposition to Hindi as a medium of instruction.

Snags in the Scheme of Navodaya Vidyalayas

1. It appears that these schools had been started in great haste, without the necessary infrastructure or operational facilities which reveals a lack of proper planning. However, these defects have been removed gradually.
2. By and large, Navodaya Vidyalayas are facing the problem of inadequate accommodation.
3. There are instances in which these schools have been set up in obscure location.
4. Another major problem has been the non-availability of experienced staff. Merited teachers are not willing to work in remote villages. Also according to the initial policy laid down by the Navodaya Vidyalaya Samiti, teachers can only join on deputation which means teachers will have very little affinity with these schools.
5. The library facilities provided are far inferior to the stipulated requirement.
6. Suitable playgrounds are not available, which is indeed sad.

Critics of the Scheme

They point out the following drawbacks in this scheme:

(i) The admission tests are anti-rural.

(ii) Children belonging to lower middle income groups find it difficult to compete for admission with the children of middle income group on account of special coaching which the latter category can provide to their wards.

(iii) They are not in consonance with the philosophy of common school concept. By setting these schools, the Government has created another category of public schools.

(iv) These schools put a heavy burden on the exchequer. In the era of liberal economy, such sort of expenditure is not justified. This money should be utilized for providing more and better facilities to ordinary primary schools.

Conclusion and Recommendations: Despite these shortcomings and criticisms which are inherent when any new institution is started, it is hoped that with the passage of time these schools will develop into truly pace-setting institutions. It is envisaged that Navodaya Schools will have far-reaching educational and socio-political implications. However, it must be ensured that schools do not become ivory towers and 'show pieces' of elitist culture. Our emphasis should be on qualitative improvements and not on opening ill staffed and ill-equipped schools. Like the scheme of Basic education in which overnight, elementary schools were converted into Basic Schools, this scheme of Navodaya Schools should not be allowed to fail. Solid work is needed to run these schools efficiently.

8.12 EXAMINATION SYSTEM

Indispensability of Examinations: It is observed that examinations are a necessary evil. Even in the idealized picture of society portrayed in H.G. Well's '*Utopia*', examinations find an important place. Examination, in one or the other form have existed from times immemorial. In the words of Secondary Education Commission (1952-53), "Nevertheless examinations—and especially external examinations—have a proper place in any scheme of education." Sir Michael Sadler, author of Sadler Commission (1917) observed, "To close down examination would be to give the signal for educational saturnalia."

Functions of Examinations: Following are the important functions served by the examinations:

1. To evaluate the achievements of the students.
2. To evaluate the achievements of the teachers.
3. To evaluate the achievements of the institutions.
4. To evaluate several aspects of personality like thinking, quickness of mind etc.
5. To acquaint parents with the achievements of their wards so that they may also take appropriate steps.
6. To act as incentives to achieve the determined goals.
7. To help in diagnosis.
8. To help in prognosis.
9. To help in guidance and counseling.
10. To provide uniformity of standards.
11. To measure fitness for admission to higher courses.
12. To help in the selection of students to various streams etc.

Defects/Limitations of Examinations

Epithets given to examinations:

(i) An enemy of true education.
(ii) An incubus.
(iii) An obstacle to learning.
(iv) A blood sucker.
(v) A bane of education system.
(vi) A glorification of memory.
(vii) A begetter of rivalry and strife.
(viii) A dead hand of education.
(ix) A growing tyranny.
(x) A presumptuous attempt to gauge the depth of human ignorance.

Drawbacks and Limitations of Examinations

1. Element of chance being very predominant on account of the limited number of questions out of the total course of a subject.
2. Lack of suitable norms of marking.
3. Indefinite and vague nature of some questions.
4. Glorification of memory—cram the only method.
5. Subjective attitude of the examiners.
6. Heavy mental strain on the students.
7. Far reaching judgment on just about 15 hours work done by the student during the whole year.
8. Stress only on academic performance.
9. Many-sided development of the personality of the student ignored.
10. Domination of the examinations over creative methods of teaching-learning.
11. Use of unfair means to score marks/grades.

Reforms in Examinations

During the last five decades or so, several attempts have been made to check the limitations and shortcomings of the examinations at various stages, especially at the secondary stage. However some defects still exist. It is also true that a foolproof system is an illusion. It can be achieved to a substantial extent if we use the objective types questions only but on account of several considerations, it is not possible to depend upon a single type. Essay type of questions, whether long answer or short answer, must find a place in the scheme of examinations. It appears some element of subjectivity is likely to exist in spite of best efforts.

Examinations cannot be ended but only can be amended. To mitigate the shortcomings of the examinations, following reforms are recommended:

1. There should be balanced mixture of essay type (Long answer) questions, Short answer and Objective type of questions. Marks of Essay type questions may not exceed 50 per cent of the total marks.
2. Questions should be thought provoking.
3. There should be no overall optional. There should be no place for such instructions; Do any five questions.
4. While asking questions, attempts should be made to cover the maximum course.

5. In place of one paper of three hours duration in a particular subject, there should be two papers, each of three hours. This would reduce chance elements to some extent.

6. Class work should be given some consideration.

7. External examinations may be supplemented by viva voce if possible.

8. Marking norms should be carefully determined and prescribed.

9. Difficult, as well as easy questions should a place in the question paper.

10. There should be no compulsory public examination.

11. The number of external examinations should be reduced

12. Cumulative record cards in respect of every child should be maintained.

13. Symbols/grades in place of numerical marking should be introduced.

14. Students may be allowed to appear in two or three subjects and complete the examination in two consecutive years or so.

Criteria of Good Examination

A good examination should have the following qualities:

1. *Validity:* By validity we means the degree to which a test or examination measures what it is intended to measure. In Geography if the aim is to test the reasoning power of the student, the questions should be framed in such a manner as to elicit replies which may assist in judging the reasoning and argumentative power of the student. Spelling or handwriting should not be taken into account while assessing the paper. Perhaps this factor of validity is the most baffling one in regard to our essay type of examinations.

2. *Reliability:* By this term we mean the degree of accuracy with which an examination measures what it seeks to measure. The greater the number of questions in an examination the more reliable is the result. New type objective tests are considered to be more reliable as the sampling is more extensive.

Total Scheme of Examinations

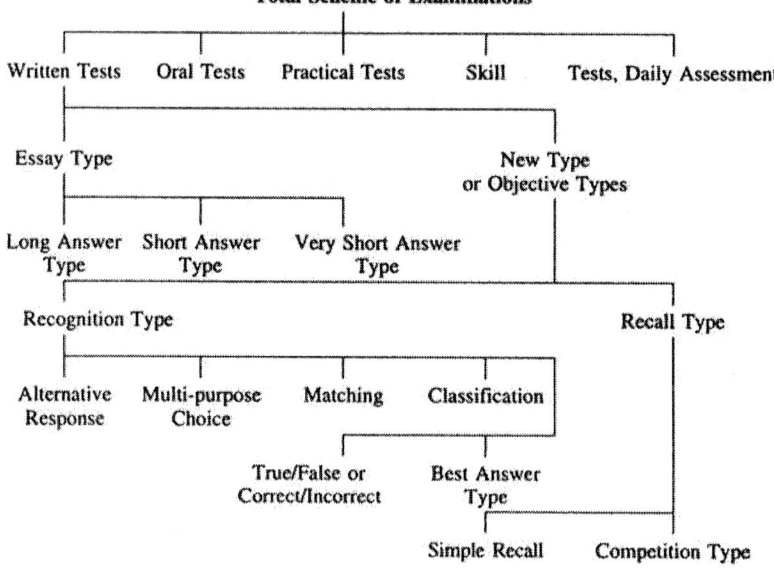

3. *Objectivity:* By objectivity we mean the degree to which personal element or judgment is eliminated in the assessment of a paper. A good test is unaffected by the mood of the examiner. At the same time, different examiners are not inconsistent in their marking of a single set of papers in a good test.

4. *Administrative Ease:* An examination should be easy to administer in all its three stages, *i.e.*, setting, answering and scoring.

Different Types of Examinations

(a) *Essay Types:* These may be classified into the undermentioned two categories:

(i) *External or Public Examinations*: These are conducted by those outside teachers who have no direct hand in the preparation of the examinees.

(ii) *Internal Examinations:* These are conducted by those teachers who are teaching the examinees. These are held quarterly, half-yearly, yearly as the case may be.

(b) *Oral or Viva Voce:* In an oral examination, evaluation regarding the capabilities of the students is made at the spur of the moment. Most of the appointments to the various posts, public or private, are made through the oral examinations. If sufficient time is devoted to these tests, there is every possibility that the evaluation may be a fair one. But in actual practice, not much attention is paid to this aspect. The subjective element also plays a dominant role. Chances of favouritism are quite high.

(c) *Practical:* Practical tests are held to evaluate the progress made by individuals in certain skills. Tests in science practicals are the well-known examples of this type in school work. Driving licences are also issued after assessing the practical skill in driving a car, a bus or any vehicle of this kind.

(d) *Modern or Objective:* Such tests are of recent origin. They may also be called by the name of short answer tests.

(e) *Systematic Observation by the Teachers:* Teachers from time to time record their observations regarding the progress of children in different spheres in their personal diaries. These may take the form of a cumulative record card.

(f) *Thesis Type:* In this type sufficient time is given to the candidate to write a thesis or dissertation after a careful study and research. Generally the candidate works under the guidance of a supervisor.

Essay Type or Objective Type Tests

Essay type examinations and objective type tests do not serve our purpose either singly or independently. A balanced combination of these two, therefore, is the first essential to be achieved in the reform of the traditional examination system.

The Indispensable Nature of Essay Tests: Essay type tests govern a wide field of learning—thinking and reasoning, study skills and work habits. Essay tests measure the functional aspects or the application of knowledge. We can evaluate through them the logical reasoning power of the students. The essay tests help us to test the power of expression, verbal facility, use of vocabulary and style of writing. They also help us to evaluate the capacity of the students to organise knowledge, to evaluate thoughts and to create new thoughts. The objective tests fail to evaluate these powers.

The Indispensable Nature of New Tests: The new type tests cover the subjects as fully as possible and they offer better and more adequate facilities of sampling knowledge than the traditional type. They also help the teacher to find out where teaching has been defective or learning inadequate. Scoring becomes very objective. Personal preferences of the examiners do not matter and subjective factor is completely eliminated and this increases reliability of the tests. In these respects these tests have an upper hand over the essay type tests.

Combination of Essay and Objective Tests: From the above it is quite evident that both type of tests are complimentary to each other. The shortcomings of the essay type of tests are overcome by the new type of tests and vice versa. Hence a judicious combination of the two is advisable. We may have the following merits of the combination of the two types:

1. The objective tests will make evaluation more reliable by eliminating the subjective element inherent in essay type tests.

2. Objective tests will cover a wide area of the subject-matter and fill up the gaps left by the essay type tests.

3. The two types of tests measure two different faculties, the essay type tests measure the functional aspect and the objective tests measure the theoretical aspect.

4. The scores obtained in the two tests can be correlated and thus the degree of reliability found. This will also check subjectivity.

Limitations of the Two: These tests are tests of knowledge. The various behaviour patterns remain untested. These fail to test the totality of the child's development of personality and character.

Conclusion: These tests should be supplemented by achievement tests, personality tests, intelligence tests etc. The views of the teachers who guide the students and watch them should be given their due place. The reproduction of the material of the text-book or the made-easy and the notes dictated by the teachers should not be valued more than the development of many-sided interests and the cultivation of all-round and well-developed personality.

Grading and Marking System

Brief Review: The Secondary Education Commission 1952-53, discussed the issue of examination and evaluation in Chapter XI of its report. It observed, "The present system of evaluating by percentiles *i.e.,* numerical marks, out of a hundred, may have certain advantages but the disadvantages seem to outweigh the advantages." The Commission pointed out the following demerits of the system of numerical marking system:—

First, it introduces too many sub-divisions which are not only useless but cumbersome.

Secondly, it is indeed difficult to distinguish between two pupils one of whom obtains, say, 45 marks and another 46 or 47.

The Commission recommended the following grading system:

'A' to indicate 'Distinction'.

'B' to indicate 'Credit'.

'C' to indicate 'Pass'.

'D' and 'E' to indicate 'Failure' or 'Cases Referred Back'.

The Commission observed that the values of the categories in terms of percentile marks may be determined by the examining authority. Individual examiners in different subjects may even use percentile system and then convert the percentile scores in terms of categories.

The Commission was emphatic that this system would work in all cases except where the distinctions are to be made for the award of scholarships and prizes.

It appears the Commission was not very clear on this issue. Its recommendations do not seem to provide the appropriate solution.

'A Monograph on Grading in Universities' (1976) published by the UGC gives the following demerits of numerical marking:

1. The standards of examiners differ very widely. There is a standard error of marking ranging from 5 to 20 marks in different subjects.
2. Examiners have a tendency to give an unusually great number of 35 marks (when 35 is passing mark).
3. Examiners in different subjects use different ranges. In some the full scale of 0 to 100 is used, while in many other subjects, scales used are all different.
4. Marks given by examiners are not scaled.
5. Marks in different subjects are added up when they should not be.

According to the *'Monograph'*, grading system fulfills the following objectives:

(a) Evaluation which is mainly judgment based on measurement is uniform if all the universities agree to adopt the 7 point scale grading system.

(b) Comparability amongst various disciplines and within various subjects in a particular discipline is possible with the grading system.

(c) In case of grading system in all universities and boards, students can move from one university or board to another.

(d) Grading system takes the emphasis away from marks.

Following grades were recommended for all subjects:

O	Outstanding	3%
A	Very Good	7%
B	Good	22%
C	Average	36%
D	Below Average	22%
E	Poor	7%
F	Very Poor	3%

Demerits of the Grading System

Prof. Atma Ram in *'Shikshak Salhi'* (May 2000) finds fault with the grading system on account of the following:

(i) It does not suit a selection situation. In view of the prevailing corruption, it can create chaotic conditions.

(ii) As the grading system does not allow ranking of the candidates, medals and prizes cannot be awarded to the deserving students.

(iii) The various appointing authorities want grades to be translated into percentage of marks.

(iv) Some education institutions are superior to others, in which case, grading of their students will not be comparable with those of others.

(v) In the grading system, there is little zeal or competition among students to strive for higher percentage of marks.

(vi) The Federation of Parents' Association, Delhi and the Delhi School Education Advisory Board, have stoutly opposed the move. They have termed it as a ploy of the NCERT to hide inefficiency. "When it (CBSE) should have worked on the revaluation system, it has embarked on a scheme to get away with its sloppy evaluation system", said Mr. Vijender Kumar, President, Delhi Abhibhavak Maha Sangh.

(vii) Some view it as a method to raise the pass percentage of government schools, to equate them with those of public schools.

He has further observed, "In terms of pure theory and academic considerations, the grading system may sound effective and desirable, but it does not suit the socio-economic conditions prevalent in the country. That it works well in several advanced countries in the world is no reason to believe that it will succeed here as well. In India, the realities of life, at the grass-roots level particularly, are different. It is not for nothing that in decades, out of 242 universities in India, only a few have opted for the grade system. We do not stress adequately the areas where revamping should be done and only hit upon short cuts and cosmetic, measures to improve the system of education or examination. At the evaluation stage, the examining body has broad-based interaction with the society. It should, therefore, take into confidence various constituents of society—students, teachers, parents, NGOs and general public. What we essentially need in education is due stress on effective teaching—220 teaching days in schools."

Concluding Observations: No system is full proof. In place of discussing the merits and demerits of marking and grading, we would do well in making teaching-learning more effective and checking the deficiency of marking system.

8.13 ADMINISTRATION OF SECONDARY EDUCATION

Role of the Central Government: Under the Constitution, secondary education remained the primary responsibility of the State till 1976. Nevertheless the Central Government was not absolved of all responsibilities in this sector of education particularly those having a bearing on the general socio-economic development of the country and the training of citizenship. It therefore, played a significant role in secondary education and to some extent in the administration of secondary education. Here, we are primarily concerned with the administration of secondary education, although administration is also linked with all educational policies and programmes. Since it has sponsored several centrally sponsored schemes of secondary education, it is closely involved in the administration. (These schemes have been given in the next chapter).

Under the Department of Education of the Ministry of Human Resource Development, Government of India, a separate Department of Secondary Education and Higher Education has been set up recently. This department monitors all educational programmes relating to this sector.

The Central Government discharges its function through the following organisations:

1. The National Council of Educational Research and Training (NCERT), a national level resource institution for the School Education Sector. It provides academic and technical support for qualitative improvement of school education through its constituents:

(i) The National Institute of Education (NIE);

(ii) Central Institute of Educational Technology—CIET;

(iii) Pt. Sunderlal Sharma Central Institute of Vocational Education (SLSCIVE);

(iv) Five Regional Institutes of Education located at Ajmer, Bhopal, Bhubaneswar, Mysore and Shillong.

2. The National Institute of Educational Planning and Administration (NIEPA), a national level resource institution, specialising in Educational Planning and Administration.

The Central Government runs, maintains and controls schools through the following:

(i) The Kendriya Vidyalaya Sangathan (KVS).
(ii) The Navodaya Vidyalaya Samiti (NVS).
(iii) The Central Board of Secondary Education (CBSE) an affiliating body.
(iv) National Open School (NOS)

Administration of Secondary Education: Role of State Government

Till recently, education being a state subject, it had been exclusively the controlling authority of all stages of education in the State. Of course, the States were expected to work under the guidance of the Central Ministry of Education (now Ministry of Human Resource Development, Department of Education, Government of India). Although education became a concurrent subject in 1976 the administration of secondary education remained almost the responsibility of the State Governments. The State looks after the secondary education through the Department of Public Instruction (DPI) or the State Department of Education. In some States, there are separate Departments for High, Secondary and Primary Education.

In the field of secondary education, the State Government performs the following functions:

(i) It opens and maintains secondary schools.

(ii) It gives grant-in-aid to private enterprise for running secondary schools.

(iii) It prescribes rules and regulations in the form of Education Codes and Acts.

(iv) It sets up Board of Secondary Education for recognition and examination purposes. Sometimes such Boards are autonomous in nature.

(v) It supervises the teaching work imparted in private schools—aided as well as un-aided.

(vi) It appoints Committees and Commissions to go into the various problems of secondary education.

(vii) It establishes State Councils of Educational Research and Training.

(viii) It sets up Districts Institutes of Education and Training.

9

Secondary Education and Its Relevance to Our Needs

9.1 SIGNIFICANCE OF SECONDARY EDUCATION TO OUR NEEDS

Undoubtedly each stage of education has its own significance in the overall scheme of things but secondary education assumes great significance in view of the following specific factors:

Terminal Stage: As observed by the Secondary Education Commission 1952-53, "We have to bear in mind that secondary education is a complete unit in itself and not merely a preparatory stage; that at the end of this period, the student should be in a position, if he wishes, to enter on the responsibility of life and take up some useful vocation". It helps individuals to become useful members of a complex modern society. Since our needs are to transform the Indian State into a democratic, secular and socialist one, the secondary education being a terminal stage must discharge this function effectively. It is of interest to note that just 5 to 6 per cent of the college age students, enter the portals of higher education. Thus a good quality of secondary education is very essential to meet the needs of the country.

Providing Teachers for Primary Schools: Secondary education provides teachers for the primary schools. Now the qualification for training in an elementary teacher training institute or school is the completion of the secondary schooling. Secondary education must fulfil this need adequately.

Mature Students for Higher Education: Secondary education leads to higher education. It is expected that students completing this stage should have the requisite maturity to pursue higher education.

According to the Secondary Education Commission, the secondary education is expected to enable the individual to meet the four-fold needs of the country which are: (i) Democratic citizenship, (ii) Vocational efficiency, (iii) Personality development, and (iv) Leadership qualities.

The Education Commission, though did not specify the specific role of secondary education in meeting the needs of the country, yet it detailed the overall needs of the country. Obviously the secondary education as an integral part of education must be geared to meet these needs. Thus secondary education should be (i) Related to productivity; (ii) Related to strengthening social and national integration; (iii) Related to consolidating democracy as a form of government and helping the country to adopt a way of life; (iv) Related to hastening the process of modernization; (v) Related to striving to build character by cultivating social, moral and spiritual values.

The National Policy on Education mentioned the following needs of the country which the secondary education should meet:

1. Secondary education should expose students to the differentiated roles of science, the humanities and social sciences.
2. It should provide children with a sense of history and national perspective.
3. It should give children opportunities to understand their constitutional duties and rights as citizens.
4. It should develop healthy work ethos.
5. It should develop the values of a humane and composite culture.
6. It should provide manpower for economic growth.

9.2 INADEQUACY OF SECONDARY EDUCATION TO MEET OUR NEEDS: THE WEAKEST LINK

The following questions in this regard arise:

Does the Prevalent System of Secondary Education Meet our Requirements? Is the Secondary Education the Weakest Link?

The answer is: Secondary education does not meet our requirements fully. It definitely is the weakest link in the chain of our system of education, although several reforms in recent years in this area have been carried out. It is generally observed that since independence, we have accorded priority to primary education as well as higher education. Secondary education has not received its due attention. A perusal of the various provisions regarding education in the Constitution would reveal that while there is Article 45 of the Constitution concerning primary education, Entries 62, 63, 64, 65 and 66 of List I included higher education and research. There was no such mention of secondary education. It is therefore, obvious that secondary education has been rather neglected, and it has remained the weakest link.

Defects of the Secondary Education

Following are the defects in the secondary education:

1. It is bookish in nature.
2. It is examination dominated.
3. It is not suited to the needs of the country.
4. It is geared to university education.
5. It prepares for clerical jobs, by and large.
6. It is not self-employment oriented.
7. It does not develop dignity of labour.
8. It does not develop necessary manpower for various industries.
9. It is restrictive in scope.
10. It is English-dominated.
11. Methods of teaching are usually dull and mechanical.
12. It fails to develop goods work habits.

9.3 SECONDARY EDUCATION COMMISSION (1952-53) AND RESTRUCTURING SECONDARY EDUCATION

Reasons for the Appointment of the Commission: India had recently achieved its political freedom and after careful consideration it had been decided to transform itself into a democratic and secular republic. This required that the educational system must contribute to the development of habits, attitudes and qualities of character which should enable its citizens to bear worthily the responsibilities of democratic citizenship. This required a review of secondary education and the Government of India set up the Secondary Education Commission in September 1952 under the Chairmanship of Dr. A. Lakshmanaswami Mudaliar, Vice-Chancellor, Madras University. Among the important recommendations, mention is made of the following:

Major Recommendations for Making Secondary Education Relevant to Our Needs

I. Needs and Aims and Objectives of Secondary Education: The Commission took note of the changed political, social and economic conditions of the country and restated the objectives of education. According to it following are the main objectives of education:

1. Development of democratic citizenship.
2. Improvement of vocational efficiency.
3. Development of personality.
4. Development of qualities for leadership.

II. Duration of Secondary Education: The Commission made the following suggestions to improve this area:

1. Under the new organisational structure, education should commence after a four or five years' period of Primary or Junior Basic education and should include: (a) the Middle or Senior Basic or Junior Secondary stage of 3 years, and (b) Higher Secondary stage of 4 years.

2. During the transitional stage, the existing High Schools and the Higher Secondary Schools should function on the lines laid down.

3. The present intermediate stage should be replaced by the Higher Secondary stage which should be of four years' duration, one-year of the present Intermediate being included in it.

4. As a consequence of the preceding recommendations the first degree course in the university should be of three years' duration.

5. For those who pass out of the High School, there should be provision for a Pre-university course of one-year, during which period the scheme of studies should be planned with due regard to the needs of the degree or the professional course to be taken by the students and special emphasis should be placed on the quickening of intellectual interests, training in methods of study at college and the study of English so long as it continues to be the medium of instruction at the University.

6. Admission to professional colleges should be open to those who have completed the higher secondary course, or have taken the one-year's pre-university course.

7. In the professional colleges, a pre-professional course of one year should be provided for the students, preferably in the professional colleges themselves. As a transitory measure, they may be given in the degree colleges where facilities exist, till professional colleges are able to provide for such courses.

III. Multi-purpose Schools and Vocational Schools: 1. Multi-purpose schools should be established wherever possible to provide varied courses of interest to students with diverse aims, aptitudes and abilities.

2. Those who have successfully completed such courses should be given opportunities to take up higher specialized courses in polytechnics or technological institutions.

3. All States should provide special facilities for agricultural education in rural schools and such courses should include Horticulture and Technical Education.

IV. Diversified Curriculum: It suggested seven groups out of which students could select anyone besides languages and core curriculum.

V. Guidance and Counselling: The Commission suggested a comprehensive programme for guidance and counselling at the secondary stage.

VI. Technical Schools: (i) Technical Schools should be started in large numbers either separately or as a part of multi-purpose schools.

(ii) A small cess to be called the 'Industrial Education Cess' should be levied on industries and the proceeds of this cess should be used for the furtherance of technical education.

Reasons for Non-Implementation or Unsatisfactory Implementation of Recommendations

1. The financial implications of the upgrading of a large number of high schools into higher secondary pattern in every State were not worked out.
2. The Commission suggested that the minimum qualifications required for teaching in the last two years of the higher secondary school were an M.A. degree or a first class B.A. degree with a degree in teaching. An adequate number of qualified post-graduate teachers were not immediately available.
3. The introduction of core-subjects like crafts and general science in the curriculum of the Higher Secondary School created further difficulties regarding staff requirements.
4. The serious difficulties in the process of implementing the recommendations of establishing multi-purpose schools could not be foreseen with the result that out of 22,581 higher secondary schools in 1983-84, there were only 2000 multi-purpose schools. The multi-purpose schools benefited neither the school-leavers nor the seekers of higher education. The scheme had to be dropped.
5. The Commission did not give a clear-cut concept of vocationalized education adequately.
6. The Commission did not suggest methods of co-ordination between growth of economy, man-power needs, employment opportunities and the output of secondary schools.
7. The selection of high schools for conversion into higher secondary schools was to be governed by strict and carefully defined conditions. However, the establishment of higher secondary schools in certain areas unfortunately became a matter of prestige for the people concerned. Social and political pressures were sometimes used for getting the necessary recognition for their institutions. This resulted in the upgrading of a number of schools which did not satisfy the minimum criteria regarding accommodation, equipment, qualification of staff, etc.

9.4 EDUCATION COMMISSION (KOTHARI COMMISSION) 1964-66 ON RESTRUCTURING SECONDARY EDUCATION

Appointment of the Commission: The Education Commission 1964-66 was appointed by the Government of India in July 1964 to advise on the national pattern of education and on the general principles and policies of development of education at all stages and in all aspects. The Commission was headed by Prof. D.S. Kothari, Chairman of University Grants Commission and the report of the Commission is therefore called the Kothari Commission Report. Shri J.P. Naik was the Member Secretary. The Commission included experts from foreign countries also. The Commission submitted its report in 1966 under the title *'Education and National Development'*.

Major Recommendations of the Kothari Commission

I. Recommendations Closely Related to Secondary Education

1. *Four-fold Objectives of Education:* The Commission suggested the following objectives of education:
   (a) To increase productivity.
   (b) To achieve national and emotional integration.
   (c) To accelerate the process of modernization.
   (d) To cultivate social, moral and spiritual values.
2. Stress on Science Education.
3. Importance of Work Experience.
4. Need for Vocationalization of Education.
5. Common School System for the Country.
6. Emphasis on Social and National Service.
7. Ten Years of Schooling of General Education.
8. Specialization in Classes XI and XII.
9. Two Years Duration of Lower Secondary and two years Higher Secondary Stage.
10. Two sets of curricula—Ordinary and Advanced.
11. Adequate Facilities for Guidance and Counselling.

II. Recommendations Related to All Stages of Education Including Secondary

12. Increased Instructional Days and Time in Schools.
13. Holidays to be minimised.
14. Academic Year to Begin on the Same Day.
15. Maximum Utilization of School Facilities.
16. College to be Related to a Number of Schools.
17. Provision of Free Textbooks at the Primary Stage.
18. Establishment of Book Banks in Schools.
19. Provision of Adequate Number of Scholarships.
20. Identification and Special Steps for the Gifted Students.
21. Residential Facilities in Some Schools.
22. Provision of Day-Study Centres.
23. Learning by Earning.
24. Education of the Handicapped—One institution in Each District.
25. Education of the Backward Classes.
26. State-Level Centres for Pre-Primary Education.
27. Development Plan for Each District.
28. Enrolment Between 360 and 450 in a Secondary School.
29. Freedom to School for Experimental Curricula.
30. Three or Four Textbooks for Each Subject.
31. Necessity of Moral and Religious Education.
32. Provision of Co-curricular Activities.

33. Evaluation a Continuous Process.
34. Establishment of School Complexes.
35. The Neighbourhood School.
36. Setting up State Evaluation Organization.
37. Setting up State and National Boards of Education.
38. Introduction of Correspondence Courses.
39. Improved Scales of Pay for Teachers.
40. Same Pay in Different Managements.
41. Liberal Assistance to States.
42. Retirement of Teachers at 60 Years of Age.
43. Constitution of the Indian Education Services.
44. Passing Education Acts by States.
45. Three Years Duration of Degree Courses.

Evaluation of the Report

Education Commission's report was an achievement, a mine of information and wisdom. The report was a synoptic survey of the entire educational situation in all its complexities. It revealed an imagination sweep not found in the excellent reports of the past. The achievement was possible partly because the Commission had faith in the key-role of education in national development implying economic growth and social transformation and partly because it was knowledgeable in the strategy and techniques of perspective planning. The Education Commission naturally hoped that the nation would be willing to pay for the reforms leading to the transformation of education so that fullest possible development of human resources might be possible. The Commission boldly assigned to education the task of transforming and modernizing existing social order so that the desired goal of a socialistic pattern of society might be realized within the foreseable future. While it may not be possible to engineer the educational revolution envisaged by the Commission with our present resources we shall have achieved a marked advance even if half the recommendations were implemented.

Following present day programmes find their origin in the Report of the Education Commission:

1. Formulation of the National Policy on Education (1968).
2. Establishment of Book Banks in Schools.
3. Increase in the duration of Secondary Stage (four years instead of three years).
4. Forerunner of the 10+2 Pattern of Education.
5. Vocationalization of Secondary Education.
6. Uniform Pattern of Education.
7. More Concern for Science and Mathematics Education.
8. Implementation of the Three Language Formula.

9.5 NATIONAL POLICY ON EDUCATION 1986 AND AS MODIFIED IN 1992 ON REFORMS IN SECONDARY EDUCATION

The NPE outlined the following priorities:

1. Access to secondary education will be widened to cover areas unserved by it. In other areas, the main emphasis will be on consolidation.
2. Emphasis will be on enrolment of girls, SCs and STs.

3. Boards of Secondary Education will be reorganized and vested with autonomy so that their ability to improve the quality of secondary education is enhanced.

4. Efforts will be made to provide computer literacy in as many secondary schools as possible.

5. Secondary stage will begin to expose students to the differentials role of Science, the Humanities and Social Sciences.

6. Secondary stage is an appropriate stage to provide children with a sense of history and national perspective.

7. Secondary stage will give students opportunities to understand their constitutional duties.

8. Secondary stage will develop work ethos.

9. Secondary stage will inculcate values of a humane and composite culture. An appropriate curricula will be formulated for this purpose.

10. Vocationalization through specialized institutions or through the refashioning of secondary education at this stage will provide valuable manpower for economic growth.

11. Vocational courses will cover 10 per cent of higher secondary students by 1995 and 25 per cent by 2000.

12. Pre-vocational courses and programmes provided at the lower secondary stage will facilitate the choice of the vocational courses at the higher secondary stage.

Programme of Action 1986 and 1992: After the formulation of 1986 policy, a Programme of Action was formulated and steps were taken to implement it. Likewise after the modification of the policy in 1992, necessary changes were introduced in the Programme of Action. (These programmes are given at the end of this chapter.)

9.6 SUGGESTIONS FOR REFORMING SECONDARY EDUCATION

Knowledge has been increasing very rapidly. At the same time population in India has also been increasing at an alarming rate. Apart from 'Knowledge Explosion', and 'Population Explosion', there is the 'Expectation Explosion'—people want more and more education. Then there are the requirements of globalisation. Therefore, a balance has to be struck against competing demands. Following are some of the suggestions to bring about qualitative and quantitative improvements in secondary education.

1. Emphasis should be laid on consolidation of secondary education and not its expansion.

2. A systematic, well planned and vigorously implemented scheme of vocationalization of education is the need of the hour.

3. Schools of general education, by and large, have failed to provide effective vocational education to students. It is, therefore, necessary that we give a second look to this aspect.

4. It is better if instead of opening ill-equipped Navodaya Schools (Pace Setting Schools), some existing schools in the rural areas are converted into model schools.

5. All the existing secondary schools must be provided with necessary staff and equipment. There is no logic in opening new schools when we are unable to provide even the basic necessities in the existing schools.

6. The present system of evaluation must be made more objective.
7. Administration and supervision of schools should be decentralized.
8. The idea of common school and neighbourhood school must be given a fair trial.
9. Provision of liberal scholarships should be made. Talent must be nurtured.
10. Facilities for part time studies should be expanded.
11. Government should open new schools in the areas inhabited by the economically weaker sections.

9.7 RECENT SCHEMES FOR QUALITATIVE IMPROVEMENT IN SECONDARY EDUCATION

The key issues in this area apart from access are: (i) Quality, (ii) Relevance, (iii) Modernization, (iv) Diversification, (v) Vocationalisation, (vi) Information Technology. Accordingly, the Central Government has sponsored several schemes for the qualitative improvement of secondary education and minimizing drop-outs, stagnation and wastage. A brief account of these schemes is given below:

1. *Vocationalisation of Secondary Education:* The scheme introduced in February 1988 aims at enhancing individual employability, reducing mismatch between demand and supply of skilled manpower and providing an alternative for those who are pursuing higher education without particular interest or purpose. Details of the scheme are given in a separate chapter.

2. *Improvement of Science Education in Schools:* The scheme has been operational since 1987-88. Under this 100 per cent assistance is provided to the States/Union Territories for provision of Science Kits to primary schools, upgradation of science laboratories and libraries in secondary/senior secondary schools and training of science and mathematics teachers. The scheme also provides for assistance to voluntary organizations for undertaking innovative projects in the field of science education.

3. *Environmental Orientation to School Education:* The scheme initiated in 1988-89 envisages grants and assistance to States/UTs and voluntary organizations for various activities related to the promotion of environmental education. The scheme includes programmes like review of textbooks and development of teaching-learning material relating to environmental education.

4. *International Science Olympiads:* With a view to identifying and nurturing talent in Mathematics and Physics at school level, India has been participating in the International Mathematical Olympiad (IMO) and International Physics Olympiad (IPO), since 1989 and 1998 respectively.

5. *Educational Technology:* Six autonomous State Institutes of Educational Technology (SIETs) have been set up in Uttar Pradesh, Bihar, Orissa, Maharashtra, Gujarat and Andhra Pradesh.

6. *Computer Literacy and Studies in Schools:* Realizing that students, who are the work-force of tomorrow, need to be exposed to utility and applications of computers, the Department of Electronics, in collaboration with the Ministry of Human Resource Development, introduced this scheme in 1984-85. However, the modified scheme since 1993-94 has the following objectives:

(a) The coverage of the new scheme will be restricted to senior secondary schools.

(b) In selected schools, instructions in Computer Literacy will be compulsory for all students of Classes XI and XII. During the Eighth Five Year Plan, 2,371 schools were covered.

7. *Strengthening of Boarding and Hostel Facilities for Girl Students of Secondary and Higher Secondary Schools:* In order to implement the modified NPE, 1992, this scheme was launched to improve the enrolment of adolescent girls belonging to rural areas and weaker sections.

10

Vocationalisation of Education at the Secondary Level

10.1 MEANING OF VOCATIONALISATION OF EDUCATION

Frequently the terms vocational education, vocationalisation of education, occupational education, job-oriented education and education for the world of work etc. are used interchangeably except where special mention is made of a particular type of education in a particular situation or environment.

For understanding the meaning and concept of vocational education, we may refer to its important definitions.

'The American Educator's Encyclopedia' (1982) defines vocational education as "a part of the school curriculum designed to make the student employable in at least one occupation."

Carter V. Good in *'Dictionary of Education'* (1973) has stated, "Vocational education is a programme of education below college grade organised to prepare the learner for entrance into a particular chosen vocation or to upgrade employed workers."

'The Encyclopedia America' (1985), defines vocational education in these words, "the preparation of young people and adults for skilled trades and semi-professional careers. It is most frequently offered at the high school or junior college level and does not normally include training for professions such as law and medicine."

UNESCO, in its recommendations of 1947 defined it as a "Comprehensive term embracing those aspects of the educational process involving, in addition to general education, the study of technologies and related sciences and the acquisition of practical skills, attitudes, understanding and knowledge relating to occupation in the various sectors of economic and social life."

Regarding the concept of vocationalisation, the Kothari Commission (1964-66) stated, "We visualise the future trend of school education to be towards a fruitful mingling of general and vocational education—general education containing some elements of pre-vocational and technical education and vocational education in turn, having an element of general education."

In the words of National Review Committee or Adiseshiah Committee (1978), "The vocationalised spectrum of the Higher Secondary School is learning of a skill or a range of skills, through study of technologies, related sciences and form or other practical work."

The National Working Group (1985) constituted by the Ministry of Education, Government of India under the Chairmanship of V.C. Kulandaiswamy, Vice-Chancellor of Anna University, explained the concept of vocational education as, "Traditionally 'vocational education' has been understood as education designed to prepare skilled personnel at lower levels of qualification for one or more groups of occupations, trade or jobs. Vocational education has been usually provided at upper secondary level."

The last definition quite fits in the present scenario.

10.2 NEED FOR VOCATIONAL EDUCATION AT THE SECONDARY STAGE

'Eat the bread at the sweat of the brow'; thus goes a Biblical injunction. What better way to follow it could there be than taking recourse to vocational education as well as vocationalisation of education!

The ratio of enrolment in vocational courses at the lower secondary and higher secondary schools in India is only 6% as compared with 20% of China, 24% in France, 29% in Italy, 59% in erstwhile USSR, 65% in U.K. and 80% or more in Denmark, Germany and Switzerland. This explains the reason for low productivity and unemployment in India.

The Education Commission pointed out, "Another programme which can bring education into closer relationship with productivity is to give a strong vocational bias to secondary education and to increase the emphasis on agricultural and technological education at the university stage."

The Adiseshiah Committee 1978 observed that special attention has to be given to the self-employment factor. It recommended 64 courses divided into 8 categories.

The National Policy on Education stressed, "The introduction of systematic, well planned and vigorously implemented programmes of vocational education is crucial in the proposed educational reorganisation."

The Policy pointed out the following merits:

1. *Enhancement of Employability*: Vocationalisation of education enhances employability.

2. *Reduction in Mismatch*: Vocationalisation of education reduces the mismatch between the demand and supply of skilled manpower.

3. *Alternative Courses*: Vocationalisation of education provides an alternative for those pursuing higher education without particular interest or purpose.

4. *Dignity of Labour*: Vocationalisation of education leads to dignity of labour.

5. *Self-Employment*: Vocationalisation of education enables individuals for self-employment.

6. *Increased Productivity*: Vocationalisation of education is related to productivity.

7. *Maximum Utilisation of Resources*: Vocationalisation of education is helpful in the maximum utilisation of the human and material resources of the country.

10.3 ACHIEVEMENT: SLOW PROGRESS IN VOCATIONAL EDUCATION

The NPE 1986 had proposed that vocational course would cover 10 per cent of the higher secondary stage by 1990 and 25 per cent by 1995. However, this target could not be achieved. The modified NPE 1992 stipulated that vocational courses would cover 10 per cent of higher secondary students by 1995 and 25 per cent by the year 2000. It also visualised that steps would be taken to see that a substantial majority of the products of vocational courses are employed or become self-employed. Achievement data in this regard is not available, '*The Annual Report 1998-99*' of the Ministry of Human Resource Development, Department of Education is silent on the data. It simply mentions, "18,719 vocational sections have been sanctioned in 6,486 schools all over the country thereby creating capacity for diversion of about 9.35 lakh students to the vocational stream which is 11 per cent of the enrolment at the +2 stages." It is interesting to note the word 'Sanctioned'. It gives no indication as to the percentage of students taking up vocational courses at the +2 stage *i.e.*, Class XI and XII.

Causes of Slow Progress of Vocationalisation: These are as under:

1. The unfavourable wage policies for middle-level skilled workers as against white-collar job operators.
2. The failure to control the expansion of general secondary education.
3. The inability to create adequate job opportunities.
4. Unfavourable prevailing social attitudes and inability to reconcile oneself to the idea of academically going into the vocational stream.
5. Lack of adequate resources for providing training to the hordes of boys and girls who would be expected to enter the vocational stream.
6. The involvement of community in providing facilities in their enterprises and establishments is a good idea but is difficult to put into practice.
7. Delinking degrees from jobs.

10.4 TARGETS AND MEASURES FOR THE PROMOTION OF VOCATIONAL EDUCATION AT THE SECONDARY STAGE: EDUCATION COMMISSION 1964-66

The Education Commission laid a great stress in vocationalisation of secondary education and pointed out, "Another programme which can bring education into closer relationship with productivity is to give a strong vocational bias to secondary education and to increase the emphasis on agricultural and technological education at the university stage." It made the following recommendations:

1. Secondary education should be vocationalised in a large measure and enrolment in vocational courses raised to 20 per cent of total enrolment at the lower secondary stage and 50 per cent of the total enrolment at the higher secondary stage by 1986.
2. A variety of part-time facilities in vocational education should be made available at both these stages to meet the needs of boys and girls, in urban and rural areas. Special sections should be set up in the Education Department to help young people who drop-out after Class VII and VIII to obtain training on a full-time or part-time basis.
3. The Central Government should provide special grants to State Governments in the Centrally sponsored sector for the vocationalisation of secondary education.

10.5 NATIONAL REVIEW COMMITTEE OR ADISESHIAH COMMITTEE (1978)

The National Review Committee was appointed by the Ministry of Education under the Chairmanship of Dr. Malcolm S. Adiseshiah, Vice-Chancellor, University of Madras. The Committee submitted its report in 1978 under the Title *'Learning to Do—Towards a Learning and Working Society'*. The report is popularly known as Adiseshiah Report after the name of its Chairman.

It is also known as National Review Committee Report for Plus Two Curriculum of School Education as its recommendations relate to the curriculum for classes XI and XII.

It is also called the Report of the National Review Committee on Higher Secondary Education with special reference to Vocationalisation of Education as it gives recommendations on vocationalisation of education.

Main Recommendations

1. *Two Broad Learning Components of the Higher Secondary Stage*: The Higher Secondary Stage should be planned as comprising two broad learning components, namely:

(i) General Education Spectrum, and
(ii) Vocational Spectrum.

2. *Vocational Spectrum*: The Committee has recommended that special attention has to be given to the self-employment factor. Vocational education at this level should, as far as possible, not duplicate, what the ITI's or Technical High Schools are at present offering. The main thrust of the proposed vocationalisation will be on rural, agricultural and related vocations. The duration of a vocational course should normally be two years in so far as the instruction in the schools in the formal system is concerned. The courses requiring lesser duration than two years may be pursued through non-formal systems such as part-time and evening courses, correspondence courses, etc., and the institutions should be free to offer such courses through non-formal channels.

Courses and Allocation of Time: The Committee has recommended the following course and allocation of time for the vocationalised spectrum:

Course	*Time Allocation*
(i) Language(s)	15%
(ii) General Foundation Course	15%
(iii) Elective Subject (60% for practical works)	70%

3. *Vocational Electives*: Any one vocational course to be offered out of 64 courses divided into 8 categories:

(i) Agricultural and Related Vocations
(ii) Business and Office Management
(iii) Para-Medical
(iv) Educational Service
(v) Local Body and other Services
(vi) Journalism
(vii) Home Science Related Vocations

(viii) Other General Services.

4. *Vocational Survey*: The Committee recommended that with regard to the offering of vocationalised courses in rural or urban schools, a vocational survey of the area—metropolitan, block, taluk, district or state—be undertaken, such surveys being done, even in cases where the vocational courses have been introduced.

5. *Selection of Schools*: The location of schools in the rural sector be given priority.

6. *Use of Available Facilities*: To economise on the financial investment on infrastructural facilities, the spare capacity in all the schools be used and the enrolment increased through running double shifts whenever it is possible.

7. *Counselling and Placement*: Counselling and Placement Officers be appointed in clusters of 3 or 4 schools, particularly in rural areas to start with.

8. *Pre-Service and In-Service Training of Teachers*: The Universities, the Teachers Training Colleges, State Councils of Educational Research and Training, State Institutes of Science Education; NCERT, Boards of Secondary Education, Agricultural Universities, institutions like ICAR, and all others should be actively involved in the programme of orientation of teachers.

9. *Teachers of Vocational Courses*: There should not be insistence on post-graduate qualifications in respect of teachers of vocational courses. Services of persons who have had actual experience of on-the-job may be fruitfully utilised to teach vocational courses. Part-time teachers may also be appointed, where necessary.

10. *Textbooks*: In order to impart instruction in vocational courses, in agricultural and related subjects, books may be written on a priority basis to suit local conditions and made available to schools.

11. *Recruitment on the Basis of Job Requirements*: The recruitment policy of the Government as well as public sector organisations should be revised and job requirements should replace the university degrees as essential qualifications. Vocationally qualified persons should be preferred to graduates.

12. *National Council of Vocational Education*: This body may be set up by the Ministry of Education and all the agencies such as the Indian Council of Agricultural Research, All India Council for Technical Education, the Nursing Council, the Dental Council, and the National Council for Training in Vocational Trades should be members of this apex body.

13. *Financial Resources*: Any expenditure on vocationalisation should be considered as a national investment and an investment for the future.

14. *Careful Preparation:* Careful preparation may be made to ensure that, many facets of the reform of Higher Secondary Education are thought through, planned for and provided as the country's stakes in this educational stage are high.

10.6 MANAGEMENT STRUCTURE FOR WORK EDUCATION, PRE-VOCATIONAL AND VOCATIONAL EDUCATION

Functions/ Levels	*Policy and Coordination*	*R&D Evaluation and Monitoring*	*Administration and Implementation*	*Examination and Certification*
National	Joint Council of Vocational Education	PSS Central Institute of Vocational Education, Bhopal	Bureau of Vocational/School Education, MHRD	Central Board of Secondary Education/Indian Council of Secondary Education
Regional	—	Regional Institutes of Education	Regional Board of Apprenticeship Training	—
State	State Council of Vocational Education	SCERT/State Institute of Vocational Education/ State Institute of Education	State Department of Education	State Boards of Examination/ Higher Secondary Council
District	District Vocational Education Committee	Vocational Training Centres/ District Institute of Education and Training	District Education/ Vocational Education Officer	—
Institute	Institute Advisory Committee	—	Principal/Head Master of Institution	—

Source: 'National Curriculum Framework for School Education', NCERT (2000).

10.7 MEASURES SUGGESTED FOR PROMOTION OF VOCATIONAL EDUCATION BY THE NATIONAL SEMINAR ON VOCATIONALISATION OF EDUCATION (1990)

(i) *Sharing Pattern of Expenditure on Vocationalisation:* It should be in the ratio of 80 : 20 between the Centre and States.

(ii) *Allocation for Construction of Sheds:* It should be enhanced by one and a half times that of the present rate.

(iii) *Course Structure:* 70 per cent of time should be utilised for vocational theory and practice.

(iv) *Standardized and Uniform Norms:* Steps should be taken to set up standardized and uniform norms for States to follow.

(v) *Training of Teachers*: Each State should identify that one or two existing teacher training colleges having adequate infrastructural facilities which could be converted into vocational teacher training colleges by supplementing with additional facilities through Central assistance.

(vi) *Orientation and Training of Vocational Officers:* Adequate arrangements should be made in this regard.

(vii) *Coverage Under Apprentice Act:* The number of vocational courses under the scheme should be increased substantially.

(viii) *Modification of Recruitment Rules:* Speedy and vigorous action is needed to enhance the chances of vocationally qualified persons to get employment.

10.8 CENTRALLY SPONSORED SCHEME OF VOCATIONALISATION OF HIGHER SECONDARY EDUCATION

The scheme introduced in February 1988, has the following objectives:

1. To enhance individual employability.
2. To reduce the mismatch between demand and supply of skilled manpower.
3. To provide an alternative for those pursuing higher education without particular interest or purpose.

The scheme is introduced through the State Governments/UT Administrations.

Following are the major steps taken to strengthen the vocational education programme:

(i) A Joint Council for Vocational Education (JCVE) was set up in April 1990 for policy formulation and coordination at the national level.

(ii) The Central Institute of Vocational Institute (CIVE), set up at Bhopal in July 1993, provides technical and academic support to the programme in the country.

(iii) Of the 150 courses introduced under the scheme, 60 vocational courses have been notified under the Apprenticeship Act.

(iv) Collaborative arrangements have been made with the Ministry of Railways etc.

10.9 CENTRALLY SPONSORED SCHEME OF PRE-VOCATIONAL EDUCATION AT LOWER SECONDARY STAGE

The scheme was introduced from the year 1993-94 primarily to impart training in simple marketable skills to the students of classes IX and X, to develop vocational interests and to facilitate students in making a choice of vocational courses at the higher secondary level.

Under the Pre-Vocational scheme, assistance has been provided to 11 States/UTs for introducing Pre-Vocational courses in 652 schools.

Table 1: State-wise Enrolment*: University Teaching Departments/ University Colleges and Affiliated Colleges: 2001-2002

S. No.	*Stage*	*University Depts./ University Colleges*	*Affiliated Colleges*	*Total (%age of Ground Total)*	*%age in Affiliated Colleges*
1.	Graduate	7,90,182	70,72,406	78,62,588 (89.13)	89.95
2.	Post-Graduate	2,77,427	5,38,908	8,16,335 (9.25)	66.02
3.	Research	55,158	5,358	60,516 (0.69)	8.86
4.	Diploma/ Certificate	43,381	38,275	81,656 (0.93)	46.87
	Grand Total	**11,66,148**	**76,54,947**	**88,21,095**	**86.78**

* Provisional.

11

Higher Education

Committees and Commissions

11.1 HISTORICAL REVIEW OF DEVELOPMENT OF HIGHER EDUCATION IN INDIA BEFORE 1947

1. *Expansion of Higher Education (1856-57 to 1901-1902)*: The development of modern higher education in India dates back to the year 1782 when the Calcutta Madrasa was founded by Warren Hastings and was for a time maintained by his friend and former tutor, Raja Nobkissen. Then came up the Hindu College in 1817.

The Wood's Despatch in 1854 led to the establishment of Universities at Calcutta, Madras and Bombay on the pattern of the London University.

The first University Entrance Examination was held at Calcutta in 1857. Out of 224 applicants who appeared, 162 were successful.

Table 1: Higher Education in 1856-1857

No. of Universities	*No. of Colleges*		*Enrolment*
	Type	*No*	
Nil	(a) Colleges of General Education	21	4,335
	(b) Colleges of Professional and other Education	13	

Thirteen candidates appeared for the first degree examination of 1858 at Calcutta University and only two were successful; one of whom was Bankim Chandra Chatterjee, the famous novelist and author of the National Song *'Vande Mataram'*.

In 1882, the Punjab University was established at Lahore. In 1887, Allahabad University came into being. All the five Universities were mere affiliating and examining bodies. They did no direct teaching work.

Table 2: Total Number of Colleges and their Students in 1901-02

Type of College	*No. of Institutions*	*No. of Students*
Arts Colleges: English	140	18,048
Oriental	05	503
Professional Colleges: Law	30	2,767
Medicine	04	1,466
Engineering	04	865
Training	05	190
Agriculture	03	70
Total	191	23,909

Note : There is slight difference in the enrolment as compared with the table in Chapter 1.

During this period, the Indian Education Commission or Hunter Commission after the name of its Chairman was appointed (Its recommendations on higher education are given in the next section).

2. *Higher Education (1902-1921)*: The University Commission of 1902 made some important recommendations (See Chapter 1). The Government Resolution on Educational Policy dated 21st February 1913 declared that a university would be established in each province. The Calcutta University Commission or the Sadler Commission (1917) made far-reaching recommendations not only with respect to Calcutta University but also with respect to university education in general.

Table 3: Expansion of Higher Education (1921-22)

(i)	No. of Universities	14
(ii)	No. of Colleges	246
(iii)	Enrolment:	
	Male	57,308
	Female	1,529
	Total	58,837

3. *Higher Education (1921-37)*: As a result of the First All India Conference of Indian Universities held at Shimla in 1924, the Inter-University Board came into being in 1925 for the coordination of the Work of Indian Universities. The number of University Departments and constituent or affiliated colleges increased from 246 in 1921-22 to 446 in 1936-37 and the number of students from nearly 60,000 to 1,20,000.

4. *Higher Education (1937-1947)*: Several new colleges and universities were opened. The large expansion was due to national awakening. The number of universities increased to 20 in 1947 (after independence). The number of colleges was 626 with nearly 2,40,000 students.

11.2 COMMITTEES AND COMMISSIONS ON HIGHER EDUCATION DURING 1800-1947

On the basis of Lord Macaulay's Minutes (1835), Governor-General Lord William Bentinck's Resolution (1835) laid down the broad parameters of the educational system in India. The Wood's Despatch (1854) led to the establishment of universities in India. There were several Government Resolutions on Education also. However, the most significant Commissions having far-reaching implications for higher education were as under:

1. Indian Education Commission (1882-83)
2. Indian Universities Commission (1902)
3. Indian Universities Act (1904)
4. Calcutta University Commission or Sadler Commission (1917-1919)

Indian Education Commission or Hunter Commission (1882-83): Lord Ripon (1880-84), the Viceroy of India, appointed the Commission with Sir William Hunter (Member of the Viceroy's Executive Council) as its Chairman and 21 members. Its important recommendations relating to higher education were as under:

1. The rate of aid to each college be determined by the strength of the staff, the expenditure on its maintenance, the efficiency of the institution and the needs of the locality.

2. The Indian graduates, especially those who have also graduated from European Universities be largely employed.

3. The Principal of Colleges may be given discretionary powers to admit those students in certain courses who have not passed the examinations required by the universities.

Indian Universities Act (1904): (i) Universities were given the rights of teaching along with conducting examinations. (ii) The number of members of the Senate of the University was fixed. (iii) Legal status was given to syndicates of the universities.

Indian Universities Commission (1902): Lord Curzon appointed this Commission. Indian members were also associated with it. Its important recommendations were:

1. Undergraduate students should be left in the main to the colleges.

2. Universities must justify their existence as teaching bodies by making better provision for advanced courses of study.

3. The proper teaching of English must be regarded as the most important matter in the curriculum.

4. A Managing Committee should be there for every college.

The Commission, failed to make any impact.

Calcutta University Commission or Sadler Commission (1917-1919)

Appointment of the Commission: On 14 September 1917, the Government of India, through a Resolution, appointed a Commission called the Calcutta University Commission, also known as Sadler Commission after the name of its Chairman, Dr. M.E. Sadler of the Leads University.

Terms of Reference of the Commission: "To enquire into the conditions and prospects of the University of Calcutta and to consider the question of a constructive policy in relation to the question it presents."

After a labour of 17 months, the Commission submitted its report in 1919. Consisting of 13 parts the report presented a comprehensive scheme of Secondary, Collegiate and University education in India. The Commission held that reform at the stage of secondary education was essential for the improvement of university education.

Important Recommendations on University Education

(i) Intermediate classes should be separated from universities and a curriculum spreading over three years should be prescribed for the degree of B.A. The stage of admission to the university should be intermediate and not matriculation examination.

(ii) Intermediate colleges should be established for the sake of completing the first stage. These colleges should conduct teaching in arts, science, medicine, engineering, education, agriculture and commerce.

(iii) A separate High School and Intermediate Board should be formed in every province, consisting of representatives of the Government, universities, high schools and intermediate colleges, for the sake of managing secondary education.

(iv) The teachers of the universities should be given more powers with a view to removing unnecessary State control over them.

(v) Regulations governing the working of universities should be made less rigid.

(vi) Provision should be made for the institution of Honours courses, as distinct from Pass course for the sake of abler students.

(vii) The duration of degree course should be three years after the intermediate stage.

(viii) For the internal administration of the university, a representative court in place of Senate and a small Executive Council in place of the syndicate should be set up.

(ix) A special Committee should be constituted for making appointments to Professorships and Readerships. The Committee should include external experts also.

(x) A full time and salaried Vice-Chancellor should be appointed.

Modern Indian Languages: The Calcutta University Commission (1917) stated: "We are emphatically of opinion that there is something unsound in a system of education which leaves a young man, at the conclusion of his course, unable to speak or write his own mother tongue fluently and correctly. It is thus beyond controversy that a systematic effort must henceforth be made to promote the serious study of the vernaculars in secondary schools, intermediate colleges and in the university."

Observations on the Report

According to *A.N. Basu,* "The report of the Commission contains the most comprehensive and authoritative study of the Indian education system from the secondary stage to the university. It is, therefore, quite natural that they have greatly influenced the subsequent course of secondary and higher education in the country." (*Education in Modern India*)

In the words of *Arthor Mathew,* "The Report of the Calcutta University Commission has been a constant source of suggestion and information. Its significance in the History of Indian Education has been incalculable." (*The Education of India*)

Though the Commission was appointed to introduce reforms in the Calcutta University, yet its recommendations exercised a tremendous influence on the functioning of universities and colleges in India.

11.3 COMMITTEES AND COMMISSIONS AND ALLIED DOCUMENTS ON HIGHER EDUCATION IN INDIA SINCE INDEPENDENCE

Following were the important documents which guided the development of higher education in a great measure:

1. University Education Commission (1948-49).
2. Constitutional Bases of Education (1950).
3. Committee to Examine the Problem of Instruction at the University Stage and Recommend Ways and Means of Securing Adequate Proficiency in English (1954).
4. Three-year Degree Course Estimate Committee (1956).

5. Examination Committee (1957).
6. National Committee on Women's Education (1958).
7. Committee on the Problem of Students Indiscipline in Indian Universities (1959).
8. Committee on Religious and Moral Instruction (1959).
9. Review Committee for Education in Indian Universities (1960).
10. Expert Committee on Correspondence Courses and Evening Colleges (1961).
11. Committee on Standards of University Education (1961).
12. Committee in Model Act for Universities (1961).
13. Committee on Emotional Integration (1961-62).
14. Committee of Members of Parliament on Higher Education (1962).
15. Committee on Some Problems of University Administration (Extent of Malpractices), 1964.
16. Education Commission (1964-66).
17. Committee on Rural Higher Education (1967).
18. National Policy on Education (1968).
19. Committee on Governance of Universities and Colleges (1969-73).
20. Development of Higher Education: A Policy Framework (1978).
21. Review Committee on University System (1985).
22. National Policy on Education (1986).
23. Programme of Action on NPE (1986).
24. National Commission on Teachers II (1983-85).
25. UGC Committee on Accreditation and Assessment Council (1988).
26. Gnanam Committee: Towards New Educational Management (1987-90).
27. Decentralization of Higher Education System (1991).
28. Revised National Policy on Education (1992).
29. UGC Committee on Funding of Higher Education (1993).

[*Note* : Other Committees and Commissions on Various Disciplines (subjects), Teacher's Salaries and other allied issues on Higher Education are not included here].

11.4 UNIVERSITY EDUCATION COMMISSION (1948-49)

Introduction

After independence the first action of a great significance to be taken by the Government of India in the field of education was the appointment of the University Education Commission under the Chairmanship of Dr. S. Radhakrishnan, a distinguished scholar and former Vice-Chancellor of Banaras University who rose to become the second President of India. The report of the Commission is a document of great importance as it has guided the development of university education in India since independence. The Commission was appointed by the Government of India to report on Indian University Education and suggest improvements and extensions that may be desirable to suit present and future requirements of the country. The Commission was inaugurated on December 6, 1948. It submitted its report in August 1949.

Major Recommendations of the University Education Commission

1. *Aims of Higher Education*: See next chapter.

2. *Teaching Staff* : (i) The importance of the teacher and his responsibility be recognised.

(ii) There be four classes of teachers—Professors, Readers, Lecturers and Instructors and accordingly their salaries be fixed.

(iii) Promotion from one category to another be solely on merit.

3. *Standards of Teaching*: (i) Admission to the University to be after 12 years of schooling.

(ii) A large number of occupational institutions be opened to divert students to different vocations after 10 to 12 years of schooling.

(iii) To avoid overcrowding in universities and colleges, the maximum number in the Arts and Science Faculties of a teaching university be fixed at 3,000 and in an affiliated college at 1,500.

(iv) The member of working days to be 180 in a year, exclusive of examination days.

4. *Courses of Study*: The relation of general and special education be worked out.

5. *Religious Education*: All educational institutions should start with a few minutes of silent meditation.

6. *Examinations*: A University degree should not be required for Government Administrative Control.

7. *Medium of Instruction*: For the medium of instruction for higher education, English be replaced by an Indian language.

Some of the recommendations are given while discussing a particular topic.

Evaluation of the Report: As already observed, the report has left its imprint almost on every aspect of higher education. The present structure of higher education derives its inspiration from the report. In a way, the present 10+2+3 pattern of education was visualised by the Commission as early as 1948-49. The 12 years of schooling and 3 years degree was recommended by it.

11.5 NATIONAL POLICY ON EDUCATION (1986 AS MODIFIED IN 1992)

Important observations are given below:

1. Urgent steps will be taken to protect the system from degradation.
2. Autonomous colleges will be helped to develop in large numbers.
3. Courses and programmes will be redesigned to meet the demands of specialisation better.
4. The UGC and the State Councils of Higher Education will develop coordinated methods to keep a watch on standards.
5. Admission will be regulated according to capacity.
6. Research in Indology, the humanities and social sciences will receive adequate support.
7. The Indira Gandhi National Open University will be strengthened.
8. A beginning will be made in de-linking degrees from jobs in selected areas.

11.6 EXPANSION IN HIGHER EDUCATION SINCE 1950-51

Table 4: No. of Universities, Deemed Universities and Institutes of National Importance

Year	No. of Universities	No. of Deemed Universities	No. of Institutes of National Importance	Total
1950-51	27	3	—	30
1960-61	45	2	2	49
1970-71	84	9	9	102
1980-81	112	11	9	132
1990-91	147	29	9	185
1994-95	164	36	14	214
1996-97	179	39	11	229
1997-98	179	39	11	229
2001-02	187	52	12	253
2003-04	213	89	13	315

There were 18 Central Universities and 195 State Universities. Their profiles varied—29 Agricultural, 3 Veterinary, 9 Medical, 8 Technological, one for Handicapped, 8 Law Universities and 9 Open Universities.

Table 5: Growth of Student Enrolment in Higher Education Since 1950-51

Year	Enrolment in Lakhs
1950-51	3.6
1960-61	6.45
1970-71	19.54
1980-81	27.52
1990-91	44.25
1996-97	67.55
1997-98	69.15
2001-02	88.20
2002-03	92.30
2003-04	99.50

Source: UGC Annual Report 2003-2004.

Table 6: No. of Colleges Since 1950-51

Year	No. of Colleges for General Education	Colleges for Professional Education
1950-51	370	208
1960-61	967	852
1970-71	2,285	99
1980-81	3,421	3,542*
1990-91	4,682	886
2003-04	9,427	1,068

* Includes Institutes for Post-Matric Courses).

Source: Economic Survey 2005-2006.

Table 7: Students Enrolment in General and Professional/Special Higher Education Since 1947 (In lakhs)

Year	*General*	*Professional*	*Total*
1947	183238 (80.06)	45643 (19.94)	228881
1957	661975 (76.79)	200100 (23.21)	862075
1967	936117 (68.39)	432686 (31.61)	1368803
1977	1829801 (78.43)	503134 (21.57)	2332935
1987	3179725 (85.28)	548882 (14.72)	3728607
1996	4983329 (90.07)	549669 (9.93)	5532998
1998	6530098 (91.97)	570344 (8.03)	7100442
2001	NA	NA	88.2

Table 8: Students Enrolment Faculty-Wise 2001-2002 (*Provisional*)

S. No.	*Faculty*	*Total Enrolment*	*Percentage to Total*
1.	Arts	40,69,632	46.13
2.	Science	17,54,110	19.88
3.	Commerce/Management	15,75,940	17.87
4.	Education	1,14,678	1.30
5.	Engineering/Technology	6,05,597	6.87
6.	Medicine	2,75,943	3.13
7.	Agriculture	52,833	0.60
8.	Veterinary Science	14,270	0.16
9.	Law	2,80,449	3.18
10.	Others	77,643	0.88
	Total	**88,21,095**	100.00

Table 9: Women Enrolment by Faculty: 2001-2002 (*Provisional*)

S. No.	*Faculty*	*Total Enrolment*	*Percentage to Total*
1.	Arts	18,20,134	51.79
2.	Science	6,99,376	19.90
3.	Commerce/Management	5,81,993	16.56
4.	Education	59,394	1.69
5.	Engineering/Technology	1,31,792	3.75
6.	Medicine	1,23,006	3.50
7.	Agriculture	9,137	0.26
8.	Veterinary Science	3,163	0.09
9.	Law	56,934	1.62
10.	Others	29,521	0.84
	Total	**35,14,450**	**100.00**

Table 10: Number and Distribution of Teaching Staff* by Designation in University Departments and University Colleges: 2001-2002

Year	*Professors*	*Readers*	*Sr. Lecturers*	*Lecturers*	*Tutor/ Demon-strators*	*Total*
2001-02	15,206 (20.22)	23,711 (31.53)	12,358 (16.43)	22,069 (29.35)	1,861 (2.47)	75,205 (100.00)

* Provisions

Notes (a) Figures in parantheses indicate the percentage of the cadres to the total staff.
(b) Part-time teachers/physical training instructors are included in lecturers.

Source: UGC Annual Report 2001-2002

12

Higher Education

Aims, Admissions, Student Unrest, Major Universities, Governance

12.1 AIM AND THEIR RELEVANCE TO OUR NEEDS

University Education Commission (1948-49) on the Aims of Higher Education in India

The University Education Commission pointed out the needs of independent India and thereafter set out the aims of higher education. It observed, "We must have a conception of the social order for which we are educating our youth ....Our educational system must find its guiding principle in the aims of the social order for which it prepares, in the nature of the civilisation it hopes to build. Unless we know whither we are tending, we cannot decide what we should do and how we should do it. Societies like men need a clear purpose to keep them stable in a world of bewildering change.

We cannot preserve real freedom unless we preserve the value of democracy, justice and liberty, equality and fraternity. It is the ideal towards which we should work though we may be modest in planning our hopes as to the results which in the near future are likely to be achieved. "Utopias are sweet dreams," wrote Kant, "but to strive relentlessly towards them is the duty of the citizen and of the statesmen as well." Universities must stand for these ideal causes which can never be lost so long as men seek wisdom and follow righteousness.

Education is a means by which society perpetuates itself. In 1852, Newman defined the function of the university thus, "If a practical end must be assigned to a university course, then I say it is training good members of society." No system of education could be directed to the weakening of the State that maintains it. But education is also an instrument for social change."

In the light of above mentioned needs, the University Education Commission laid down the following aims of higher education:

1. To awaken the innate ability of the students to live life with wisdom.
2. To teach the students that life has a meaning.
3. To train students for democracy.
4. To acquaint students with the social philosophy which governs all our institutions.
5. To develop in the students values like fearlessness of mind, strength of conscience and integrity of purpose.
6. To train students for self-development.
7. To develop understanding of the present as well as of the past.
8. To acquaint students with cultural heritage and its regeneration.
9. To enable the students to know that education is a life-long process.

10. To impart professional and vocational training to students.

Laying emphasis on high ideals as the aims of higher education, the Commission observed, "The greatness of a country does not depend on the extent of its territory, the length of its communications or the amount of wealth, not even on widespread education or equitable distribution of wealth important as all these things are. If we wish to bring about a savage upheaval in our society, a *raksasa raj*, all that we need to do is to give vocational and technical education and starve the spirit. We will have a number of scientists without conscience, technicians without taste who find a void within themselves, a moral vacuum and a desperate need to substitute something, anything, for their lost endeavour and purpose. Society will then get what it deserves. If we claim to be civilized we must develop thought for the poor and the suffering, chivalrous regard and respect for women, faith in human brotherhood regardless of race or colour, nation or religion, love of peace and freedom, abhorrence of cruelty and ceaseless devotion of the claims of the justice."

Education Commission (1964-66) on the Aims of Higher Education

The Education Commission suggested the following aims in the light of the Preamble of the Constitution which envisages a democratic, secular, socialist and modern India.

1. To enable the students to seek and cultivate new knowledge and to interpret old knowledge and beliefs in the light of new needs and discoveries.
2. To enable the students to engage vigorously and fearlessly in the pursuit of truth.
3. To enable the students to provide the right kind of leadership in all walks of life.
4. To enable them develop their full potential by cultivating physical fitness, developing the powers of the mind and cultivating right interests, attitudes and moral and intellectual values.
5. To develop in the students a sense of social purpose.
6. To develop professional efficiency and prepare them to take up responsibility in agriculture, arts, medicine, science and technology and various other professions.
7. To enable them to strive for promoting quality and social justice and reducing social and cultural differences.
8. To foster in the students and through them in the society generally, the attitudes and values needed for developing the 'good life' in individual and society.
9. To encourage individuality, variety and dissent, within a climate of tolerance.

National Policy on Education (1986 and 1992) on the Aims of Higher Education

1. To imbue the students to develop a strong commitment to humane values.
2. To imbue the students with ideals of social justice.
3. To enable them to refine sensitivities and perceptions that contribute to national cohesion, a scientific temper and independence of mind and spirit—thus

furthering the goals of socialism, secularism and democracy enshrined in our Constitution.

4. To enable the students to contribute to national development.

To develop the ability to internalise new ideas constantly and creatively.

5. To prepare the students for taking up professions at the different levels of economy.

6. To enable the students to develop new designs of human resource development needed in the new environment.

7. To enable the students to reflect on the critical social, economic, cultural, moral and spiritual issues facing humanity.

12.2 PROBLEMS OF ADMISSION

The problem of admission to higher education presents a very paradoxical situation. On the one hand, the access to higher education in India is very limited as compared with advanced and developed countries (see Table below) and on the other hand there is the problem of educated unemployed. Another disturbing factor is that quite a substantial number of educated who have received professional education in India migrate to foreign countries. The problem of admission has also to be viewed in the context of a considerable demand for and expansion of education due to the (i) Aspirations of the people after the adoption of the democratic, socialistic pattern of life; (ii) Growth of industries and the corresponding need for skilled manpower; (iii) Liberalisation of the economy and demand on education for new knowledge and technology leading to better employability; and (iv) New directions in manpower development activities provided by higher education.

Table 1: Some Select Countries with their Enrolment Ratios per 1,00,000 Population

S. No.	*Country*	*Enrolment*
1.	Canada	7,000
2.	Australia	5,400
3.	U.S.A.	5,301
4.	Korea, Republic of	5,000
5.	New Zealand	4,600
6.	India	68

Table 2: No. of Students in India in Higher Education per One Lakh

Year	*No. of Students Per 1 Lakh*
1901	1.2
1951	4.8
1961	12.6
1971	36.0
1981	40.2
1991	54.6
1995	68.0

Table 3: Percentage of Students Enrolled in Higher Education in Selected Countries

S. No.	*Country/Region*	*% Enrolled in the Age Group 18-23 years*
1.	U.S.A.	75
2.	Western Europe	40
3.	South-East Asian Countries	20
4.	India	6

Education Commission (1964-66) on Admission Policy in Higher Education

Selective Admissions

Three main elements needed for operating a programme of selective admissions in higher education are:

1. the determination of the number of places available in an institution in relation to teachers and facilities available to ensure that standards are maintained at an adequate level;
2. prescription of eligibility criteria by the universities; and
3. selection by the institution concerned of the best students from amongst those who are eligible and seek admission.

Part-Time and Own-Time Education: The opportunities for part-time education through programmes like evening colleges, and for own time education through programmes like correspondence courses, should be extended as widely as possible and should also include courses in science and technology (either at the degree or diploma level). They will help reduce the capital costs of expanding higher education and down even the recurring costs to a substantial extent, especially as enrolments grow.

Open University and Students Benefiting from the Open University in India: The Open University is expected to benefit the following:

1. Students who could not get admission in colleges for want of finance or because of employment and the consequent dislocation;
2. Students who, having been admitted, had to leave their studies to take up jobs;
3. Students of regular colleges who might require after-hour guidance;
4. Women who could not get higher education due to paucity of teachers or due to marriage;
5. Employees who wish to improve their professional skill; and
6. The older generation who might seek this instruction to secure better academic qualifications as the fulfilment of a life dream.

National Policy on Education on Admission Policy

The NPE observed, "In view of the need to effect an all-round improvement, it is proposed that, in the near future, the main emphasis will be on consolidation of and expansion of facilities in existing institutions."

12.3 STUDENT UNREST

While discussing the problem of student unrest in India, following are the important facets which must be kept in view:

1. Student unrest has existed since the establishment of universities in the world. Of course its magnitude was very insignificant in earlier times.

2. As the University Education Commission (1948-49) observed the problem of student indiscipline is world-wide.

3. The fact that the university is a sub-system of the society, and hence it reflects its value and norms of conduct and behaviour, is not an *'alibi'* for the present state of indiscipline in the universities and institutions of higher education.

4. In recent years, the 'teacher unrest' has become more pronounced than student unrest.

University Education Commission on Student Indiscipline

The University Education Commission observed that indiscipline arises from world and local conditions. It stated, "Some of the unrest in college now appears to start from world conditions. Ferment is international and continental, a condition that follows in the wake of wars, and is more acute now than ever before. We should not forget that we are living in a period of confusion and conflict. This is a world-wide phenomenon. This has an unsettling effect upon the youth of every country."

The Commission listed the following causes of student unrest:

(i) Some political cliques and even anarchical elements exploit college students for their purposes;

(ii) Meager finances and consequent lack of amenities required for healthy life;

(iii) Lack of adequate facilities *i.e.,* playgrounds and cooperative activities etc.;

(iv) The masses of students;

(v) The failure of parents at times to support the college authorities;

(vi) The inability of the teachers to cope with confused thinking, admission of students without the intelligence or industry requisite for successful study;

(vii) Tensions over examinations which unfortunately dominate the educational system; and

(viii) Financial worry caused to poor students by the cost of university education.

All these contribute to the difficulties of maintaining the best conduct and welfare of students.

The Universities Education Commission recommended the following measures for checking student unrest:

1. Universities should be divorced from party politics.

2. Constructive approaches to the solution of disciplinary and allied problems should be adopted. Reliance should not be placed on a multitude of restraints and reprimands or in the infliction of continuous penalties.

3. The National Cadet Corps is a very useful form of developing discipline and orderly habits among students.

4. Opportunities for recreation, athletics, sports etc., should be provided on an extensive scale.

5. Amenities for social life should be made available in a large measure.

6. The problem of discipline requires cooperative efforts on several sections of population.

Prof. Humayun Kabir's View on Student Unrest

Prof. Humayun Kabir in a pamphlet entitled *'Student Indiscipline'* (1955), published by the Ministry of Education listed the following four causes of student unrest:

1. The loss of leadership by teachers who, in general, did not involve themselves on a large scale in the freedom struggle.
2. Growth of economic difficulties of the students to pursue higher education.
3. Defects in the existing system of education.
4. General loss of idealism in the society and its reflection on students.

Multiple Caurses of Student Unrest

Academic	*Administrative*	*Political*	*General*	*Teacher*
(i) Lack of proper academic environment in institutions.	(1) Double standard of authorities and corruption.	(i) Political inter-ference in admissions, appoint-ments etc.	(a) Lack of ideals in society.	(i) Frequent strikes by teachers.
(ii) Uninspiring curriculum.	(2) Lack of under-standing about student problems.	(ii) Political interference in student union elections.	(b) Ideological frustration.	(ii) Lack of devotion to work.
(iii) Defective examination system.	(3) Non-involve-ment of students in university affairs pertaining to student issues.		(c) General lack of respect for parents, authorities etc.	(iii) Absenteeism and neglect of work.
(iv) Raise in tuition fees.	(4) Lack of amenities.		(d) Lack of employment opportnities.	
(v) Lack of individual contact between the teacher and the taught.	(5) Lack of finances.		(e) Increase in bus fares etc.	
(vi) Defective admission policy.				
(vii) Lack of motivation among students.				

University Grants Committee on Student Indiscipline (1960)

It made the following recommendations:

1. Students should be admitted to the university after careful selection. Admissions to the universities and colleges should be made strictly with reference to qualifications and merit.
2. Every effort should be made by universities to raise the minimum age of entry from +16 to +17.
3. No college should ordinarily be allowed to have more than 1,000 students, so that opportunities for organized community life can be developed.
4. Universities and colleges should take appropriate steps to bring about increasingly close touch between teachers and pupils so as to secure a full impact of the mature teachers' personality on the not yet mature students.

5. The salary of a lecturer in a college or university should be similar to that of a Class I Government servant in the Government of India or the State Government.

6. There should be a very careful selection of teachers. In addition to their academic qualifications, it is necessary to see that the men and women recruited to the profession are persons of the highest integrity and of sound character.

Overall Recommendations on Checking Student Unrest

The words of wisdom of the University Education Commission (1948-49) are as relevant today as they were at that time. The Commission felt, "The key to the successful handling of young people is not found nowadays in a multitude of restraints and reprimands or in the infliction of continuous penalties. These devices may have to be resorted to in extreme cases but wholesome student attitude and life cannot be created by negative and repressive measures. The true sanction of discipline lies in the development of the social conscience of the undergraduate body as a whole rather than in punitive measures of precautionary vigilance. As in society so in the university laws are observed because they are approved by reason rather than because they are imposed by force. Indiscipline should be terminated by the good sense of the students.

We recommend that students be given the opportunity to develop self-respect and self-reliance through an attitude of trust rather than live in an atmosphere of suspicion and fear. Good Student government integrates the college community, imparts a wholesome social atmosphere, fosters common ideals and loyal pride in an institution but most important, provides training for good citizenship and social responsibility. It gives scope for the right types of student political activity, which helps to develop the capacity to play the role of citizens in a republican form of Government and a democratic society. It replaces the undesirable tendencies towards undermining respect for constituted authority and leaving youth a prey to propaganda of conflicting ideologies."

Recommendations of Committees and Commissions on checking student unrest may be summarised as:

1. Cooperative efforts at various levels may be made to understand student ethos and necessary concern shown.
2. Institutions of higher education should be divorced from party politics.
3. Students should be involved in the framing of policies that affect them.
4. Welfare measures on an extensive scale should be undertaken.
5. Curriculum should be reconstructed to meet the changing needs.
6. Overcrowding in classes should be checked.
7. Admission process should be made more fair.
8. Student Advisory Bureaus should be constituted.
9. Appropriate liaison with industries should be established.
10. Teachers should take more interest in their work.
11. Social service activities should be planned on a large scale.
12. Adequate number of scholarships should be provided to the deserving students.

Concluding Observations: The major responsibility lies on the political leaders—leaders in power and leaders in opposition—and the administrators. They must set high ideals before students. This seems to be the only solution for making the students devoted to their academic pursuits.

12.4 MAJOR UNIVERSITIES AND PRESENT POSITION

The Education Commission (1964-66) made the following recommendations on Major Universities. It observed, "The most important reform in higher education is the development of some 'major universities' where first-class post-graduate work and research would be possible and whose standards would be comparable to the best institutions of their type in any part of the world. The UGC should select, as soon as possible, from amongst the existing universities, about six universities (including one of the IITs and one Agriculture University) for development as major universities."

Main Features of a Major University

A major university should have a 'critical mass' of students and teachers of outstanding capacity and promise. From this point of view,

1. Each major university should be assigned a number of scholarships for the undergraduate stage which will provide it with enough talented students for its post-graduate classes. Of these scholarships, about half should be from outside the area of the university;

2. Each department or faculty of a major university should have a specially appointed personnel advisory committee, which should work in close collaboration with the appointing authorities of the university. The search for staff, instead of being limited to the State or the region, should be made nation-wide and, in a sense, world-wide. Where necessary, the selected candidates should be offered advance increments. What is even more important, they should be assured of research opportunities, opportunities for study leave and the possibility to achieve professional excellence. There should be room for flexibility in the appointments and promotions. The UGC should place at the disposal of each university a contingency fund which may be used to provide more attractive salaries to persons of exceptional promise and performance.

3. It is necessary to establish 'clusters' of advanced centres in the major universities. They will add strength to, and enrich one another and be specially helpful in promoting interdisciplinary research. About fifty such centres should be established, including some in modern Indian languages. At least one of them should concentrate on developing an interdisciplinary approach to education. Other important areas to be covered are agriculture, engineering and medicine.

4. The administration of a centre, subject to the overall supervision of the university's Executive Council, should be the responsibility of its director assisted by a small but representative committee of his colleagues.

5. The original selection of a university department as a centre should be made on the basis of the quality and extent of work already done by it, its reputation for good teaching, its contribution to research and its potentiality for further development. The process of selection should be so devised that it will win the confidence of the universities and the academic community generally.

6. The privilege of being a centre of advanced study should be continually earned and deserved. Each centre of advanced study should have, say, once in three to five years, a visiting committee, consisting of outstanding Indian and,

where possible and necessary, foreign experts who will conduct a review and appraisal of the accomplishments of the centre.

7. The centres within a university should function in close collaboration with other centres and departments which are not centres of advanced study and measures should be adopted to involve the entire staff of the university in functioning as an intellectually effective community.

8. The major universities should constantly strive to enlarge the area of their excellence. For this purpose, they might be given a grant in proportion to the number of centres they already possess, to be used for the purpose of raising other departments within the university to their level.

9. Centres for advanced study should seek to bring the relevant teachers of their affiliated colleges into closer contact within their work.

10. The recurring and capital costs of the major universities should be met by the UGC.

11. The major universities should be utilized to provide teachers of quality to other universities and to the affiliated colleges. From this point of view:

(i) Every effort should be made to induce talented students from the major universities to join the teaching profession and to place a majority of them in universities and colleges, other than their own, so that they can help to raise standards;

(ii) The UGC should sponsor a scheme for instituting a number of fellowships at three levels—lecturers, readers and professors. Outstanding persons, who may otherwise be lost to the profession, should be granted these fellowships and seconded to work in suitable departments of universities.

Present Position: The UGC assists a large number of centres as national facilities. There are 6 Inter-University Centres and 11 other centres as national facilities/information centres assisted by UGC. The Inter-University Centres are namely, Nuclear Science Centre, Delhi; Inter-University Centre for Astronomy and Astro-Physics, Pune, Inter-University Consortium for DAE facilities, Indore; National Assessment and Accreditation Council, Bangalore; Information and Library Network (INFLIBNET), Ahmedabad and Consortium of Educational Communication, New Delhi.

The scheme of major universities has not materialized. Nevertheless nearly 20 Central Universities have been established for promoting excellence in education. These Central Universities, for this purpose are given special grants and assistance.

12.5 GOVERNANCE OF HIGHER EDUCATION

Constitutional Provisions: The Constitution of India placed education in the State List subject to some provisions relating to higher education. However with the Constitutional Amendment in 1976, education became a concurrent subject.

Indian Universities are Statutory Bodies established under Acts of Parliament or State Legislatures. The sources of their funding are grants from the public sector.

The following chart explains the organization and governance of higher education.

Chart showing Organisation and Governance of Higher Education

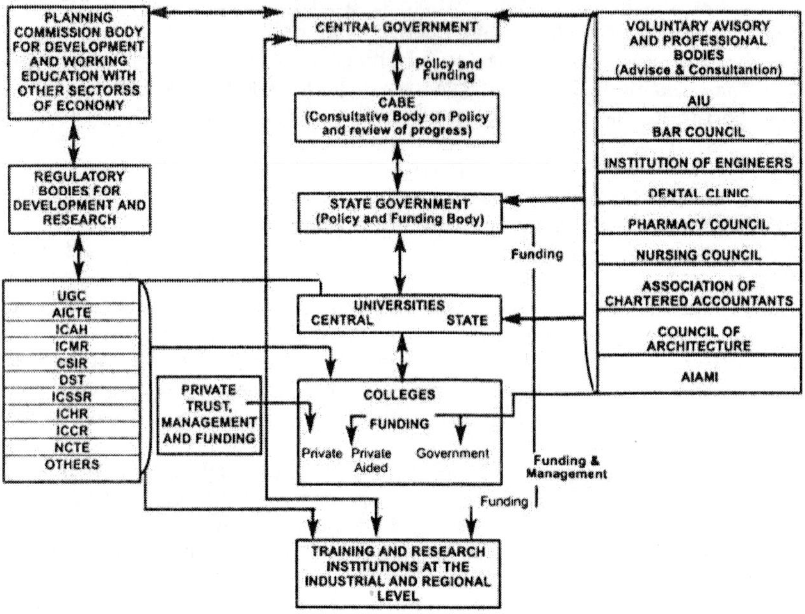

Major Institutions and Organisations set up by the Government of India

The Government of India has set up the following institutions (subordinate as well as autonomous) to discharge its functions in higher education.

UGC : University Grants Commission
ICMR : Indian Council of Medical Research
DST : Department of Science & Technology
ICHR : Indian Council of Historical Research
CABE : Central Advisory Board of Education
NCTE : National Council of Teacher Education
AIAMI : All India Association of Management Institutions
ICAR : Indian Council of Agricultural Research
CSIN : Council of Scientific & Industrial Research
ICSSR : Indian Council of Social Science Research
ICCR : Indian Council of Cultural Relations
AIU : Association of Indian Universities
AICTE : All India Council for Technical Education

Sources: UGC Annual Report, '95-96
Prof. K. Sudha Rao, *New Frontiers in Education'*. Vol. XXVIII, No. 4, Oct-December, 1998, New Delhi.

12.6 UNIVERSITY GRANTS COMMISSION (UGC)

The University Grants Commission was set up by the Government of India under an Act (3 of 1956) of Parliament in 1956. The functions of the Commission in Section 12 of the Act are: "It shall be the general duty of the Commission to take, in consultation with the universities or other bodies concerned, all such steps as it may think fit for the promotion and coordination of university education and for the determination and maintenance of standards of teaching, examination and research in universities." For the purpose of performing its functions under the Act, the Commission takes up the following measures:

1. Inquires into the financial needs of the universities;
2. Allocates and disburses the grants to the universities;
3. Recommends to any university the measures necessary for the improvement of university education and advises the university upon the action to be taken for the purpose of implementing such recommendations.
4. Advises any authority on the establishment of a new university or on proposals connected with the expansion of the activities of the university;
5. Collects information on all matters relating to university education in India and other countries as it thinks fits and makes the same available to any university; and
6. Performs such other functions as may be prescribed or as may be deemed necessary by the Commission for advancing the cause of higher education in India or as may be incidental or conductive to the discharge of the above functions.

The Chairperson of the UGC is nominated by the Government of India, Ministry of Human Resource Development, Department of Education.

The UGC Act was amended in 1972 with a view to regulating the unplanned proliferation of universities by adding a proviso which said, "No grant shall be given by the Central Government, the Commission, or any other organisation receiving any funds from the Central Government, to a university which is established after the commencement of the UGC (Amendment) Act, 1972, unless the Commission has, after satisfying itself as to such matters as may be prescribed, declared such university to be fit for receiving grants." As a result of this proviso, the State Governments started consulting the UGC before establishing new universities.

Another important power invested in the Commission under the Act is to enquire into the financial needs of the universities to allocate and disburse grants for the maintenance and development of universities and to recommend to any university the measures necessary for the improvement of university education, concerned upon the action to be taken for the purpose of implementing such recommendations.

The Commission has, under the amended Act referred to above, now got the power to allocate and disburse, out of the funds of Commission, grants for maintenance to the universities, other than Central universities, for any specified activities of such universities, or for any other general and specified purpose.

The University Grants Commission Act was further amended in September, 1984. The two main features of the amended Act which came into force with effect from 1.10.1984, are: (1) to enlarge the functions of the Commission so as to enable it to establish, in accordance with the regulations made under the Act, institutions for providing common facilities, services and programmes for a group of universities or for the universities in general and maintain such institutions or provide for their maintenance by allocating and disbursing out of its funds such grants as it may deem necessary, and (2) to empower the UGC to determine the scales of fees charged by college and to deny grants to and de-recognise the colleges, which violates the provision so that it cannot send up any candidate for the examinations.

The UGC Act authorized the Central Government on the advice of the Commission to declare by notification in the Official Gazette that any institution for higher education other than a university, shall be deemed to be a university for the purpose of this Act, and on such a declaration being made, all the provisions of this Act shall apply to such institution as if it were a university.

12.7 REFORMS IN HIGHER EDUCATION ADMINISTRATION

The UGC appointed a Committee in 1987 to suggest reforms in higher education administration after the formulation of NPE. The Committee popularly known as Gnanam Committee after the name of its Chairman Prof. A. Gnanam, Vice Chancellor, Bharathidasan University, submitted its report in 1990. Its important recommendations on higher education administration and management are given below.

1. The Parliament may enact a law (Model Act) setting out the basic structure of the university governance and ensuring that all related legislations by the State Governments conform to the core provisions of this law;

2. The UGC Act to be reviewed and revised:

(a) To empower the Commission for greater involvement in the overall development of higher education in the country;

(b) to make prior concurrence of the Commission obligatory for opening new universities; and

(c) To provide for consultation with the State level machinery.

3. *University Grant Commission* to establish 4-5 regional offices for effective implementation and monitoring of the Commission's programmes and its funding to universities and colleges.

4. *State Governments:* (i) To constitute the State Council for Higher Education to assist and coordinate the functioning of the universities and for effective liaison with the State Government and the UGC.

5. *Universities:* (i) Large universities, with 40 or more colleges affiliated to it, to establish regional centres to compensate for the infrastructural deficiencies in colleges in rural and semi-urban areas; and

(ii) To start building up endowment funds so that total dependence on government grants is reduced.

6. *Colleges:* (i) To constitute a Planning and Evaluation Committee to formulate the specific/distinctive goals of the Institution, periodically review its personnel and material resources, administrative patterns, and

(ii) To review and revamp administrative structure.

Autonomous Colleges

The concept of autonomous colleges is aimed at providing academic freedom by way of designing their courses, evolving new methods of teaching, research and learning, framing own rules for admission and conducting examinations. The college evaluates the students for the award of degrees which will be accepted by parent university. The number of autonomous colleges in India is 123. These are spread over eight States, viz., Tamil Nadu, Andhra Pradesh, Uttar Pradesh, Gujarat, Maharashtra and Himachal Pradesh.

13

Adult Education

13.1 MEANING OF ADULT EDUCATION

Adult education is the key that unlocks the door to modernization. Nevertheless, the concept of adult education is like a chameleon; its appearance *i.e.,* its concept and methods etc. changing with every observer from country to country and even from region to region, depending upon the nature of development—a developed, developing and underdeveloped economy.

There is no internationally accepted definition of adult education. In 1952, it was stated in UNESCO's *'International Directory of Adult Education'*, "In essence, adult education is so closely related to the social, political and cultural conditions of each country that no uniform or precise definition can be arrived at."

The meaning of adult education has to be seen in the cultural context. However, following definitions throw a lot of light on the meaning of adult education.

Elsinore Conference, the First International Conference on Adult Education (1949), stated the following meaning of adult education, "Adult education has the task of satisfying the needs and aspirations of adults in all their diversity."

'Blond's Encylopaedia of Education' (1969) states, "Adult education is the provision of learning situations to enable mature men and women to enlarge and interpret their own experiences."

A Handbook of Adult Education Instructors' (1980) in India stated the meaning of adult education as "Adult education is a package of educational programmes for adults outside the formal educational system aiming at providing more information and both knowledge and skills for improving their life-style, and also their earning capacity."

UNESCO in an International Conference on the Development of Adult Education (1976), has explained the meaning of adult education in these words, "The term adult education denotes the entire body of organised educational process, whatever content, level and method, whether formal or otherwise, whether they prolong or replace education in schools, colleges and universities as well as in apprenticeship, whereby persons regarded as adults by the society to which they belong develop their abilities, enrich their knowledge improve their technical or professional qualifications and bring about changes in their attitudes or behaviour in the two-fold perspective of full personal development and participation in balanced and independent social, economic and cultural development. It is an integral part of life-long education and learning."

Adult Education, Adult Functional Literacy, Basic Education (In the World Context), Community Education, Continuous Education, Fundamental Education, Life Long Education, Non-Formal Education, Professional Upgrading and Social Education, All these terms, by and large, connote the same meaning. In a wider context, all these terms are used to prepare the adult for an appropriate civic, economic, political and social role. In adult education, 'learning', 'working' and 'living' are inseparable. Adult education is not co-terminus with schooling but takes place in work and life situations.

13.2 NEED FOR ADULT EDUCATION: OBJECTIVES OF ADULT EDUCATION

Adult education is needed on account of the following considerations:

1. Preservation and promotion of culture.
2. Enrichment of life of an individual.
3. Promotion of values like give and take, mutual appreciation and tolerance.
4. Constructive participation in social life.
5. Development of vocational efficiency.
6. Development of basic and upgraded skills.
7. Improvement in the quality of followership and leadership.
8. Deriving benefit from new knowledge.
9. Development of basic essentials for a healthy life.
10. Development of worthy leisure time pursuits.
11. Development of values of emotional integration and national unity.
12. Development of awareness regarding the work done during Five Year Plans.
13. Liquidation of elements of fatalism and superstitions.
14. Inculcation of scientific temperament.

13.3 SCOPE OF ADULT EDUCATION

The revised National Policy on Education (1992) has set out the scope of adult education in India in Paras 4.12, 4.13 and 4.14. It is to be so planned and implemented that it is "geared to the national goals such as alleviation of poverty, national integration, environmental conservation, observation of the small family norms, promotion of women's equality universalisation of primary education, basic health care, etc. It will also facilitate energisation of the cultural creativity of the people and their active participation in development process." The NPE also observed that the 'critical development issue is the continuation upgradation of skills so as to produce manpower resources of the kind and the number required by the society. Special emphasis will, therefore, be laid on organisation and employment/self-employment oriented and need and interest based vocational and skill training programme."

From above it is quite clear that the scope of adult education is as vast as life itself. In fact, scope of adult education covers all the dimensions of education. Of course, there would be differences in content, approach and methods of adult education which suit the adults.

The scope of adult education, thus, includes the following dimensions:

1. Liquidation of illiteracy *i.e.*, giving a reasonable mastery of the tools of learning—reading, writing, simple arithmetic and to create an interest in knowledge. The target according to the NPE is the eradication of illiteracy, particularly in the age group 15-35.

2. Providing comprehensive programmes of post-literacy and continuing education for neo-literates and youth who have received primary education with a view to enabling them to retain and upgrade their literary skills.

3. Undertaking programmes for developing a proper sense of rights and duties of citizens in democracy.

4. Programmes for enabling the adults to understand the functions of the Government at all levels *i.e.*, from Village Panchayats to the Central Government.

5. Programmes providing a brief outline of our cultural heritage and activities.

6. Programmes related to citizenship training.

7. Programmes related to cooperative movement and values of cooperative work.

8. Programmes related to development of skills in various areas concerning the adult's occupations and vocations.

9. Programmes related to health and sanitation.

10. Programmes related to the development of scientific temperament.

11. Organising recreational activities.

12. Environmental education.

13. Population education.

14. Sex education.

15. AIDS education.

16. Prohibition.

17. International understanding.

18. Latest developments in science and technology which affect them in particular.

13.4 THE ROLE OF SCHOOLS AND UNIVERSITIES IN ADULT EDUCATION

The Role of Schools in Adult Education

From time to time attempts have been made to involve students in adult education programmes but results are not very encouraging primarily because plans in this regard were sporadic, lacked commitment and direction. It is a matter of great concern that we have not made concerted efforts to channelise the energy of the students towards this constructive work.

The Central Board of Secondary Education, Delhi has made a valuable contribution to this area. In pursuance of the objectives of National Literacy Mission (NLM), Government of India, the Central Board of Secondary Education took up a programme from the academic session 1991-92 beginning with classes IX and X as a special measure to remove illiteracy through mass involvement of students. This has been termed as Special Literacy Drive (SALD). The SALD has been made an integral part of the prescribed curriculum and incorporated in work experience as an essential component.

Role of Universities in Adult Education

The Education Commission (1964-66) made significant remarks about the changed role of the universities: "The walls which divide the 'gown' and the 'town' have crumbled and the life of the university and the community can be vitally linked for their mutual enrichment." In this regard it further observed, "Universities in our country must take upon themselves much larger share in the community for educating adults."

The UGC Policy Statement of 1977 clearly underlined this need. In 1982, it revised its guidelines on continuing and Adult Education and observed that the universities and colleges should launch a national campaign for eradicating illiteracy which was the first step in rural development. By way of illustration, UGC has suggested the following target groups for adult literacy.

(i) Women in particular.

(ii) Scheduled Castes and Scheduled Tribes.

(iii) School Drop-outs.

(iv) Unemployed and out of school groups.

(v) Workers in the unorganised sectors.

The country's large number of universities and equivalent institutions and colleges are an important part of the voluntary efforts to eradicate illiteracy. Some of the universities like the Gujarat Vidyapith and Rural Institute of Gandhigram have done a considerable amount of work in this area.

In 1986, the Government of India launched a programme involving students under the National Service Scheme (NSS) in adult literacy and education programmes.

13.5 ROLE OF VOLUNTARY ORGANISATIONS IN ADULT EDUCATION

The Education Commission 1964-66 recognised the vital role of voluntary agencies in the field of adult education and recommended that they should be given every encouragement, financial and technical. The National Literacy Mission envisages a big role of the voluntary agencies in the adult education programmes. The Ministry of Human Resource Development, Government of India expects that voluntary agencies would play an important role in adult education through the following programmes and accordingly provides financial grant and other help.

1. Running of TLC, PLPs and continuing education programmes.
2. Establishing Jana Shikshan Nilayams (Libraries for Neo-literates).
3. Organising functional literary component in developmental programmes like health care, women's development, environmental conservation, SC and ST development.
4. Organising vocational and technical programmes leading to development of such skills as may be relevant to the needs of the adults.
5. Undertaking programmes of innovation, experimentation, learner evaluation etc., in this field.
6. Helping in the creation of environment conducive to adult learning through support to mass media, folk and traditional media and Vigyan Jathas etc.
7. Training youth and animators to facilitate implementation of NLM.
8. Taking up varied programmes for women's development and eradication of female illiteracy.
9. Organising conferences, seminars and symposia on adult education.
10. Undertaking publication of literature on adult education.
11. Undertaking such other activities as may be appropriate for the achievement of NAM.

During 1998-99, the Ministry of Human Resource Development, Government of India provided grant-in-aid exceeding Rs. one lakh each to nearly 70 Voluntary Organisations working in the field of adult education. Grant-in-aid below Rs. one lakh was given to several other organisations working in this field.

Pattern of grant is as under:

Administrative costs	75 per cent
Programme costs	100 per cent

A Word of Caution About Voluntary Agencies: A few years ago, an official evaluation of the Voluntary Agencies/Non-government Organisations working in the field of adult education came up with the disturbing fact that out of the 382 agencies, the work of only 27 could be rated as "entirely satisfactory." The work of 116 other agencies was "also satisfactory but required improvements to be made." The bonafides of several agencies were found to be doubtful.

13.6 CAUSES OF SLOW PROGRESS AND MEASURES TO LIQUIDATE ILLITERACY

Causes of Slow Progress

Since independence, the Government of India, has evolved several strategies to spread country-wide literacy but unfortunately the results are not very encouraging. The following table illustrates the state of literacy in India since independence.

Table 1: Showing Literacy Rates Since Independence (%)

Category	*1951*	*1961*	*1971*	*1981*	*1991*	*2001*
Males	24.95	34.44	39.45	56.50	64.13	75.85
Females	7.93	12.95	18.69	29.85	39.29	54.16
Total	16.67	24.02	29.45	43.67	52.21	65.38

Source: 1. 'Selected Educational Statistics 1998-99'. Department of Secondary Education and Higher Education, Government of India, 2000
2. For 2001- Census of India 2001.

(*See also* Table 13.9 India *vis-a-vis* some select countries)

Following are the important reasons for slow growth:

1. Apathy of adults towards adult education programmes as they do not seem to be convinced that such programmes can bring about appreciable changes in their earnings.
2. Feeling among the uneducated adults that it is too late to learn to read and write. They feel shy of learning at an advanced age.
3. The problem of earning being so acute that the adults do not have sufficient time or energy to come to the class for receiving instruction. They are too occupied with their own problems and find it extremely hard to get out of this cobweb.
4. The adults are very often indifferent towards adult education. They consider it as useless, sheer waste of money, time and energy.
5. Social customs and traditions put such demands upon the time of adults that they are unable to attend classes regularly.
6. The rural uneducated adults are submerged in superstitions and ignorance.
7. There is a dearth of suitably trained, sincere and selfless workers in the field.
8. Government has also failed to arouse consciousness among the people. People's participation is also conspicuous by its absence.
9. There is a great shortage of appropriate literature and equipment on the subject.
10. The officers and workers lack the spirit of social service. Even its organisation is faulty.
11. The funds earmarked for adult education are too inadequate, and whatever little has been set aside, it is not being utilised profitably.
12. The scheme has been enforced from top to bottom, from the government to the people. It does not originate with the people.

13. There is lack of research in basic vocabulary and methodology for educating the adults.

14. Caste system is proving a great hindrance. People need different centres for various castes. This is not possible.

15. Very little coordination exists among the different agencies engaged in adult education work. Very often there is duplication of work at most of the places.

16. No follow-up work is being taken up by any organisation with the result that in its absence the people lapse into illiteracy again.

17. A large number of the centres exist in name only.

18. Lack of interest in adult education by political parties with the result that they themselves do not organise adult education programmes and take little interest in it.

Measure for the Promotion of Adult Education

1. Giving top priority by the Central and State Governments to adult education.
2. Creation of proper environment in the country for adult education.
3. Involvement of students on a large scale in literacy programmes.
4. Fixing responsibility of industrial establishments—big and small to provide literacy to their workers. Likewise agricultural farms may be made responsible.
5. Making obligatory on the national and state political parties to run a number of literacy centres and on this basis also giving them recognition.
6. Preparing adult literacy booklets in regional languages and including appropriate instructional material.
7. Establishment of reading rooms and libraries for adults at suitable places.
8. Use of electronic media on a large scale.
9. Providing some sort of incentives to neo-literates.
10. Giving functional literacy training to adult education personnel.
11. Fixing flexible timings for adult literacy classes.
12. Monitoring effectively all adult literacy programmes.
13. Ensuring that enrolment data are genuine so that a pragmatic policy is evolved.
14. Cutting down top-heavy bureaucratic establishment and making the optimum use of funds earmarked for adult literacy.
15. Financing only adult literacy centres and not adult education centres involving heavy expenditure. Social education centres in general have failed to generate appropriate environment.
16. Involving Village Panchayats in adult literacy work and making them responsible for giving grant-aid to voluntary organisations. All funds earmarked for this purpose should be put at the disposal of the Village Panchayats. No financial grant to voluntary organisations should be given directly by the Central Government.

13.7 NATIONAL LITERACY MISSION (NLM)

The NLM was set up in 1988 with the objective of imparting functional literacy to 80 million adult illiterates in the age group 15-35 by 1995. It was extended to cover 100 million by 1997 i.e. by the end of 8th Plan. Now the target for full literacy is the year 2005.

The following diagrammatic structure indicates the role and functions of various functionaries at different levels at the Centre.

NATIONAL LEVEL STRUCTURE

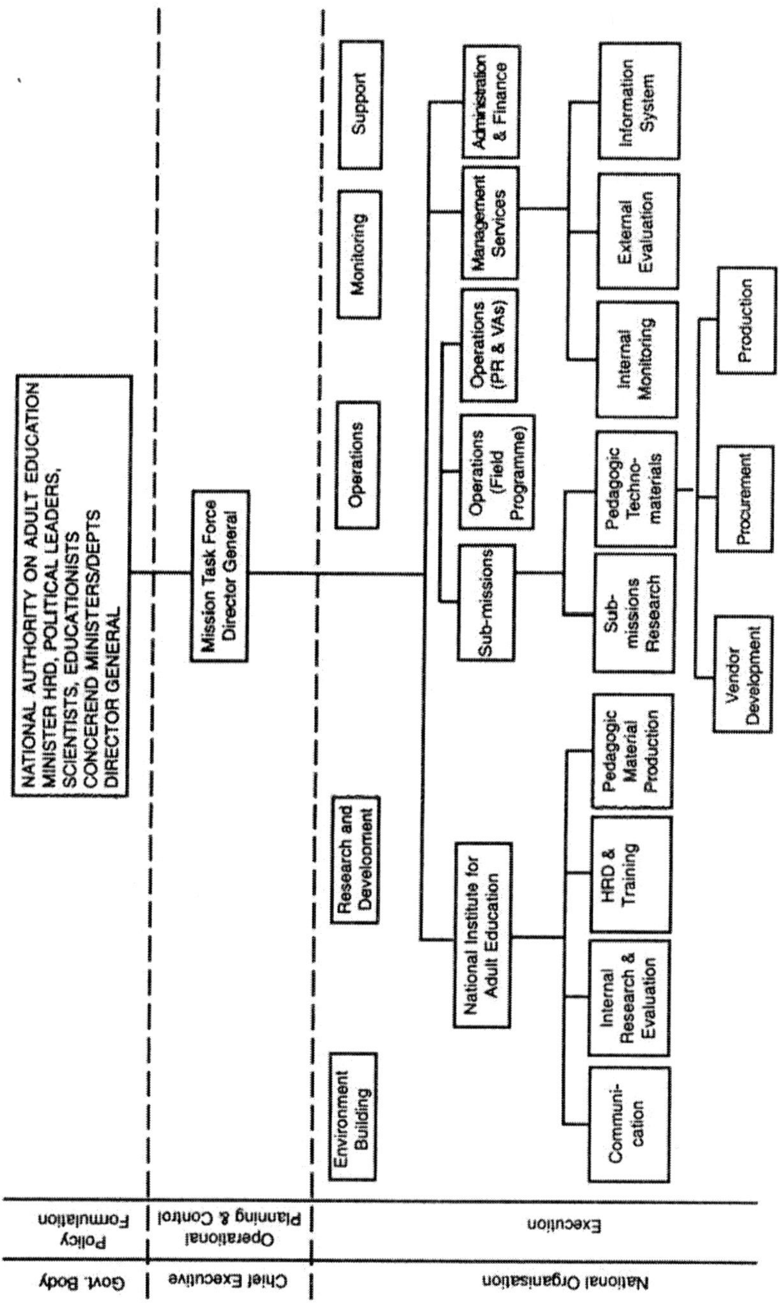

13.8 SPECIAL PROJECTS FOR ERADICATION OF LITERACY TAKEN UP BY THE MINISTRY OF HRD, DEPARTMENT OF EDUCATION

1. Zila Sakashtra Samitis (ZSS) funded by the Government of India and the States in the ratio of 2 : 1. (4 : 1 for districts in the Tribal Areas). They take up Total Literacy Campaigns (TLC) and Post Literacy Campaign (PLC). In 2001 TLC were in progress in 172 districts and PLC in 292 districts.

2. Continuing Education (CE) Centres for life long education were in progress in 95 districts in 2001. The scheme came into operation in 1996-97.

3. Shramik Vidyapeeths (SVPs), a programme of Polyvalent (multi-faceted) Adult Education for workers and their families in urban and industrial areas, started in 1967 increased to nearly 60 in 16 States and 1 UT.

4. National Literacy Resource Centre (NLRC), set up by NLM at the Lal Bahadur Shastri Academy of Administration, Mussorie serves as resource Centres for adult education functionaries.

5. Rural Functional Literacy Project, initiated in 1978 has been in operation in a few states.

6. Assistance to voluntary agencies is being provided for taking up adult education work.

7. The Directorate of Adult Education (DAC), a subordinate office of the Department of Education has been functioning as the national resource centre. It is considered as the functional arm of NLM.

8. The National Institute of Adult Education (NIAE), Delhi, set up in 1991, is an autonomous organisation and it acts as the National Level Resource Centre for Adult Education.

9. The district of Ernakulum (Kerala) was declared the first district of total literacy in 1990. Since then TLC has become the principal strategy of NLM.

13.9 COMPARATIVE DATA ON ADULT EDUCATION. SOME SELECT COUNTRIES INCLUDING INDIA (1980 and 2000)

S. No.	*Country*	*Adult Literacy Rate*				
		1980		*2000*		
		M	*F*	*M*	*F*	*Total*
1.	Afghanistan	30	6	51	21	36
2.	Bangladesh	41	17	49	30	40
3.	Bhutan	41	15	61	34	47
4.	Canada	99	99	99	99	99
5.	China	78	51	92	78	85
6.	Denmark	99	99	99	99	99
7.	France	99	99	99	99	99
8.	Germany	99	99	99	99	99
9.	India	55	25	68	45	57
10.	Japan	99	99	99	99	99
11.	Myanmar	86	66	89	81	85
12.	Nepal	38	7	59	24	42
13.	Pakistan	41	14	57	28	43
14.	Russian Federation	99	93	99	99	99
15.	Sri Lanka	91	79	94	87	90
16.	Switzerland	99	99	99	99	99
17.	United Kingdom	97	97	97	97	97
18.	Unites States	99	99	99	99	99

Source: 'The State of the World's Children 2004' UNICEF.

Note : Adult Literacy Rate implies the percentage of persons aged 15 and above who can read and write.

14

National Integration

14.1 MEANING

National integration has been defined as a feeling of oneness which may transcend all groups or cultural differences and synthesize the different religions, castes, linguistic communities emotionally into a compact whole. It implies a feeling among citizens of India that India is 'One' and we belong to it culturally and emotionally. "What is in the interest of India, it is in our interest." Country comes first and other loyalties are subservient to it. We must share and respect common objectives, purposes or ideas and give them a higher place over sectional, linguistic, racial and other loyalties.

14.2 WHY NATIONAL AND EMOTIONAL INTEGRATION

India is a land of so many faiths, creeds, castes, languages etc. It is very essential that people of different faiths and creeds, etc. think in terms of nationalism and place the welfare of the country above such narrow considerations. In the words of the Emotional Integration Committee, "One of the hardest problems before us today is the building up a national mind by curbing the religious, linguistic and communal conflicts which tend to disunite us." Jawaharlal Nehru observed that national integration would weld Indian people into one and make India into "one strong national unit maintaining at the same time all our wonderful diversity."

14.3 ROLE OF EDUCATION IN DEVELOPING NATIONAL INTEGRATION

In the words of Dr. Radhakrishnan, "National integration cannot be built by brick and mortar, it cannot be built by chisel or hammer. It has to grow silently in the minds and hearts of men. The only process is the process of education."

14.4 EMOTIONAL INTEGRATION COMMITTEE (1961) IN THE ROLE OF EDUCATION IN EMOTIONAL INTEGRATION

At the Conference of the Education Ministers held in November, 1960, the distressing frequency with which disruptive tendencies were making themselves in the country was discussed. It was felt that such tendencies, if unchecked, might threaten the unity of the country. In the circumstances, the importance of the role of education in counteracting such divisive trends and in fostering unity was stressed. The Conference recommended that a Committee be set up to study the problem and to suggest positive educational measures for promoting integration. This was followed by the appointment of the Committee in May 1961 by the Ministry of Education.

Dr. Sampurnanand was the Chairman of the Committee. Among the other nine members, Shrimati Indira Gandhi, who after a few years became the Prime Minister, was also a member of the Committee.

Terms of Reference

(a) To study the role of education in considering and promoting the processes of emotional integration in national life and to examine the operation of tendencies which come in the way of their development; and

(b) In the light of such study, to advise on the positive educational programmes for youth in general and students in schools and colleges in particular, to strengthen in them the processes of emotional integration.

14.5 ROLE OF EDUCATION AND MAJOR RECOMMENDATIONS/MEASURES FOR THE PROMOTION OF NATIONAL INTEGRATION AS SUGGESTED BY THE EMOTIONAL INTEGRATION COMMITTEE

The Committee observed, "Education can play a vital role in strengthening emotional integration. It is felt that education should not only aim at imparting knowledge but should develop all aspects of a student's personality. It should broaden the outlook, foster a feeling of oneness and nationalism and a spirit of sacrifice and tolerance so that narrow group interests are submerged in the larger interests of the country. The Committee gave the following suggestions:

1. *Re-orientation of the Curriculum*: The school and college curriculum should be re-oriented to suit the needs of a secular State.

At the primary stage the importance of stories, poems, folklore and teaching of social studies, national anthem and other national songs should be emphasized. Daily morning prayer has also been recommended.

At the secondary stage the curriculum should include, among other things, the study of language and literature, social studies, moral and religious instruction and co-curricular activities.

At the university level the study of different social sciences, languages and literature, culture and art and also the exchange of teachers and students should play an important role.

2. *Co-curricular Activities*: The place of co-curricular activities in the curriculum is considered to be very important. These activities include common observance and celebration of festivals and events of national importance, sports, educational excursions, tours, and picnics, military training like the NCC, ACC, scouts and guides, student camps, debates, symposia, dramatics, and youth festivals. The use of audio-visual aids like films, pictures, radio and TV has also been recommended.

It is felt that participation in co-curricular activities helps in the growth of a well-balanced and well-adjusted personality. It creates a group feeling of oneness and brotherhood, broadens the outlook and develops a catholicity of spirit and tolerance which are necessary for good citizenship.

3. *Special Stress on the Teaching of Social Studies*: The teaching of social studies has been recommended at all levels *i.e.*, the primary, secondary and university stages. This would impart knowledge of the geographical, historical and cultural background of the country and of the world as a whole. Books on social studies should include reference to the lives and works of the great men

of India and of the world and also stories from ancient books like the *Ramayana* and the *Mahabharata*.

4. *Textbooks*: In order that the textbooks play their legitimate role in strengthening of emotional integration, it is necessary that they be re-oriented and improved. In the preparation of history textbooks special care needs to be taken to see that facts are not misrepresented, distorted or exaggerated to create prejudice.

The get-up and the content of textbooks require a change.

At the primary level the textbook writers should make a liberal use of pictures and illustrations so as to create interest in the child at the very outset.

5. *Language and Script*: (i) The use of the Roman script may be permitted in certain areas for an interim period to enable persons to improve their acquaintance with Hindi.

(ii) Throughout India the international numerals must be used.

(iii) To reduce the burden of three scripts, Hindi may be learnt in the non-Hindi areas in the regional script.

(iv) To popularise the study of Hindi in non-Hindi speaking areas, a beginning may be made with the publication of Hindi books in the Roman script and the compilation of simple dictionaries in Hindi—other languages, also in the Roman script.

(v) Hindi books may be published in the regional scripts and the compilation of Regional Language—Hindi dictionaries should be encouraged.

(vi) At the high school stage Hindi must be taught in the Devnagri script, keeping in view the constitutional provisions.

(vii) The two link languages—Hindi and English should be effectively taught at university level so that conditions of emotional and intellectual isolation are not created.

(viii) It is necessary to ensure that in implementing any language policy the rights of minorities are adequately projected.

6. *Uniform for School Children*: It is desirable to have a uniform for school children; one common uniform for the whole of India is not necessary; schools may have their own preference in regard to colour and pattern.

7. *Singing of National Anthem*: Children should be taught to sing the National Anthem in unison and behave in a disciplined way when it is sung. They should also be the taught meaning of the verses.

8. *Reverence for National Flag*: Students should be told the history of the National Flag and taught at the earliest stage to show reverence for the National Flag.

9. *Celebration of National Days*: National Days—January 26, August 15 and October 2—should be celebrated in schools with the full participation of the teachers, the students and the community.

10. *Special Talks on the Unity and Oneness of the Country*: Special meetings of the school assembly should be held from time to time and the speakers speak to the children on topics dealing with the unity and oneness of the country.

11. *Taking Pledge*: Students may be asked to repeat a pledge twice a year dedicating themselves to the service of their country. A draft of such a pledge in English is given below:

India is my country, all Indians are brothers and sisters.

I love my country, and I am proud of its rich and varied heritage,

I shall always strive to be worthy of it.

I shall give my parents, teachers and all elders respect and treat everyone with courtesy. I shall be kind to animals.

To my country and my people, I pledge my devotion. In their well-being and prosperity alone lies my happiness.

12. *Open-Air Dramas*: Open-air dramas emphasising the ideals of national unity may be staged four times a year by every school.

At least one play should be based upon a theme derived from the classic or from the history of ancient India. In predominant Hindu areas there should be some plays dealing with non-Hindu lives and *vice versa.*

13. *Student Exchange and Tours*: Such tours should be conducted from one State to another. The inter-state visits if properly organised should do much to acquaint both teachers and children with different parts of the country.

A network of youth hostels should be set up by all the States in selected places.

14. *School Improvement*: Students should be associated with the cleanliness of the school premises. This would not only increase their pride in it and loyalty to the school but would also help in improving the school for future students.

15. *Admissions*: Admissions to schools, colleges and other educational institutions should not be given on the basis of caste but be on the basis of means and merits.

16. *Recognition of Institutions*: Recognition should not be given to institutions where divisive tendencies are encouraged.

17. *Freeship and Scholarships*: These should be awarded only on the basis of means and merit.

18. No Domiciliary Restrictions: Domiciliary restrictions in regard to migration of students between one State and other should be removed.

19. *Suitable Handbooks for Teachers*: Suitable handbooks for teachers in the social studies and languages should be published.

20. *All-India Award*: An annual all-India award for the best general essay on different States in India should be instituted.

21. *Educational and Travel Documentaries*: Educational and travel documentaries with particular emphasis on various aspects of Indian scenery, flora and fauna, on various developmental and reconstruction programmes should be produced for use in schools and these should form a regular feature of the schools.

22. School Projects: Schools may conduct several projects which improve their general knowledge of the country. For instance 'Know Your Country' project can be undertaken during which children may share in the collection of information about a State in the Indian Union other than their own.

23. *Exchange of Professors*: Distinguished professors should also be deputed periodically to different universities so that a large range of students can benefit from their experience.

24. *All-India Youth Council*: An all-India youth council should be set up to coordinate all the youth programmes taken up by the Central and State Governments and also to help various agencies to extend their efforts.

25. *Teachers*: The Union Ministry of Education should implement a scheme providing for a national minimum scale of salaries for teachers in the primary, middle and secondary schools.

26. *A Pay Revision Committee*: A Pay Revision Committee consisting of representatives from the Planning Commission, the Ministries of Education and Finance and representatives from the teaching profession, should be immediately set up to work out the full financial implications and operative details of implementing the scheme for a national minimum scale of salaries for teachers with the help of a sub-committee at State levels, if necessary. This work should be completed as expeditiously as possible.

14.6 NATIONAL INTEGRATION COUNCIL (1962)

With a view to promote values of national and emotional integration, the Government of India set up the National Integration Council which includes prominent persons representing all shades of opinion. It is a guiding force in matters of importance in this area. It is headed by the Prime Minister.

14.7 RECOMMENDATIONS OF THE EDUCATION COMMISSION (1964-66) ON NATIONAL INTEGRATION

1. A reasonable quality of good education should be made available to all irrespective of any consideration.
2. A common school system should be established, all over the country.
3. A uniform educational structure should be established.
4. Public schools should not be permitted as they breed inequality.
5. Equal educational opportunities should be provided to all.
6. Three language formula should be followed.
7. All parts of the country should be provided with suitable educational institutions.
8. Social and national service should be made an integral part of education as its absence is also responsible for increasing the gulf between the educated and the uneducated classes.
9. Recommendations of the Emotional Integration Committee should be followed.
10. The use of regional languages as media of education from the lowest to the highest stage was a matter of 'profound importance for national integration'.

14.8 NATIONAL POLICY ON EDUCATION (1986 AND MODIFIED IN 1992) ON NATIONAL INTEGRATION

The NPE provides for a common core curriculum including the History of Indian Freedom Movement, the constitutional obligations and other content essential to national identity. These contents are expected to cut across subject areas and designed to promote values such as India's common cultural heritage, egalitarianism, democracy and secularism, equality of the sexes, protection of the environment, removal of social barriers, etc.

14.9 COMMITTEE TO GIVE SUGGESTIONS TO TEACH FUNDAMENTAL DUTIES TO THE CITIZENS OF THE COUNTRY (1999)

The Committee appointed by the Government of Indian under the Chairmanship of Justice J.S. Verma, former Chief Justice of India, to give suggestions to Teach Fundamental Duties to the citizens of the country, made some suggestions. It may be stressed that the Fundamental Duties included in the Constitution "include, to uphold and protect the sovereignty, unity and integrity of India", "To promote harmony and the spirit of common brotherhood amongst all the people transcending religious, linguistic and regional or sectional diversities to renounce practices derogatory to the dignity of women"; "To defend the country and render national service when called upon to do so."

The suggestions include reorienting approaches to school curriculum and teacher education programmes.

14.10 BARRIERS TO NATIONAL INTEGRATION

1. Casteism.
2. Linguism.
3. Regionalism.
4. Provincialism.
5. Religious Bias.
6. Uneven regional development.

14.11 PROGRAMMES UNDERTAKEN FOR PROMOTING NATIONAL INTEGRATION

1. Setting up of the National Integration Council.

2. Setting up of National Integration Samitis in universities and colleges for the purpose of promoting mutual understanding and appreciation among persons coming from different parts of India. At present there is a total number of 105 Samitis functioning in the country.

3. Formation of committees composed of members drawn from various fields of national life to act as spearheads for a mass movement in the cause of national integration.

4. Survey of textbooks and elimination of biased and prejudiced material leading to hatred among different communities.

5. Establishing planning forums for disseminating information.

6. Organisation of writers' camps.

7. National Integration Inter-State Student-Teacher Camps.

8. Celebration of Centenaries.

9. *Community Singing*: A National Integration Project as a national movement has been launched by the Ministry of Human Resource Development for the promotion of community singing. NCERT has been organising community singing camps for music and musically inclined teachers drawn from different States and Union Territories of the country. Several Camps of State and National levels on community singing have been organised and several thousand music and musically inclined teachers drawn from States have been trained in community singing. Under the scheme every trained teacher is given an illustrated book entitled, "Let's Sing Together". A recorded cassette containing 15 songs in different Indian languages and a tape recorder is also given to each teacher.

Concluding Observation: In the end, it must be stressed that the major responsibility for the promotion of values of national integration among the people of India rests with the political and religious leaders. Here also, political leaders have the most prominent role to play. It is they who, by and large, are responsible for sowing the seeds of disintegration. However, this is not to minimise the role of education in this respect.

15

Religious and Moral Education

15.1 CONTROVERSY ON RELIGIOUS AND MORAL EDUCATION IN SCHOOLS

There has been a great controversy regarding imparting of religious education in schools. Statesmen like Rajagopalachari have strongly advocated the introduction of religious education in schools. Ross has also advocated for a religious basis of education. He advocated that religion should become a compulsory subject in schools. The protagonists of religious education argue that religious education makes man God fearing and develops humane values.

The antagonists of religious instruction are of the view that in a secular state like India, religious education in schools should not be imparted. They argue that this would lead to bigotry, disunity, hatred and narrow mindedness. It is also felt that there is dearth of truly religious teachers to impart religious education.

15.2 MEANING AND COMPONENTS OF RELIGION

Religion etymologically means something that helps to bind man to man or man to God. (*'Religase'* means to bind). Broadly speaking, every religion has six aspects:

1. *Personality of the Founder*—dealing with the greatness and holiness of the founder of the faith.
2. *Genesis*—seeking to give an account of the Creator and the Universe created by Him.
3. *Rituals*—prescribing some outward forms which the followers adopt and follow. (worship etc.)
4. *Spiritualism*—oneness with God.
5. *Religious Books*—dealing with various aspects—sacredness of books.
6. *Ethical and Moral Code*—telling what is right and what is wrong.

Greatness and holiness of the founder of every faith should find place in curricular programmes. Likewise the last aspect of religion which consists of ethical and moral code is universally valid and it should be included in all aspects of school life.

The following illustration makes it very clear.

The Golden Rule, a universal ethic, is part of the spiritual heritage of humankind. It is taught in one form or another in all the world religions and systems of belief and can be found among the traditions of the world's most ancient societies:

Baha'i Faith: "He should not wish for others that which he doth not wish for himself, nor promise that which he doth not fulfil." *Gleanings from the Writings of Baha'u'llah.*

Buddhism: "Hurt not others in ways that you yourself would find hurtful" *Udana-Varqa,* 5 : 18.

Christianity: "As ye would that men should do to you, do ye also to them likewise." *Luke* 6 : 61.

Confucianism: "Surely it is the maxim of loving-kindness: Do not unto others that you would not have them do unto you. *Analects XV, 23.*

Hinduism: "This is the sum of all true righteousness: deal with others as thou wouldst thyself be dealt by. Do nothing to thy neighbour which thou wouldst not have him do to thee after." *The Mahabharata.*

Islam: "No one of you is a believer until he desires for his brother that which he desires for himself." *Sunnah.*

Jainism: "In happiness and suffering, in joy and grief, we should regard all creatures as we regard our own self,...." *Yoga-Sastra.*

Judaism: "What is hateful to you, do not to your fellow men. That is the entire Law, all the rest is the commentary." *The Talmud, Shabbat,* 31a.

Sikhism: "Be thou not estranged from another. For in every heart pervades the Lord." *Guru-Granth Sahib,* Vol. 1, p. 250.

Taoism: The good man "ought to pity the malignant tendencies of others; to regard their gains as if they were his own, and their losses in the same way." *The Thai-Shang.*

Zoroastrianism: "That nature only is good when it shall not do unto another whatever is not good for its own self." *Dadistan-i-Dinik,* 94 : 5.

15.3 TRUE MEANING OF RELIGIOUS EDUCATION

A true religious spirit makes us God-fearing. It inculcates in us the virtues of unselfishness and love for all. The spirit of religion instills in us a desire to stick to the moral and ethical codes when we are faced with a grave situation. In the case of irreligious persons these codes are reduced to mere crap of paper in times of stress.

Religion does not consist in certain rites and rituals. It is a very narrow view of religion. "Unselfishness is the test of religion. He who has more of this unselfishness is nearer to Shiva. And if a man is selfish even though he has visited all the temples, seen all the places of pilgrimage, and painted himself like a leopard, he is still farther off from Shiva," writes Swami Vivekananda. At some other place he writes, "I do not care for liberation, I would rather go to a hundred thousand hells doing good to others (silently) like the spring, this is my religion." True religion is the motive power behind all ethical and moral codes. No boy or girl can be counted as properly educated unless he or she knows the religious interpretation of life.

15.4 COMMITTEES, COMMISSIONS AND OTHER DOCUMENTS ON RELIGIOUS AND MORAL EDUCATION

The need for value education has been emphasised by Education Commissions in the past.

1. *Radhakrishanan Commission (1948)*: "If we exclude spiritual training in our institutions we would be untrue to our whole historical development."

2. *The Secondary Education Commission (1952-53)*: It observed regarding religious instruction; "In view of the provision of the Constitution of the Secular State, religious instruction cannot be given in school hours; such instruction should be given to the children of the particular faith and with the consent of the parents and the management concerned. In making the recommendation we wish to emphasize that all unhealthy trends of disunity, rancour, religious hatred and bigotry should be discouraged in schools".

3. *Sri Prakasa Committee on Religious and Moral Instruction (1959-60)*: "Every effort must, therefore, be made to teach students true moral values from the earliest stages of their educational life."

4. *Kothari Commission (1964-66)*: "A serious defect in the school system is the absence of provision for education in social, moral and spiritual values. A national system of education that is related to life, needs and aspirations of the people cannot afford to ignore this purposeful force."

5. *National Policy on Education (1986)*: "The growing concern over the erosion of essential values and an increasing cynicism in society has brought to focus the need for readjustments in the curriculum in order to make education a forceful tool for the cultivation of social and moral values."

6. *Programme of Action NPE (1992)*: "The framework emphasised value of education as an integral part of school curriculum. It highlighted the values drawn from national goals, universal perception, ethical considerations and character building. It stressed the role of education in combating obscurantism, religious fanaticism, exploitation and injustice as well as the inculcation of values."

Sri Prakash Committee on Religious and Moral Instruction (1959-60)

Among the several recommendations made by the Committee, the following indicate a broad, frame-work of instruction in moral and spiritual values at different stages of education:

1. *Elementary Stage*: The School Assembly should be held for a few minutes in the morning for group singing. Simple and interesting stories about the lives and teachings of prophets, saints and religious leaders should be included in the syllabus for language teaching. Two periods a week should be set aside for moral instruction.

2. *Secondary Stage*: The Morning Assembly should observe 2 minutes' silence followed by readings from the scriptures or great literature of the world or an appropriate address. The essential teachings of the great world religions should be studied. One hour a week should be assigned to moral instruction.

3. *University Stage*: Students should be encouraged to meet in groups for silent meditation in the morning. In the first year of the degree course, lives of the great religious and spiritual leaders, in second year, some selections of universalist character from the scriptures of the world and in the third year, the central problems of philosophy of religions should be studied. A fairly long period of social service should be introduced.

Education Commission (1964-66) on Religious Education

The adoption of a secularist policy, no doubt, means that no religious community will be favoured or discriminated against, and the instruction in religious dogmas will not be provided in State schools. Such a secularist policy is not an irreligious or anti-religious policy. It does not belittle the importance of religion. This policy gives to every citizen the freedom of religious beliefs and worship, and promotes not only religious toleration but also an active reverence for all religions. It is necessary for a multi-religious democratic State to promote a tolerant study of all religions so that its citizens can understand each other better and live amicably together.

The Commission has recommended: "There will be natural points of correlation between the moral values sought to be inculcated and the teachings of the great religions.... All religions stress certain fundamental qualities of character, such as honesty and truthfulness, consideration for others, reverence for old age, kindness to animals, and the compassion for the needy and the suffering. In the literature of every religion, the story or parable figures prominently as a means of impressing an ethical value on the followers. The narration of such stories by the teachers at the right moment in the programme of moral education would be most effective, particularly in the lower classes. At a later stage, accounts of the lives of great religious and spiritual leaders will find a natural place. Similarly the celebration of festivals of different religions will afford opportunity for the narration of incidents from the life history of the leaders of these religions. In the last two years of the secondary school, a place should be found for the study of the essential teachings of the great religions."

15.5 MEANING OF SECULARISM

The essence of secularism is aptly expressed in the two great Vedic sayings of which we can all be proud. *Mata Bhoomihi putro aham Prithivya.* (The whole world is our motherland; we are all children of the earth.)

Second saying is: *Ekam Brahma Viprah Bahuda Vadanti* (God is one, but wise men call Him by different names.)

15.6 CONSTITUTIONAL PROVISIONS ON SECULARISM AND RELIGIOUS EDUCATION

Constitutional Provisions—Article 25: Subject to public order, morality and health and to other provisions of this part, all persons are equally entitled to freedom to conscience and the right freely to profess, practise and propagate religion."

Article 27: "No person shall be compelled to pay any taxes, the proceeds of which are specifically appropriated in payment of expenses for the promotion or maintenance of any particular religion or religious denomination."

Article 28(1): "No religious instruction shall be provided in any educational institution wholly maintained out of State funds."

(2) Nothing in clause (1) shall apply to an educational institution which is administered by the state but has been established under an endowment or trust which requires that religious instructions shall be imparted in such institution.

(3) No person attending any educational institution recognised by the State or receiving aid out of State funds shall be required to take part in any religious institution or to attend any religious worship that may be conducted in such institution or in any premises attached thereto unless such person, or if such person is a minor his guardian has given his consent thereto."

Article 30(1): "All minorities whether based on religion or language, shall have the right to establish and administer educational institutions of their choice.

(2) The State shall not, in granting aid to educational institutions, discriminate against any educational institution on the ground that it is under the management of a minority, whether based on religion or language.

Dr. B.R. Ambedkar has explained the concept of secular state as "All that a secular state means is that this Parliament shall not be competent to impose any particular religion upon the rest of the people."

Dr. Rajendra Prasad, the first President of India has very clearly observed that by becoming secular, India has not been anti-religious or irreligious. He stated, "There are some who think that because we are a secular state we do not believe in religion or spiritual values. Far from being so, it really means that in this country all are free to profess or preach the faith of their liking and that we wish well of all religions and want them to develop in their own way without any hindrance."

Jawaharlal Nehru, the first Prime Minister of India has explained the secular nature of our State as, "It means while religion is completely free, the state includes in its wide fold various religions and cultures, gives protection and opportunities to all and thus brings about an atmosphere of tolerance and cooperation."

The secular state is one which guarantees individual and corporate freedom of religion, deals with the individual as a citizen irrespective of his religion, is not constitutionally connected to a particular religion, nor does it seek either to promote or interfere with religion.

Although the word secularism was introduced only in 1976 in our Constitution, our secularism is historical in its development. We had great breadth of vision, a liberal universalism expressed in the above two great Vedic sayings of which we feel proud.

15.7 MORAL VALUE EDUCATION

Human values or moral values are sets of beliefs or principles of behaviour accepted by groups or societies, especially democratic societies and are deemed to be universally acceptable and desirable. They broadly may be classified under the following seven heads:

1. Values related to democracy and human rights.
2. Values related to co-operation and solidarity.
3. Values related to the preservation and promotion of culture.
4. Values related to self and others.
5. Values related to the protection of the environment.
6. Value related to internationalism.
7. Values related to spirituality.

Emphasis through practical activities should be laid on the development of these values in the students. Besides these values, skills and attitudes relating to ethical, moral and spiritual aspects should be developed through relevant school programmes.

1. *Values related to human rights and democracy:*

- Dignity;
- Equality;
- Justice;

- Protection of the rights of all peoples;
- Freedom of participation;
- Freedom of speech and expression;
- Freedom of religious belief.

2. *Values related to co-operation and solidarity:*

- The belief in peace and harmony;
- Interdependence of all people;
- Conflict resolution by peaceful means;
- Mutual understanding, co-operation and respect among individuals and societies;
- A culture of peace and co-operation.

3. *Values related to the preservation and promotion of cultures:*

- Respect for the family and all of its members;
- Appreciation of one's own culture;
- Appreciation of the world's cultural heritage and human achievement;
- Awareness of social and cultural change.

4. *Values related to the self and others:*

- Self-awareness, self-reliance, self-esteem and self-discipline;
- Respect and empathy towards others; a considerate and caring attitude;
- Moral courage;
- Open-minded, trustworthy, truthful, tolerant, self-possessed and reconciliatory;
- Inquisitive and creative.

5. *Values and attitudes related to the protection of the environment:*

- The interdependence of people and nature;
- Appreciation and commitment to maintenance and improvement of the environment so as to favour the survival of all species;
- Promotion of a sustainable environment.

6. *Values related to internationalism:*

- Awareness of the rights and duties of citizenship;
- Respect of and equality among nations;
- Harmony between nationalism, regionalism and internationalism;
- Awareness of global issues and their peaceful resolution.

7. *Values and attitudes related to spirituality:*

- Aspiring to inner-peace;
- Freedom of thought, conscience and creed;
- Freedom of religious practice;
- Mutual respect for the religious observances of others;
- Equality of treatment of religions by the State.

Skills and Attitudes

It is expected that students will develop the skills and attitudes necessary to be active and effective. These skills can be summarized under the headings of 'Thinking skills', 'Communication skills' and 'Personal skills'.

Thinking Skills

- *Critical Thinking:* the ability to distinguish among fact, opinion and belief; to recognize bias and prejudice; to identify true issues and problems, as

well as personal assumptions employed in an argument; to reason correctly.
- *Information Handling:* to be able to form a hypothesis and to put it to the test; to know where to look for answers and how to select and reject information; to weigh up evidence; to hypothesize about eventual outcomes and consequences in order to choose the most appropriate action.
- *Creative Thinking:* to seek novel solutions and answers; to think 'laterally' and to approach problems from multiple perspectives.
- *Reflection:* to stand back from a problem and identify its component parts; to understand thought processes and produce appropriate strategies for dealing with any particular problem.
- *Dialectical Thinking:* thinking about more than one point of view; understanding points of view other than one's own; being able to construct an argument from either point of view— sometimes contradictory—based on knowledge about the other.

Communication Skills

- *Presentation:* to be able to explain ideas to others in a clear and coherent manner.
- *Active Listening:* to listen carefully, and to understand and acknowledge the views of others.
- *Negotiation:* to recognize the role and limitations of compromise as a tool for the cessation of conflict; to conduct a productive dialogue towards the resolution of a dispute.
- *Non-verbal Communication:* recognizing the meaning and significance of body language.

Personal Skills

- *Co-operation:* to work effectively with others towards a common goal.
- *Adaptability:* to be prepared to change one's opinion in the light of evidence and reason.
- *Self-discipline:* the ability to conduct one's self appropriately in different contexts and to manage time effectively.
- *Responsibility:* to begin and complete tasks in an appropriate manner; being willing to assume one's share of the responsibility.
- *Respect:* listening carefully to others; making decisions based on fairness and equality; recognizing that others' beliefs, views and ideas may differ from one's own.

Concluding Observations

In the ultimate analysis it must be admitted that no amount of sermons on religion and morality can achieve worthwhile results. The materialistic concept of life is a great contributory factor in making our lives corrupt and destroying our peace and happiness. Moral values must permeate our daily lives. Elders must set good examples before the youngers to follow. Example is better than precept.

16

Women's Education

16.1 HIGH STATUS AND WIDESPREAD EDUCATION OF WOMEN IN ANCIENT INDIA

The 'Vedas' accord a very honourable and respectable status to women. Accordingly they were not only eligible for education but also received higher education and status. They could occupy administrative and other important jobs mostly performed by men. It was only during the middle ages that their education and status began to decline. Here we are giving a few quotes from the Vedas and other ancient literature which bring out the factual position of the status and education of women in earlier times in this country.

Just as boys acquire sound knowledge and education by the practice of 'Brahmacharya' and then marry girls of their own, who are young, well educated, loving and of like temperament, so should a girl practice 'Brahmacharya', study the Vedas and other sciences and thereby perfect her knowledge, refine her character, give her hand to a man of her own choice, who is young, learned and loving. (A.V. XI. 16.3.18).

In the battlefield, in the absence of the king, the queen should take command of the forces and should inspire them. (R.V.X. 159.2).

O Learned Lady! All life is dependent upon you because you impart education to all. (R.V. 2, 49.17).

From the point of view of reverence due, a teacher is ten-fold superior to mere lecturer, a father a hundred fold to teacher, and a mother a thousand fold to father. *'Vashisht Dharmsutra'* (13.480)

Where women are respected, there the Gods delight, and where they are not, there works and efforts come to naught, there is no hope of rise for that family or country where they live in sadness. (*'Manusmriti'*)

What can the fire not burn.
What cannot merge into the ocean
What can the weaker section not achieve
And what can escape death (*'Ramcharitmanas', 'Ayodhyakand'*)

16.2 IMPORTANCE OF WOMEN'S EDUCATION

Women play a prominent role in the cultural, economic, political, religious and social life of a country. The ancient people of India fully realised this fact and accorded a reasonable status to women and encouraged their education. According to Vedas, women should have opportunity to attain knowledge of the Vedas from all the four courses (Rig. Veda 14.9.64).More than 400 verses in the Vedas are ascribed to 24 women seers. In the Vedas, women have been called '*Updeshtri*' of knowledge and this indicates women working as teachers (Rig Veda 1.3.11).

Swami Vivekananda has emphasized, "If you do not raise the women who are living embodiment of the divine mother, don't think that you have any other way to rise."

Gandhiji stated the importance of women education in these words, "I am strongly of the opinion that women should have the same facilities as men and even special facilities where necessary."

Jawaharlal Nehru very rightly observed, "Education of a boy is the education of one person, but education of a girl is the education of entire family."

In view of the importance of women education in national development, the University Education Commission 1948-49 remarked, "There can't be an educated people without education of women. If general education had to be limited to men or to women, then opportunity should be given to women, from them it would more surely be passed to the next generation."

Similarly, the Kothari Commission 1964-66, stated, "For full development of human resources, the improvement of human beings and for moulding the character of children during the most impressionable years of infancy, the education of women is of great importance than that of men."

16.3 PROGRESS OF WOMEN EDUCATION SINCE INDEPENDENCE

Table 1: Women Literacy Rates Since 1950-51 (%)

Category	*1951*	*1961*	*1971*	*1981*	*1991*	*2001*
Total	**16.67**	**24.02**	**29.45**	**43.67**	**52.21**	**65.38**
Females	7.93	12.95	18.69	29.85	39.29	54.16
Males	24.95	34.44	39.45	56.50	64.13	75.85

Table 2: Percentage of Girls Enrolment to Total Enrolment by Stages Since 1950-51

Year	*Primary I-V*	*Middle VI-VIII*	*Sec./Hr. Sec.*	*Hr. Education*
1950-51	28.1	16.1	13.3	10.0
1955-56	30.5	20.8	15.4	14.6
1960-61	32.6	23.9	20.5	16.0
1965-66	36.2	26.7	22.0	20.4
1970-71	37.4	29.3	25.0	20.0
1975-76	38.1	31.3	26.9	23.2
1980-81	38.6	32.9	29.6	26.7
1985-86	40.3	35.6	30.3	33.0
1990-91	41.5	36.7	32.9	33.3
1991-92	41.9	38.2	33.8	32.3
1992-93	42.6	38.8	33.9	33.2
1993-94	42.7	39.1	34.3	33.5
1994-95	42.8	38.9	34.4	34.0
1995-96	43.2	39.0	35.3	37.2
1997-98	43.6	40.1	37.1	34.8
1998-99	43.5	40.5	37.8	38.4
1999-00	43.6	48.4	38.9	39.9
2001-01	43.7	40.9	38.6	36.9
2001-02	44.1	41.8	39.5	39.9

Table 3: Gross Enrolment Ratio of Girls at the Primary Stage Since 1950-51

Year	*Primary (I-V)*		*Upper Primary (VI-VIII)*		*Elementary (I-VIII)*	
	Girls	*Total*	*Girls*	*Total*	*Girls*	*Total*
1950-51	24.8	42.6	4.6	12.7	17.7	32.1
1960-61	41.4	62.4	11.3	22.5	30.9	48.7
1970-71	60.5	78.6	20.8	33.4	44.4	61.9
1980-81	64.1	80.5	28.6	41.9	52.1	67.5
1990-91	85.5	100.1	47.0	62.1	70.8	86.0
1991-92	86.9	100.2	49.6	61.35	73.2	87.7
1992-93	73.46	84.6	48.94	67.5	65.7	77.15
1993-94	73.1	81.9	45.4	54.2	63.7	72.3
1994-95	92.6	104.0	55.0	67.2	78.8	90.7
1995-96	93.3	104.3	55.0	67.6	79.3	90.9
2000-01	85.9	95.7	49.9	58.6	72.4	81.6
2001-02	86.9	98.3	52.1	60.2	73.6	87.4
2003-04	95.67	98.31	57.69	62.49	81.51	84.91

Table 4: Sex-wise Enrolment by Stages/Classes Since 1951 (in Million)

Year	*Primary*			*Middle/Upper Primary*			*High/Hr. Secondary,*		
	Boys	*Girls*	*Total*	*Boys*	*Girls*	*Total*	*Boys*	*Girls*	*Total*
1950-51	13.8	5.4	19.2	2.6	0.5	3.1	1.3	0.2	1.5
1955-56	17.1	7.5	24.6	3.8	1.0	4.8	2.2	0.4	2.6
1960-61	23.6	11.4	35.0	5.1	1.6	6.7	2.7	0.7	3.4
1965-66	32.2	18.3	50.5	7.7	2.8	10.5	4.4	1.3	5.7
1970-71	35.7	21.3	57.0	9.4	3.9	13.3	5.7	1.9	7.6
1975-76	40.6	25.0	65.6	11.0	5.0	16.0	6.5	2.4	8.9
1980-81	45.3	28.5	73.8	13.9	6.8	20.7	7.6	3.4	11.0
1985-86	52.2	35.2	87.4	17.7	9.6	27.1	11.5	5.0	16.5
1990-91	57.0	40.4	97.4	21.5	12.5	34.0	12.8	6.3	19.1
1991-92	58.6	42.3	100.9	22.0	13.6	35.6	13.5	6.9	20.4
1992-93	57.9	41.7	99.6	21.2	12.9	34.1	13.6	6.9	20.5
1993-94	55.1	41.9	97.0	20.6	13.5	34.1	13.2	7.5	20.7
1994-95	62.3	46.8	109.1	24.5	15.8	40.3	16.0	8.4	24.4
1995-96	62.4	47.4	109.8	25.0	16.0	41.0	16.1	8.8	24.9
1996-97	62.5	47.9	110.4	24.7	16.3	41.0	17.2	9.8	27.0
1997-98	61.2	47.5	108.7	23.7	15.8	39.5	17.08	10.16	27.24
1998-99	62.7	48.2	110.9	24.0	16.3	40.3	17.26	10.50	27.56
2000-01	64.4	49.8	113.8	25.3	17.5	42.8	16.9	10.7	27.6

Table 5: Drop-out Rates Sex-wise at Primary and Middle Stages Since 1960-61

		1960-61	*1970-71*	*1980-81*	*1990-91*	*1997-98*	*2000-01*	*2002-03*
Class I-V	Boys	61.7	64.5	56.2	40.1	38.23	39.7	36.0
	Girls	70.9	70.9	62.5	46.0	41.34	41.9	33.9
	Total	64.9	67.0	58.7	42.6	39.58	40.7	35.1
Class I-VIII	Boys	75.0	74.6	68.0	59.1	50.72	50.3	52.3
	Girls	85.0	83.4	79.4	65.1	58.61	57.7	53.5
	Total	78.3	77.9	72.7	60.9	54.14	53.7	52.8

The total enrolment at primary stage (Classes I to V) during the period 1950-51 to 2000-01 increased by 6 times while for the girls the increase was nine times. At the upper primary stage of education, the increase during this period was more than 13 times while that of girls, the increase was more than 32 times, which is quite appreciable. At the secondary and senior secondary stage the total increase was more than 18 times and that of girls the increase was about 50 times.

The participation of girls at all stages of education has been increasing steadily over the time as may be seen from the above tables. However, the percentages are still much below fifty per cent at all stages of education.

Table 6: Teachers by Sex and Type of Schools Since 1951

(in '000)

Year	*Primary*			*Upper Primary*			*High/Hr. Secondary*		
	Boys	*Girls*	*Total*	*Boys*	*Girls*	*Total*	*Boys*	*Girls*	*Total*
1950-51	456	82	538	73	13	86	107	20	127
1955-56	574	117	691	132	19	151	155	35	190
1960-61	615	127	742	262	83	345	234	62	296
1965-66	764	180	944	389	139	528	368	111	479
1970-71	835	225	1060	463	175	638	474	155	629
1975-76	955	283	1248	554	224	778	559	200	759
1980-81	1021	342	1363	598	253	851	669	257	926
1985-86	1094	402	1496	663	305	968	793	339	1132
1990-91	1143	473	1616	717	356	1073	917	417	1334
1991-92	1152	492	1644	714	365	1079	931	450	1381
1992-93	1137	514	1651	709	376	1085	941	454	1395
1993-94	1110	513	1623	723	406	1124	953	492	1445
1994-95	1181	533	1714	732	390	1122	956	490	1446
1995-96	1187	553	1740	756	409	1165	982	511	1493
2002-03	1166	746	1912	936	645	1581	1157	620	177

* Provisional.

In 2000-01 the percentage of female teachers to total was about 55% in primary schools, 62% in Upper Primary Schools and 54% in High and 42% in Sr. Secondary Schools.

Table 7: No. of Women Universities, Women Vice-Chancellors Etc. (2003)

No. of Women Universities	*No. of Women Vice-Chancellors*	*% of Women as Professors/ Heads of Deptt.*
5*	20	2%

* 1. S.N.D.T. Women's University.
2. Mother Teresa Women's University.
3. Shri Padmavati Mahila Vishwavidyalaya.
4. Avinashilingam Institute for Home Science and Higher Education for Women.
5. Banasthali Vidyapeeth.

Table 8: No. of Women Colleges Since 1986-87

Year	*No. of Women's Colleges*
1986-87	780
1987-88	786
1988-89	824
1989-90	851
1990-91	874
1991-92	950
1992-93	994
1993-94	1033
1996-97	1195
1997-98	1230
2001-02	1625
2002-03	1651
2003-04*	1798

* Provisional.

Table 9: Percentage of Women Students in Higher Education in Select States (2002-2003)

States	*% of Women Students in Higher Education*
Bihar	23.8
Uttar Pradesh	38.4
Kerala	60.0
Punjab	52.8
Goa	58.5
Delhi	46.0
Pondichery	52.6
Manipur	44.3
Jammu & Kashmir	47.3
Gujarat	44.2
Tamil Nadu	45.1
Overall Percentage	40.1

16.4 PROGRESS BUT SLOW: PROBLEMS AND CAUSES OF SLOW PROGRESS: COMMITTEES AND COMMISSIONS

From the figures given above, it is quite clear that there has been phenomenal progress on women's education since Independence but still there is a wide gap between female education and male education.

Following Committees and Commissions have discussed the various issues relating to women's education:

1. The University Education Commission (1948-49).
2. Smt. Durgabai Deshmukh Committee (1959).
3. Smt. Hansa Mehta Committee (1962).
4. M. Bhaktvatsalam Committee to look into the causes of Public Support Particularly in Rural Areas for Girls Education and to enlist Public Cooperation.
5. Education Commission (1964-66).
6. Resolution on the National Policy on Education (1968).
7. Report of the Committee on the Status of Women in India (1974).
8. Challenge of Education 1985.
9. National Policy on Education 1986.
10. Programme of Action 1986.

Causes of Slow Progress

Usually following causes of slow progress are mentioned:

(i) Lack of proper social attitudes in the rural and backward areas for the education of girls.
(ii) Lack of educational facilities in rural areas.
(iii) Economic backwardness of the rural community.
(iv) Conservative nature and co-educational aspects.
(v) Lack of suitable curriculum.
(vi) Lack of proper incentives to parents and children.
(vii) Lack of women teachers.
(viii) Lack of proper supervision and guidance due to inadequate women personnel in the Inspectorate.
(ix) Uneducated adult women and lack of social education.
(x) Social Ills.
(xi) Inadequate systematic publicity.
(xii) Indifference of Panchayats.

Measures for the Promotion of Women's Education

Following measures are suggested:

I. Creating Proper Social Attitude in the Rural and Backward Areas for the Education of Girls: Following measures may be taken:

1. To study the problems relating to women's education and to get detailed scientific data, a thorough research should be taken up by the Institutes of Education and allied institutions in different States and co-ordinated at the national level.
2. Separate schools for girls at the middle and high school stages should be established where needed.
3. School Mothers in co-education primary schools should be appointed.
4. Creches and nursery classes wherever possible should be opened.
5. Public opinion in favour of girls' education should be created.

II. Providing Adequate Educational Facilities in Backward and Rural Areas: The target should be to have at least one primary school within a radius of one kilometer from every home which is within the walking distance of a child. Following steps are needed :

1. Hostel for girls at the middle and high school stages.
2. Maintenance stipends to girls residing in hostels for meeting their board and lodging expenses, at least in part.
3. Subsidised transport facilities, wherever necessary and possible.
4. All priority to be given to the construction of suitable buildings for girl's schools.
5. Free education for girls.

III. Removing Economic Backwardness of the Rural and Backward Areas: The girls are very useful at home for carrying out domestic duties and so mothers are reluctant to send them to school. A large number of children in the rural areas are under-nourished. They hardly have a square meal a day. Unless the parents are given some kind of economic relief, it will be impossible to achieve the targets.

Following measures should prove very useful.

1. Free uniforms and free books to the needy and deserving children should be provided.

2. Attendance scholarships which serve as a compensation to the parents should be given. This will also ensure reduction of wastage and stagnation.

3. Mid-day meals should be made available free of charge.

IV. Conservative Nature of Parents and Co-education: Parents in rural areas and backward communities tend not to send the girls to co-educational schools. Their apprehensions have to be removed with a thought-out plan of educating them in this regard (see next part)

V. Provision of Suitable Curriculum: Curriculum, by and large, has not met the requirements of women.

Following suggestions made by Smt. Hansa Mehta Committee (1962) deserve careful consideration:

1. No differentiation should be made in the curricula for boys and girls at the primary and middle stages of education.

2. Steps should be taken to improve the instruction of home economics.

3. Steps should be taken to improve the teaching of music and fine arts and liberal financial assistance should also be made available to girls' schools for the introduction of these courses.

4. Universities should review periodically the provision they have made for the courses designed to meet the special needs of girls and take necessary action to remove the deficiencies discovered.

VI. Proper Incentives to Parents and Girls: The following measures have been suggested:

1. The number of attendance scholarships should be doubled in the ninth Plan.

2. The allowance of the School Mothers should be enhanced so that qualified women may be attracted to take up the work.

3. The number of maintenance stipends should be doubled in the ninth Plan and the rate of such stipends should be adequately increased in view of the rising prices all over the country.

4. The number of sanitary blocks in co-educational primary schools be adequately increased during the ninth Plan.

5. Larger allocation of funds should be made in the budget for construction of hostels for girls during the ninth Plan.

VII. Provision for Providing Adequate Number of Women Teachers: Following steps are suggested:

1. A large number of training institutions have to be provided for women, especially in the backward States. These institutions should generally be located in rural areas and they should generally recruit their trainees from that area.

2. Condensed course centres should be started in these backward areas to open up avenues to adult unqualified women for employment as teachers. Wherever possible such centres should be attached to the training institutions.

3. A large number of quarters for women teachers should be provided, particularly in rural areas. Our target should be to provide at least 50 per cent of the women teachers with quarters in primary schools.

4. All women teachers employed in rural areas should be given adequate rural allowance.

5. Special stipends should be given to girls in high and higher secondary schools with aptitude for teaching.

6. Whenever possible husbands and wives should be posted in the same place even if they work in different departments of the Government.

7. Free training should be imparted with stipends to all candidates of training institutions.

8. In-service education training should be given to untrained women teachers who have put in at least two years of service. The period of training of education should be treated as on duty.

VIII. Proper Supervision and Guidance: For providing proper guidance and supervision, following steps should be taken:

(a) Increase in the number of women inspecting officers, particularly in the backward States, at different levels including State level and Directorate level.

(b) Provision of adequate transport for all district women inspecting officers.

(c) Adequate office staff and equipments.

(d) Residential facilities to all women officers at all levels.

(e) Adequate funds at the disposal of the State Council for closer contact with rural areas.

IX. Facilities for Education of Adult Women: Girls education and education of adult women suffers on account of lack of social education. This problem can be tackled in the following ways:

1. By opening adult literacy classes in large number.

2. By teaching simple skills like sewing, knitting, handicrafts etc., and knowledge of basic principles of health and food habits.

3. New attitudes towards community living, family planning, superstitions, caste, etc.

This programme can be tackled effectively with the help of the Education Department in co-operation with other departments concerned like the Community Development, Health and Social Welfare.

X. Eradicating Social Ills: The Purdah system (in some States such as in Orissa, Uttar Pradesh, Bihar and Rajasthan) and certain other harmful social customs in these States and in others stand in the way of the development of girls' education. In some places caste barriers also contribute to this. Social reformers and other voluntary organisations may be motivated to take up this work.

XI. Wide Systematic Publicity: For educating the parents to take interest in the education of girls, press and electronic media may be used extensively.

XII. Awards to Panchayats: Panchayats should be given some motivation to take up work in this area.

Concluding Remarks: The role of women outside the home has become an important feature of the social and economic life of the country and in the years to come this will become still more significant. From this point of view greater attention will have to be paid to the problems of training and development of women. The education of girls, therefore, should be emphasised not only on grounds of social justice, but also because it accelerates economic and social transformation.

16.5 RECOMMENDATIONS—WOMEN EDUCATION IN SCIENCE TECHNOLOGY AND MANAGEMENT (1997)

The Institute of Advanced Studies in Education, Rohilkhand University, Bareilly organised in February-March 1997, "A National Seminar on Women Participation in Science, Technology and Management Education." The Seminar was sponsored by the All India Council for Technical Education (AICTE), University Grants Commission (UGC) and Department of Science and Technology (DST), Govt. of India and Rohilkhand University. After detailed discussion, the following recommendations emerged in areas of education, and entrepreneurship and employment :

1. Regular interactions of parents and teachers to encourage, promote and reinforce girls/women education should take place.
2. In order to promote girls education in areas like science, technology and management, it was essential to have their counselling at high school so that after 10+2 level, they could get the opportunity to avail of engineering, technical and management education.
3. Counselling for encouraging girl students to study the subjects, *e.g.*, science, math's, computers etc., could be arranged with faculty members from universities/colleges, engineering and management institutions, industry personnel, etc.
4. The constitutional provisions of free and compulsory education up to 14 years and prohibition of child labour be enforced effectively.
5. Provision of scholarship on the basis of merit-cum-means be introduced for deserving girl students at secondary and tertiary levels particularly in technical, medical, management and other professional fields.
6. Separate Engineering Institutions be opened for women in Ninth Five Year Plan with emphasis on courses like computer science, electronics and management etc.
7. 30% seats may be reserved for girl candidates in technical, management, medical and other professional courses.
8. There was an urgent need to develop and produce special programmes for electronic media (TV, Radio), to change the attitude of the society towards women's education, gender bias, segregation of sexes, gender roles, etc. and importance of women participation in the nation building and development.
9. With the help of both print and electronic media, the awareness must be generated among masses about use of innovations of science and technology in improving the human life (health and hygiene, population management, energy and environmental protection, etc.) and easier means to carry out their work (household, agricultural, business, etc.).

With regard to *Enhancing Women's Participation in Entrepreneurship and Employment Sectors*, the seminar recommended as under:

1. There should be horizontal reservation in open and reserved categories (SC, ST and OBC) for women to the extent of 50% depending upon the availability of suitable candidates.
2. Vocational counselling and guidance cell be established in universities/ colleges so that women/girls could get information about career prospects and courses of studies.

3. With the help of National Social Service Scheme, awareness about women's participation in entrepreneurship be created.

4. The seminar felt the necessity of mass awareness regarding legal rights of women in different spheres of life.

5. Media, both electronic and print, may be used by the Government to change attitudes of masses towards women's entrepreneurship and employment in scientific, technical, professional and managerial spheres. (*University News*, March 31, 1997)

16.6 CO-EDUCATION

Meaning of Co-education: Co-education has been defined in *'Encyclopaedia Britannica'* in these words, "Co-education means that boys and girls should be taught the same courses at the same time, in the same place, by the same faculty, with the same methods and under the same regime." However, such a rigid concept of co-education is hardly applicable to Indian situation.

Conflicting views have been expressed by thinkers and Education Committees and Commissions on this issue.

Merits of Co-education. Following merits are claimed:

1. It is economical as separate buildings, staff etc., are not needed when the number of students is small.
2. It has a humanising effect on both the sexes.
3. It is helpful in the sublimation of some instincts.
4. It prepares to adjust oneself in a world in which men and women work shoulder to shoulder.
5. It helps to have a fuller and richer development.
6. It solves the problem of shortage of women teachers in some subjects.
7. It motivates the students to achieve better in order to impress someone of the opposites sex.
8. It enables the students to understand the psychology of sex. Haward writes, "Future mothers should not have to confess with tears that they do not understand boys."
9. It helps in reducing mental diseases. Dr. Freud believed that co-education alone could keep young people 'free from diseases of mind'.
10. Coeducation helps to have a sophisticate as well as homely environment.
11. Addison once said, "Female friendship is necessary for intellectual development." Co-education may serve this purpose.

Demerits and Limitations of Co-education

1. *Separate Needs of Men and Women*: Dr. Joad has remarked, "Girls tend to be more interested in their immediate surroundings, in what is pretty and ornamental, boys in what is more remote from them, in what is useful, in what is general and what is abstract. Boys seek expression in investigating, exploring, constructing, girls through artistic and emotional channels."

2. *Unhealthy Effects on Intellectual Pursuits*: "Men cannot study when women are around and that if women are let into a college, they are likely to get round some of the professors and marry them and then bid good-bye to research and higher thought."

3. *Less Attention to Girls*: Girls usually suffer. It is generally seen that in co-educational institutions adequate facilities are not provided for girls.

4. *No Thorough Cleansing of the Mental Make-up*: Co-education is a farce in many cases as we have not taken to this business in the right spirit. There must be a sane attitude and proper and healthy outlook.

5. *Trouble in Free Mixing*: Dr. Stanley Hall writes: "During the early years of adolescence when the body is rapidly changing and a sense of an awkwardness and reticence is felt, the two sexes should not intrude upon each other." Since in our tropical country sex consciousness develops at an early age, free mixing is fraught with danger.

6. *Distraction of Attention*: Co-education distracts the attention of boys and girls in attending to lectures as sometimes they go on booking at each other.

7. *Separate Code of Discipline*: Discipline that is suitable for girls may not be suitable for boys.

8. *Too much Emphasis on Make-up*: It is felt by some thinkers that girls tend to use too much make up to attract boys and *vice versa*.

9. *Physiological Differences*: Physiological considerations demand separate type of activities. A common curriculum is not suited to both the sexes.

10. *Anti-tradition*: Conservative elements in the society consider co-education as anti-tradition and anti-culture.

11. *Purdah System*: It is felt that on several occasions the purdah system does not allow the women to take the full advantage of facilities and also creates hindrances in the display of their talents.

On the issue of co-education the Secondary Education Commission observed, "It seems to us, therefore, that there can be no hard and fast policy with regard to co-education. We are of the opinion that where it is possible, separate schools for girls should be established as they are likely to offer better opportunities than in mixed schools to develop their physical, social and mental aptitudes and all states should open such schools in adequate numbers. But it should be open to girls, whose parents have no objection in this matter, to avail themselves of co-educational facilities in boys schools."

Suggestions for Making Co-education Successful

1. Co-education should be adopted as the general policy at the primary level.
2. At the middle and secondary stages separate schools should be provided in areas where there is a demand for them. But the effort to pursue co-education as a general policy at these stages should continue side by side.
3. At the university level, co-education should be the general policy and opening of new colleges exclusively for girls should be discouraged.
4. There should be no bar on admission of girls to boys' institutions.
5. Whenever separate schools/colleges for girls are provided, it has to be ensured that they maintain required standards in regard to the quality of the staff, provision of facilities, relevant courses and co-curricular services.
6. Acceptance of principle of mixed staff should be made a condition of recognition for co-educational institutions.
7. Where there are co-educational institutions separate toilet facilities and retiring rooms for girls should be provided.
8. The lady teachers as well as male teachers must be appointed in these schools.
9. There should be adequate provision for those subjects as are liked by girls, *i.e.*, Music, Home Craft, Drawing and Painting, etc.

10. Separate rooms, play-fields and sanitary conveniences should be provided for girls according to their specific needs.

11. There should be at least one woman teacher in a rural school even if the number of girl students is less.

12. Special co-curricular activities suited to girls like Home Nursing, Needle Work and Girls Guiding should be introduced.

13. The women representatives should be taken on the management so that they could plead for providing necessary facilities for girls.

16.7 NO DIFFERENTIATION OF CURRICULA FOR MALES AND FEMALES

The Hansa Mehta Committee on Differentiation of Curricula for Boys and Girls (1961-64), appointed by the National Council for Women's Education, in consultation with the Ministry of Education considered the issue of providing suitable curricula for women and observed, "In the ultimate democratic and socialistic pattern of society, education will be related to individual capacities, aptitudes and interests which are not related to sex. Therefore, 'there would be no need in such a society to differentiate curricula on the basis of sex." It, however, further felt, "But it will be some years before this new social order is created. In the transitional phase, certain psychological differences between men and women as well as certain divisions of social functions based on them will have to be accepted as matters of fact and as practical basis for building up the curricula for boys and girls. It is on these fundamental assumptions that the proposals for a differentiation of curricula between boys and girls are based."

1. *Primary Stage*: (a) No differentiation should be made in the curricula for boys and girls at the primary stage.

(b) Women should be appointed on the staff of all primary schools.

2. *Middle School Stage*: (a) The curriculum of general education should be common to boys and girls and no differentiation should be made therein on the basis of sex.

(b) In all middle schools it is desirable to have mixed staff but where girls do attend school ordinary meant for boys, appointment of women teachers on staff should be obligatory.

3. *Secondary Stage*: (a) The accepted policy at the secondary stage is to provide diversified curricula to meet the aptitudes and capacities of all adolescents. If properly implemented, this programme could provide for all the special needs of girls. Diversified courses such as those for home science, fine arts, music, etc., should be increasingly introduced at the secondary stage to meet the special needs of girls. These electives should not, however, be made compulsory for them.

(b) The introduction of home science in the secondary school curriculum has come in for a good deal of criticism, due mainly to bad implementation resulting from inadequacy of textbooks, lack of teachers, lack of the recognition by universities and defective designing of courses. Steps should be taken to improve the implementation.

(c) Sex education is essential at the middle and secondary stage.

(d) Special encouragement should be given to girls who study mathematics or science at the secondary stage, and special efforts should be made to prepare women teachers of mathematics and science.

4. *Vocational Education*: (a) Immediate attempts should be directed to expand the provision of vocational courses at the secondary and higher stages of education, and to relate these courses with manpower and womanpower requirements of society.

(b) The possibilities of employing women on a larger scale on a part-time basis in as many vocations as possible have to be explored.

16.8 EDUCATION FOR WOMEN'S EQUALITY

The NPE stipulates that "Education will be used as an agent of basic change in the status of women. In order to neutralise the accumulated distortion of the past, there will be a well conceived edge in favour of women." For achieving this, "The National Education System will play a positive, interventionist role in the empowerment of women." The NPE's programme includes the following dimensions:

1. Redesigning of courses to develop new values.
2. Redesigning of textbooks to eliminate all sex bias.
3. Training and orientation of teachers for developing sensitiveness to women's issues and their empowerment.
4. Orientation of decision makers and administrators to women issues.
5. Active involvement of educational institutions in enabling women in the process of empowerment of women.
6. According priority to the removal of illiteracy among women through provision of special support services, setting of time-targets and effective monitoring.
7. Increasing participation of women in vocational, technical and professional education at all levels.
8. Following policy of non-discrimination to eliminate stereotyping in vocational and professional courses.
9. Promoting women's participation in non-traditional as well as in existing and emergent technologies.

Mahila Samakhya (MS) Programme

The programme launched in support of Women's education mandated in the NPE revolves around the *'Sangha'* (Village Level Women's Collective) which is considered as the nodal point. The process of mobilising women and creating an environment for women participation in learning is facilitated by a *'Sahayogni'* (a cluster coordinator in charge of 10 villages). She is a crucial link between the village *'Sangha'* and the district implementation unit of the programme. The district implementation unit provides resource support and inputs to meet the needs of women. The district units in turn are supported by a state office.

'Mahila Samakhya' has expanded its coverage to 40 districts and over 6,876 villages.

The *'Sangha'* the nodal point of the programme addresses a wide range of issues relating to the livelihood of women, their education, health etc. It has taken an active lead in enrolling children primarily girls in the village schools.

The *'Sangha'* has encouraged thrift and credit among women to better their economic condition.

Women s Studies Centres

The UGC has been assisting more than 20 universities and a dozen colleges to set up women's studies centres. Institutions are also encouraged to take up research projects relating to women. These women's studies centres have played an important role in highlighting crucial issues relating to women's status and education.

Empowering Women for Educational Management

Although women can play a significant role in educational management at the higher level, yet their number at higher posts is insignificant. The following table illustrates the position.

Table 11: Women Administrators in Indian Universities

Administrative Position	*Number*
Chancellors	3
Vice Chancellor	12
Pro-Vice Chancellors	3
Registrars	7
Deans	72
Directors	11

Source : *AIU Handbook 2000*, AIU, New Delhi

17

Social Service in Education

17.1 MEANING AND IMPORTANCE OF SOCIAL SERVICE: SOCIAL SERVICE AN INTEGRAL PART OF EDUCATION

The essence of social service education may be expressed in the words 'Caring for Others', Concern for Others', 'Compassion' and 'Selflessness'.

The report of the National Commission for Teachers I *i.e.,* School Teachers (1983-85) stated the following goals of the Indian society.

1. A United Secular India.
2. A Modern Nation.
3. A Productive People.
4. A Humane and Caring Society.

While elucidating the goal of "Humane Society" the report recalled the beautiful and sublime words of the *'YajurVeda'* (XXXVI. 8), which sound so fresh and current today, "May all beings look on me with the eye of a friend: may I look on all beings with the eye of a friend."

Caring for people is necessary. There is a deep and genuine 'compassion' in our Constitution that is unique in its prescription to 'care' for the disadvantaged sections of society and to restore to them equality of status and opportunity. Our humane traditions enjoin upon us to be 'caring' for others.

The Committee for Review of National Policy on Education (1990), popularly known as Ramamurti Committee entitled its report *'Towards an Enlightened and Humane Society'*. This shows its concern for the development of a humane society.

In the *'Bible'* the same sentiment has been expressed," No man lived unto himself., we are all parts of one another."

The International Commission on the Development of Education entitled its report *'Learning to Be'* (1972). This also emphasized social service aspect of education.

A UNESCO International Symposium organised with the caption *'Foreseeable Demands in the Twenty-first Century'* (1991) laid stress upon the need to pay attention to many aspects of caring including:

- Caring for one's family and peers.
- Caring for other people.
- Caring for the social, economic and ecological welfare of one's society and nation.
- Caring for human rights.

The National Policy on Education has observed, "The growing concern over the erosion of essential values and an increasing cynicism in society has brought to focus the need for readjustment in the curriculum in order to make education a forceful tool for the cultivation of social and moral values."

Swami Vivekananda, one of the greatest exponents of Indian philosophy has observed, "So long as the millions live in hunger and ignorance, I hold every man a traitor, who, having been educated at their expense, pays not the least heed to them... I call him a 'Mahatma' who feels for the poor. Let the people be your God—think of them, work for them " This indicates that the educated persons must render social service to the needy. This is the appropriate example of social service education.

A renowned poet Shaikh Saadi has stated the difference between a man of worship (*Abid*) and a man of knowledge (*Alim*'-educated). "The 'Abid' tries to retrieve his own garment in the storm. The *'Alim'* struggles to save those who are drowning."

17.2 UNIVERSITY EDUCATION COMMISSION ON SOCIAL SERVICE IN EDUCATION

Regarding the drawbacks of the educational system the Commission observed, "The present educational system is also responsible for increasing the gulf between the educated and the uneducated classes, between the intelligentsia and the masses." To remove this, the Commission stated, "The intelligentsia should try to become a real service-group striving to uplift the masses and should resist the temptation to become a parasitical group living for itself and perpetuating its own privileged position." There is a great need for the development of 'social conscience.'

For the above mentioned purpose, the University Education Commission recommended "some form of social and national service to be made obligatory for all students and also to make it an integral part of education at all stages." The Commission was of the view that "This can become an instrument to build character, improve discipline, inculcate a faith in the dignity of manual labour and develop a sense of social responsibility."

The University Education Commission made the following suggestions in this regard:

— encouraging and enabling students to participate in community living on the school or college campus; and

— providing opportunities of participation in programmes of community development and national service.

17.3 MERITS OF SOCIAL SERVICE PROGRAMMES IN EDUCATION

Social service programmes in education are very helpful in the following ways:

1. Sublimation of several significant instincts of students.
2. Providing social training.
3. Developing the 'Art of Living' among students.
4. Promoting values of civic training.
5. Developing moral values.
6. Providing worthy recreational interests.
7. Inculcating sentiment of loyalty and 'oneness'
8. Developing disciplinary values.
9. Developing qualities of leadership.

10. Helping physical development.
11. Strengthening and supplementing class work.
12. Bringing the community and the educational institution closer to each other.
13. Solving the thorny issue of adult education/literacy.
14. Developing dignity of labour.
15. Saving funds.
16. Doing an act of merit.

17.4 DIAGRAMMATIC PRESENTATION OF SOCIAL SERVICE ACTIVITIES IN EDUCATION

(1)	(2)	(3)	(4)	(5)	(6)	(7)	(8)	(9)
Community living in schools and colleges	Participation in programmes of Community Development	Red Cross Society	Scouts and Girl Guides N.S.S.	Social service in fairs and community functions	Social service during natural calamities like floods etc.	Social service during war or war like situation	Social service to the needy	Adult Literacy Programme

17.5 IMPORTANT PROGRAMMES AND ACTIVITIES IN SOCIAL SERVICE: RECOMMENDATIONS OF THE KOTHARI COMMISSION

1. *Community Living in Schools and Colleges*: Every educational institution should try to develop a rich community life of its own and provide adequate and satisfying opportunities for students to participate in it and help in organizing it. Various opportunities for such work exist in the classroom, on the campuses of the schools and the colleges, in the hostels and on the playgrounds. For instance, instead of utilizing servants and hired labour for educational institutions and their hostels, it is possible to have much of the work done by students, not primarily to save money, but to provide valuable experience. Japan has followed this practice in her national system, and many schools in India (including some schools for well-to-do children) are also doing so to some extent. This type of work-experience would cultivate in students the habit of work and a sense of the dignity of labour. If this is done on a nation-wide scale, it will incidentally effect some saving in expenditure which could be utilized for providing certain basic amenities for students. Pattern of hostel life should be introduced in schools and colleges so far as possible. The practice of making self-help and manual work a part of the daily life and training in all types of educational institutions—as was the case in many of the old Ashrams and Academies—would yield good educational results. It is not possible to totally re-create the conditions of the past in our educational institutions; but we can certainly profit from the useful elements in past experience.

2. *Participation in Programmes of Community Development*: It is essential to make participation in meaningful programmes of community service an integral part of all education from the primary to the undergraduate stage. Such participation can help to create positive attitudes towards social service and to develop closer ties between the educated persons and the rest of the people. It can also help in building up a sense of social purpose and

self-confidence and giving students a sense of participation in community life and activities.

The organization of the programmes will naturally vary from stage to stage:

1. At the primary stage, it will take the form of bringing the school closer to the community with an accent on serving the community in suitable ways.

2. At the secondary stage, such programmes can be more ambitiously designed, and have a greater impact on young minds. Every secondary school should develop carefully planned programmes for promoting good school community relations and suitable forms of service to the community. About ten days a year (or a total of 30 days at the lower secondary stage and 20 days at the higher secondary stage) may be fully devoted to such programmes. Where this is not possible, it should be obligatory for the students to participate in the Labour Service Camps for secondary school students to be organized by the State Education Departments on a district basis.

3. Similarly, it should be obligatory for every college student, before he is awarded his first degree, to put in at least 60 days of national service in one to three stretches. Each college should develop its own programme, suited to its objectives, its resources and the age and competence of its students. Participation in Labour and Social Welfare Camps or the NCC should also be regarded as alternative forms of such service.

The NCC programme, at the university stage, has shown some good results. It has possibilities of promoting national development by building-up closer ties between the people and the defence services. It also helps to lessen the difference between the so-called 'martial' and other classes and inculcates the idea of the defence of freedom in all classes of people. It may not be easy to organise an effective programme of social service for all the secondary schools in the country. Its implementation should, therefore, be carried out in stages. To begin with, selected schools of high quality may organize the national service programme on a voluntary basis; and to help them, the Department should draw up model plans of social and community services. The training schools and colleges may take the lead in this regard and help to build up a suitable list of activities for the neighbouring schools. As experience is gained in executing the programme, it may be extended to cover a larger number of schools and students.

Advantages of Community Activities

(i) These inculcate in students the spirit of community service.
(ii) These inculcate in the students the spirit of self-sacrifice.
(iii) These give children a scope for the exercise of initiative.
(iv) They build up an attitude of co-operation and fellow-feeling.
(v) They build a co-operative atmosphere in the home and the outside world.
(vi) They train students in leadership.
(vii) They give children training in citizenship and in the art of self-government.
(viii) They develop wider outlook.
(ix) These activities help in the many-sided development of the pupil—physical, mental, moral, religious and social.
(x) These activities foster dignity of labour.
(xi) These directly and indirectly impart moral education.

In short, these activities develop virtues of give and take, co-operation, participation in social life, sharing responsibilities, cooperative endeavour, mutual adjustment, internal self-discipline friendly disposition, ideals of service, proper attitudes, etc.

3. *Labour and Social Service Camps*: While every encouragement should be given to each secondary school to develop its own programme of social service on the lines indicated above, it is realized that it will not be possible for many schools to do so, at least for some years to come. It is, therefore, recommended that labour and social service camps which will run throughout the year (except during the monsoon season when outdoor work will not be possible), should be organized in each district, and each secondary school which does not have a social service programme of its own should be under an obligation to participate in such camps and provide this rich and valuable experience to its students. For this purpose, a special organization should be set up in each district under the direct control of the district educational officer. It will be the responsibility of this organization (1) to select one or more specific projects on which students can work all the year round; (2) to provide the necessary community contacts; (3) to assist in providing residential arrangements, implements, utensils, etc; and (4) where possible, to provide a part of the expenditure of the entire organization of the camps. The schools will be responsible for drawing up the programme for their participation, in consultation with this district agency, for taking the students to the camp, and for guiding the students in carrying out the projects assigned to them.

Great care should be taken in selecting the projects for the camp. The idea should be to take up a project which could be completed within the time given. This would make the students and teachers feel that they are doing something worth while, something which results in a lasting benefit to the community. The co-operation of the Community Development Administration should be sought for the purpose and the project should be connected with the five year plans for the area.

During the period of the camp, students would be expected to put in 8 hours of work per day and the general routine would be as follows:

2 hours—personal time in morning.
2 hours—intellectual work not connected with school studies.
6 hours—manual work.
2 hours—intellectual work not connected with school studies.
2 hours—rest and recreation.
2 hours—personal time in the evening.
8 hours—sleep.

A part of the funds for the programme could be obtained from the local Rural Works Programme. All the overhead charges—which will come to a very small amount—should be met by Government. The students should be required only to bear (1) transport charges to the camp site and back, and (2) food charges during the stay at the camp. Even these could be subsidized to some extent on the basis of the work that the students put in. A student who holds freeship or half freeship should be given similar concessions in the camp. Adjustments could also be made by requesting the students to bring some articles of foodstuffs etc. from home. On the whole, an attempt should be made to keep the cost of this camp down to the minimum for each period. Moreover, camps for boys and girls may have to be organized separately.

4. *Labour Weeks—School Improvement and Neighbourhood Improvement Programmes*: Regarding this type of work, K. G. Saiyidain writes, "I feel strongly that not only in this country, but in the whole world, we have to make an earnest and concentrated effort to give a new orientation to the social ideology of our children and youth particularly in the direction of inculcating a sense of the dignity of labour and cultivating the capacity to work together for constructive and socially worthy causes. I cannot think of any better method of doing so than by bringing all school children together into a fellowship of work and service where the meanest work will be undertaken in a spirit of adventure and comradeship because it is useful and provides healthy outlet for their energies and talents." Following types of work may be done during a labour week:

(a) Cleaning and white-washing the school building.

(b) Decorating the rooms.

(c) Removing stones, iron nails, waste paper, etc. from the school compound, playground, lanes and streets.

(d) Filling pits in the streets and lanes, and cleaning roads.

(e) Organising first-aid centres for the public.

(f) Teaching adults.

(g) Improving drainage of selected localities and drying marshy land created by open drains.

(h) Turfing school compounds.

(i) Propaganda amongst the public regarding the importance of personal cleanliness and social sanitation in order to ward off common diseases.

To make this programme a success, the teachers themselves should take an active part in activities stated above. This will give incentive and encouragement to the students.

5. *Adult Education/Literary Centres*: Traditionally in India, imparting of education is considered as an act of merit as well as social service. The students, if properly motivated can be used very conveniently and profitably for this purpose. Out of nearly 3 crores of students at the secondary stage and 70 lakhs at the college stage, even if one-fourth of them are involved during vacations, substantial success in spreading adult literacy can be achieved. All funds earmarked for the voluntary agencies for this purpose should be diverted to this proposed programmes. Students' boarding and lodging arrangement could be made with this fund. The State Education Departments and the universities should be allotted these funds. We have so far failed to make use of this huge manpower. The duration of the academic session could be extended just by one month for only one year. For launching such a type of programme, necessary political will and administrative reorientation are needed. The all round development of an individual as the aim of education requires that an individual must imbibe a spirit of social service. Our education, therefore, must include an element of social service in all its manifestations.

18

Diverse Issues

18.1 MODERNISATION AND INDIANISATION OF EDUCATION

Meaning of Modernisation: While discussing the issue of modernisation and Indianisation, it must be kept in view that modernisation and Indianisation are not incompatible terms and modernisation is also not synonymous with Europeanisation.

Following three quotes illustrate this point:

Pt. Jawaharlal Nehru said, "Can we combine the progress of science and technology with the progress of mind and spirit also? We cannot be untrue to science because that represents the basic fact of life to-day. Still less can we be untrue to those essential principles for which India has stood in the past throughout the ages. Let us then pursue our path to industrial progress with our strength and vigour and at the same time remember that material riches without toleration and compassion and wisdom may well turn to dust and ashes!'

The Education Commission (1964-66) observed, "We believe that India should strive to bring science and the values of the spirit together in harmony and thereby save their way for the cultural emergence of a society which would cater to the needs of the whole man and not only to a particular fragment of personality"

The NPE (1986 and modified in 1992) has clearly stated, "The existing schism between the formal system of education and the country's rich and varied cultural traditions needs to be bridged. The preoccupation with modern technologies cannot be allowed to sever new generations from the roots in Indian history and culture. Deculturalisation, de-humanisation and alienation must be avoided at all costs. Education can and must bring about the fine synthesis between change-oriented technologies and the country's continuity of cultural traditions."

We must, of course have engineers, technicians and other personnel needed for development and bringing Indian agriculture, economy, commerce, industry etc. at par with the developed nations, but they must be imbued with the true humantistic spirit, traditions and values of worthy life that our country prides. It should be the object of modernisation of education to maintain a correct balance between what is valuable in the legacy inherited from the past and the needs and requirements of the present day.

Main Features of Modernisation: Following are the main features of modernisation:

1. *Science Based Technology*: The most distinctive feature of a modern society in contrast with a traditional one is in its adoption of a science based

technology. It is this which has helped modern societies to increase their production rapidly.

2. *The Explosion of Knowledge*: The last few decades witnessed a great explosion of knowledge. In a traditional society, the stock of knowledge is limited. In a modern society on the other hand, the stock of knowledge is far greater and the pace of its growth is infinitely quicker.

3. *Rapid Economic, Social and Cultural Changes*: Another feature of a modern society is the quick, almost breath-taking rate at which changes take place.

What Modernisation is !

1. Modernisation is a progressive change in all areas of life.
2. Modernisation signifies progress.
3. Modernisation is the outcome of the development and application of scientific and technological knowledge.
4. Modernisation implies feeling for others.
5. Modernisation signifies mobility.
6. Modernisation is rational thinking and rational actions.
7. Modernisation signifies changes in traditional attitudes and development of new attitudes towards work, wealth and saving.
8. Modernisation signifies achievement.
9. Modernisation signifies individualistic tendencies.

What Modernisation is Not!

1. Modernisation is not Westernisation.
2. Modernisation is not out and out industrialisation.
3. Modernisation is not just superficial acquisition of certain values.
4. Modernisation is not anti-moral or anti-religious.

Modernisation and Westernisation

It is a wrong notion to equate modernisation with Westernisation and Westernisation with all that is against traditional Indian culture. As a matter of fact, the rapid development of means of communications, science and technology have narrowed down considerably the difference between eastern and western values. Westernisation should not be understood as something which is to be hated. Are British people not hard working? Are they not patriots? Similarly, we have to learn several lessons from the German people. Americans have made tremendous progress in different areas.

Modernisation and Education

Studies conducted on the relationship of modernisation and education report that "Education is the most powerful factor in making nations and Indians modern." It is also revealed that education itself is greatly influenced by modernisation. One of the most significant research done in this are is the Harward Project which covered Argentina, Chili, India, Pakistan, Israel, and Nigeria. (Inkeles, Alex 1969). Similarly studies conducted by F. B. Waisannen and Hideya Kumata (1972), which were based on 5 national probability samples of adult age 20 and older, drawn from the U.S.A, Finland, Japan, Mexico and Costa-Rica revealed positive correlationship between education and various indicators of modernity."

Studies conducted in India by M. S. Gore, I.P. Desai and Suma Chitnis (1970) pointed out, "The state, sex and educational level of the respondents were all important variables in determining the modernity of student population."

The study done by S. L. Sharma and published by Indian Council of Social Science Research (1979) revealed inverse relationship between the level of higher education and the student modernity.

Major Changes Affecting Modernisation of Education

1. Globalisation and increasing economic integration across the world.
2. The advent of new communications and information technology on a large scale.
3. The changes in the labour market.
4. The changing structure of the economy of the nation as a whole.
5. The changes related to public finances.
6. The changes in the family finances.
7. The social and cultural changes.
8. The changes in the demographic patterns.
9. The environmental changes.
10. The changes that are to be effected in the school and further education.
11. The developments in education elsewhere in the world.

Education and Modernisation in India

As already observed that modernisation of education and Indianisation of education are compatible terms. The significant point in this regard is that modernisation of education in India cannot be envisaged without a happy and harmonious blend of science and technology with spirituality.

Following are the important features of modernisation and Indianisation of education.

1. *Modernisation and Aims of Education*: In the light of the above features of modernization, the very aim of education has to be viewed differently—It is no longer taken as concerned primarily with the imparting of knowledge or the preparation of a finished product but with the awakening of curiosity, the development of proper interests, attitudes and values and the building up of such essential skills as independent study and the capacity to think and judge for oneself without which it is not possible to become a responsible member of a democratic society.

2. *Modernisation and Science and Technology based Education*: We are at a crucial stage in the process of development and transformation and in this context the role of science (using the word in its broadest sense) is of the utmost importance. Science education must become an integral part of school education and ultimately some study of science should become a part of all courses in the humanities and social sciences at the university stage.

The quality of science teaching has also to be raised considerably so as to achieve its proper objectives and purposes, namely promoting ever-deepening understanding of basic principles to develop problem solving, analytical skills and the ability to apply them to the problems of the material environment and social living and to promote the spirit of enquiry and experimentation.

3. *Vocationalisation of Education*: The need to provide some correctives to the over-academic nature of formal education has been widely recognised. In the curricula of most contemporary school systems particularly in the socialist countries of Europe, a place is found, for what is variously called, 'manual work' or 'work experience'. At present, the intelligentsia consists predominantly of the white-collared professions and students of humanities, while the proportion of scientists and technical workers in its rank is quite small. To achieve this, greater emphasis must be placed on vocational subjects, education and research.

4. *Mass Education*: The proportion of persons who have so far been able to receive education is very small. This will have to be increased. It is very essential to produce educated and skilled citizens and train an adequate and competent intelligentsia to modernize society quickly. N.A.E.P. (National Adult Education Programme) is likely to go a long way in modernization of Indian education.

5. *Education for Social and National Integration*: Social and National integration is crucial to the creation of a strong, united country, which is an essential pre-condition for modernization.

6. *Development of Skilled Manpower*: There can be no hope of modernizing the agricultural economy of the country unless the farmer is ready to adopt techniques that increase yields and move out of his age-long conservatism. The same is true of industry. The skilled manpower needed for the relevant research and its systematic application to agriculture, industry, and other sectors of life can only come from a development of scientific and technological education.

7. *Study of Foreign Languages*: It is important to encourage the study of important foreign languages on more extensive scale for a variety of academic and practical purposes. Russian, French, German, Japanese, Spanish and Chinese besides English are important world languages of communication and for acquiring knowledge and culture.

8. *Dynamic Methods of Teaching*: In a modern society, knowledge inevitably ceases to be something to be received passively. It is something to be actively discovered. If this is rightly understood, it would involve a revolution in traditional education where 'to know' has come to mean 'to know by heart', where respect for all inherited knowledge is vigorously cultivated and where the assimilative facilities tend to be emphasized to the neglect of the 'critical and creative' ones. India, as in other countries where similar conditions prevail, this would require the introduction of dynamic methods of teaching and learning.

9. *Harmony between Science and Spirituality*: The pursuit of material affluence and power should be harmonized with the higher values. The concept of the mingling of 'science and spirituality' is of special significance for Indian education.

Concluding Observations

India is on the move with the promise of a new renaissance and industrialisation in the making and the most powerful tool in this process of modernisation is education based on moral and spiritual values on the one hand and on the other on science and technology.

18.2 STANDARDS/QUALITY IN EDUCATION

Although standards in education have become the touchstone of education, especially higher education, yet they have not been defined. Terms like standards quality, efficiency and effectiveness in education are very bewildering and deny all attempts to define them in a uniform way. It is said, "You can not define these terms but you know when you observe." Quality or standard of education is not the same as satisfying a customer with, for example, the latest model of a motor car." In the document produced by the Higher Education Quality Council, it is observed, "Quality in higher education embraces, but is not synonymous with effectiveness, efficiency and accountability." Sometimes it is said that in the education sector much of the discussion and debate which was hitherto focused on standards has now shifted to quality. Standards of education is a very ambiguous term and has connotations of both quality and excellence and vice verse also. Some thinkers consider all such terms as synonymous.

The term standard usually means a basis for measurement or a 'yardstick' to describe a required characteristic or a parameter and this would vary from country to country, from time to time and even from institution to institution over a period of time. However, it is also true that once the standards are set, the institutions and individuals can try to achieve quality so as to attain excellence.

Wider Concept of Standards in Education: The standards in education need to be defined in the wider sense of the overall aim of education as the all round development of the individual and his commitment to social objectives; and viewed in this context, there is no doubt that vigorous efforts will have to be made to improve these to suit the changing needs of the country. It has become increasingly evident that the relevance of education, its significance, its validity for personal aspiration, its link with societal needs and goals, its efficiency and impact are the basic parameters of every educational system.

Narrow View of Educational Standards: According to narrow interpretation, educational standards are judged from examination results. An educational institution that shows high pass percentage is considered to be an institution of great standard or quality.

No Single Measure to Assess the Quality/Standards in Education: Educational output unlike industrial outputs which are tangible and standardized, is extra-ordinarily an imprecise and slippery connotation. Since outputs vary with variation in institutional objectives, there can be no single measure of outputs and consequently of their quality. Outputs include all the residual learning's, skills, insights attitudes, styles of thinking—all the developed aptitudes and capabilities that a student carries from the educational system beyond what he brought to it, initially from home or elsewhere. Taking students coming out of an educational institution as its outputs, their quality can be considered from the following variable or characteristics.

1. Percentage of passing students in terms of divisions and distinctions secured.
2. The magnitude of wastage and retention.
3. The age earning profiles of the qualified students.
4. Achievement of students in the domain of co-curricular activities like athletics, dramatics, debates etc.

5. Admission of students into reputed institutions or professions etc.

Quality of what students learn or more correctly, what they carry with them out of an institution, is largely dependent upon the variables like (i) students—their ability, interest, level of motivation, family background, attitudes, expectancies etc., (ii) teachers —their qualities and qualifications, and (iii) equipments which students and teachers, are given to work with. Given the same level of other facilities to an identical group of students in two different institutions, one institution significantly excels the other because of its teachers competencies, caliber and professional responsibility.

Factors Affecting Standards in Education

Quality of education is dependent upon the following : (i) Quality of the staff. (ii) Quality of the curricula. (iii) Quality of the students. (iv) Quality of the infrastructure. (v) Quality of the management. (vi) Quality of systematic evaluation. (vii) Quality of regulation. (viii) Quality of funding. (ix) Forms of co-operation.

Quality of the Staff. This implies:

(a) Acceptable social and financial status of teachers.

(b) A will to reduce inequalities such as relating to gender.

(c) A concern to manage the staff in accordance with the merit principle.

(d) A desire to provide them with the in-service training they need to fulfil their role in a changing society.

(e) A system of the establishment of incentives and structures to encourage research to work in multidisciplinary teams and thematic projects, thus breaking with the habit of exclusively solitary scientific work.

Quality of Curricula. This implies:

(a) Taking special care in the definition of the objectives of the training provided in relation to the requirements of the world of work and the needs of the society.

(b) Adaptation of teaching methods to make students more active and to develop an enterprising spirit in them.

(c) Expansion and greater flexibility in training so as to make the full use of the possibilities afforded by information technology (IT).

(d) Internationalization and networking of curricula, students and teachers.

Quality of the Students who Constitute the Raw Material of Higher Education: It is dependent upon:

(a) Giving special attention to their problems of access in the light of the criteria related to merit (abilities and motivation).

(b) Adopting proactive policies for the benefit of the disadvantaged.

(c) Undertaking exchanges with secondary education and with the bodies involved in the transition from secondary to higher education to ensure that education is an unbroken chain.

Quality of Infrastructure: This implies that the infrastructure connected especially with the use and development of IT must be taken care of.

Quality of Management: The management of the institutions should be such as they do not exist in isolated enclaves.

Systematic Evaluation and Regulation: This entails inculcating a culture of evaluation within the institution, *i.e.*, a concern for setting up systems for the gathering of relevant, valid, reliable data so as to improve activities and outcomes.

It entails developing culture of autonomy, responsibility and accountability.

Quality of Education and Financial Constraints: Monetary inputs are indispensable for qualitative improvement of programmes. But monetary inputs are very often rendered infructuous without the support of non-monetary inputs such as insightful planning and human effort. Therefore, a climate of dedicated and sustained hard work needs to be maintained. Quality of an institution is a function of investment on teaching force as well as on instructional and supporting materials. The apportionment of resources varies from institution to institution on the basis of their needs, priorities and programmes. The case studies stressing the hazards of unbalanced resource allocation reported: "If the amount spent on teachers and the amount spent on the tools are seriously out of balance, teacher productivity and quality of education will suffer."

At a time when education is faced with fiscal stringency and it has to encounter a stiffer and a gloomier future, costs of education have to be weighted against the benefits it accrues. In other words, educational planners and administrators are to be cost and quality conscious.

Concluding Observations

Ours is a duel/multiple society by and large and in it economic as well as political power is mainly concentrated in the hands of a small class or classes at the top. This reflects in a dual or multiple educational system in which the access to the best institutions and the second best institutions etc. at all stages of education is limited to the small group of the top in every section according to means, mostly economic or economic/political power etc. It is this feature of the educational system which strengthens and perpetuates our dual society or multiple society. If this vicious circle is to be broken, action on the educational front alone will not be enough and will not succeed. What we need is a radical, simultaneous and complementary action for educational as well as socio-economic transformation.

18.3 IMBALANCE IN EDUCATION

Meaning of Imbalance in Education: Imbalance in education implies variations in the standards of education and expansion in education in different dimensions. The development of education in India since independence is a picture of both light and shade of some outstanding achievements along with dismal failures. Following data, broadly illustrates the imbalance in education as regards quantitative expansion. It is just one dimension of imbalance in education.

Table 18.1: Rural-Urban and Sex-wise Literacy Rates (1951-1997)

Year	*Male*	*Female*	*Persons (Total)*
1951(a)			
Rural	19.02	4.87	12.10
Urban	45.06	22.33	34.59
Total	**24.95**	**7.93**	**16.67**
1961(b)			
Rural	29.10	8.55	19.10
Urban	57.49	34.51	46.97
Total	**34.44**	**12.95**	**24.02**

Year	*Male*	*Female*	*Persons (Total)*
1971(c)			
Rural	33.76	13.17	23.74
Urban	61.27	42.14	52.44
Total	**39.45**	**18.69**	**29.45**
1981(d) (7 Years and above)			
Rural	49.69	21.77	36.09
Urban	76.83	56.37	67.34
Total	**56.50**	**29.85**	43.67
1991(e) (7 Years and above)			
Rural	57.87	30.62	44.69
Urban	81.09	64.05	73.08
Total	**64.13**	**39.29**	**52.21**
1997 (f) (7 Years and above)			
Rural	68.0	43.0	56.0
Urban	88.0	72.0	8.0
Total	**73.0**	**50.0**	**62.0**

Notes: (a) For Rural/Urban : Census of India 1951 C-IV Table.
(b) Census of India 1961, Part II-C (i) Social and Cultural Tables.
(c) Census of India 1971, Part II-C (ii) Social and Cultural Tables
(d), (e) Census of India 1991 Paper 2 of 1991 Vol. II excluding J & K.
(f) Literacy rates for December 1997, according to 53rd Round of NSSO.

Source: *'Selected Educational Statistics: 1998-99'*. Ministry of Human Resource Development, Government of India.

Five Major Imbalances in Indian Education

Following are the five major balances in education in India:

1. *Imbalance Between Formal and Non-Formal Education*: It still continues to be dominated by models and value-systems adopted during the colonial regime. For instance, it lays greater emphasis on narrow individualism, unhealthy competition to the neglect of social good, verbal fluency (especially in English), and mere acquisition of information, while it neglects social objectives, co-operation, manual work, training in skills and building up of character. It places an almost exclusive emphasis on formal school (with its single-point entry, annual sequential promotions, insistence on full-time attendance, and almost exclusive use of full-time teachers), and neglects both non-formal and recurrent education. The educational institutions function in isolation from the community as well as from one another.

2. *Institutions of Double Standards*: The system maintain a set of double standards. A small minority of educational institutions at all levels is of good quality and compares favourably with those in developed countries. But access to them is selective and is mostly availed of by the top social group, either because they can afford the costs involved or because they show merit which, on the basis of the existing methods of selection, shows a high correlation with social status. But this core of good institutions is surrounded by a large number of institutions where although there is open door access, the standards are poor. Consequently, it is in these institutions that the large majority of the people including the weaker sections receive higher education. This dualism leads to

undesirable social segregation and to a perpetuation and strengthening of inegalitarian trends in our society.

Following are the broad categories of schools in India.

1. Public Schools (various categories)
2. Government/State schools.
3. Local body schools.
4. Government aided schools, popularly called private schools.
5. Central schools.
6. Navodaya vidyalayas.
7. Sainik schools.
8. Army schools.
9. Schools run by linguistic minorities.
10. Schools run by religious minorities.
11. Schools run by cultural organisations.
12. Other types of Schools.

Imbalance: Gulf in the Education of the Classes and Masses: Even in quantitative terms, it is mainly the upper and the middle classes that are the beneficiaries of this system. Sixty per cent of the population (age 10 and over) which is still illiterate, has obviously received none of its benefits. Of every 100 children of six years of age, nearly 56% drop-out at an early stage, so that only about 44 complete class VIII. 70 per cent of the seats in secondary schools and 80 per cent of the seats in higher education are taken by the top 20 per cent of income groups.

4. *Regional Disparity*: There is a great disparity in the expansion of education in different States and regions.

5. *Disparity in Women's Education*: Women's education has greatly lagged behind. (*For details See Chapter 16*)

Transformation of the Education System

What the system needs, therefore, is drastic overhaul: a transformation of its character, through the introduction of a modern scientific outlook and other essential measures, to suit our national needs and aspirations; a substantial improvement of standards; an extension of its coverage so that the education of the people becomes not a peripheral pursuit but a central objective. It is in these main directions that educational reconstruction in India will have to be vigorously pursued in the years ahead.

Perhaps the most urgent and significant reform needed is to transform the value system, the basic structure and processes of the educational system, to make it flexible and dynamic, and to move in the (ultimate) direction of providing opportunities for lifelong learning to every individual. This transformation will emphasize ethical values and human welfare enriched by science and technology. It will also imply the shifting of emphasis from teaching to learning, from the individual to social objectives, and from mere acquisition of information to the development of skills and character formation based on knowledge. There would be multiple points of entry, flexible and student oriented curricula, an equal emphasis on all the three channels of study (full-time, part-time or own-time), use of all the teaching resources of the community (both human and institutional) rather than depending only on the schools or professional teachers. It would imply the provision of every facility for recurrent education so that an individual can join or step off the formal systems as and when necessary, adopt any channel of study that suits him, and learn at his own best pace and from whomsoever he chooses; work and education (which will be closely linked to productivity) would run concurrently throughout the life of an individual; and education and development would be linked together; education assisting socio-economic transformation and participation in programmes of such transformation becoming a medium of education itself.

18.4 INEQUALITY OF EDUCATIONAL OPPORTUNITY

Dimensions of Inequality of Opportunity: The problem of inequality of educational opportunity may be considered at several levels and with reference to different sections of society, as follows:

(i) Inequality that exists between one State and another.

(ii) In a State the prevailing inequality between one district and another.

(iii) In a district, unequal educational opportunity in different areas.

(iv) Inequality of educational opportunity between boys and girls.

(v) Inequality of educational opportunity that now prevails between the different sections of society; advanced castes *vs.* scheduled castes and scheduled tribes; upper and middle classes *vs.* lower classes; economically better off classes *vs.* poorer sections, etc.

Causes of Inequality of Educational Opportunity: On the basis of the experience reported in the different States, the following causes which now tend to create inequality of educational opportunity may be listed:

1. Varying economic conditions. Some States are economically advanced while others are lagging behind.
2. Social and psychological reasons, *e.g.*, apathy towards girls' education, particularly in socially backward groups of people.
3. Varying literacy levels in States, districts, and localities.
4. Existence of inaccessible and isolated small habitations particularly in hilly and forest areas.
5. Varying occupational opportunities prevailing in different areas.
6. Lack of suitable and adequate accommodation for running schools.
7. Dearth of suitably qualified teachers, particularly women teachers and teachers for tribal areas.

Recommendations for Popularising Education in the Backward and Tribal Areas

1. *Training of Teachers*: Those teachers working in these areas who do not possess enough knowledge about the tribal life and culture may be given training in these aspects. The teachers posted in tribal areas should also acquire knowledge of tribal dialects.
2. *Provision of Hostels and Extension of Ashram Schools*: Wherever possible the schools functioning in these areas, may be provided with hostels which will solve many problems. Extensions of Ashram schools, use of youth dormitories may also solve some of the problems.
3. *Provision of Suitable School Accommodation*: All the schools functioning in these areas should be provided with suitable accommodation.

4. *Encouragement of Participation of Tribal Parents*: Participation of parents in the educational programmes may also be encouraged. The awareness and interest regarding the utility of education for the children should be created among the parents.

5. *Provision of Audio-Visual Aids*: Provision of audio-visual aids for the development of education of children is essential and may be made available as soon as possible.

6. *Introduction of Tribal Dialects and Medium of Instruction*: In tribal areas, having a large population where people do not understand the regional language, tribal dialects may be introduced as the medium of instruction where possible in the initial stages and then they should be integrated with the general educational system and may be taught regional languages. But in the tribal areas where the children understand the regional language it can be used as medium of instruction. Such practices will reduce the rate of wastage and stagnation and also create interest among the children.

7. *Suitable Curriculum for the School*: There is a need for evolving a suitable curriculum for the school functioning in these areas. This curriculum may be science-oriented but culture based. The curriculum should be so framed as it should include the various aspects of tribal life and culture.

8. *Economic Incentive to Parents*: Since people are economically backward and the children have to take part in different activities of the economic pursuits, the parents do not care for the education of their children because this sustains economic loss. Thus some economic incentive may be given to the students but not to parents to prosecute their studies. Timing of the schools may be adjusted according to the local needs.

9. *Special Training for Talented Students*: A scheme to help the talented students may be started. They may be given different types of training and they may be asked to work in tribal areas.

10. *Improvement in Teacher Community Relationships*: Steps to improve the Ashram School education may be taken. The teacher community relationship may be improved. The cleanliness of the buildings and discipline in the Ashram Schools may be improved and adequate freedom to students for participation in various games may be given. Some courses to train these teachers may be organised.

19

Organisational Set-up at Various Levels of Education

19.1 INTRODUCTION

Education in India remained a State subject for several decades after independence. However higher education was under the Central list. With the amendment in the Constitution, education became a concurrent subject. The Central Government has accepted a larger responsibility to reinforce the national and integrative character of education to maintain quality and standards and to monitor the educational requirements of the country. Since the states play a dominant role in education, there is no uniform organisational set up at various levels.

Private enterprises also exists side by side.

The Constitution of India makes an elaborate distribution of governmental powers—legislative, administrative and financial— between the Central Governments and State Governments. Adequate mechanisms exist for sharing of resources and responsibilities, between the Union and the States, for harmonious exercise of their powers in larger national interest. The National Development Council (NDC) imparts a national character to the entire process of planning. In the education centre, the Central Advisory Board of Education (CABE) plays a lead role in the evolution and monitoring of policies and programmes.

Problems of various levels of education at the pre-primary level, primary level, upper primary level, secondary level, senior secondary level and higher education level have been discussed separately in relevant chapters.

19.2 EDUCATIONAL ENTERPRISES: TYPES OF MANAGEMENT

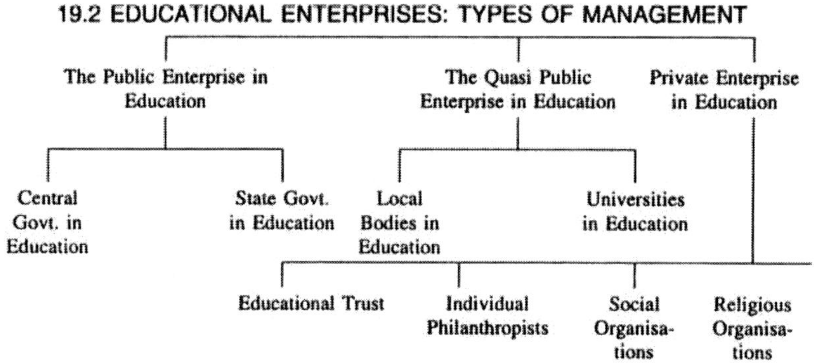

19.3 SET-UP OF THE STATE DEPARTMENT OF EDUCATION

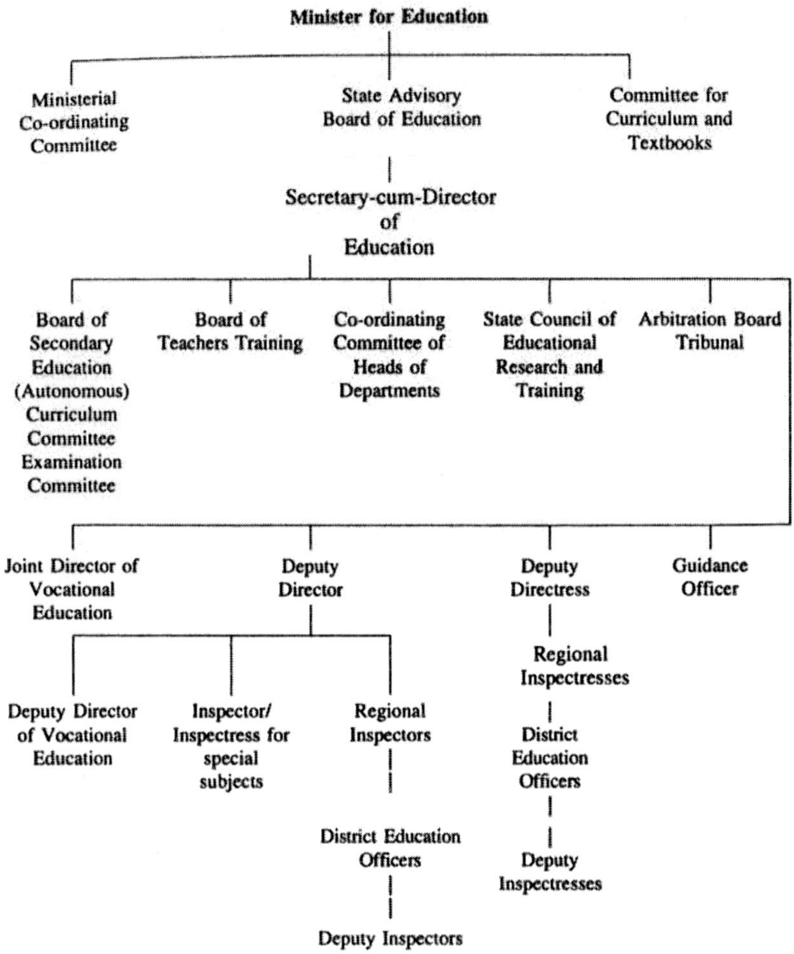

Note: This is the broad set-up. Variations exist in States.

19.4 DIAGRAMMATIC REPRESENTATION OF EDUCATIONAL STRUCTURE AT VARIOUS LEVELS IN INDIA

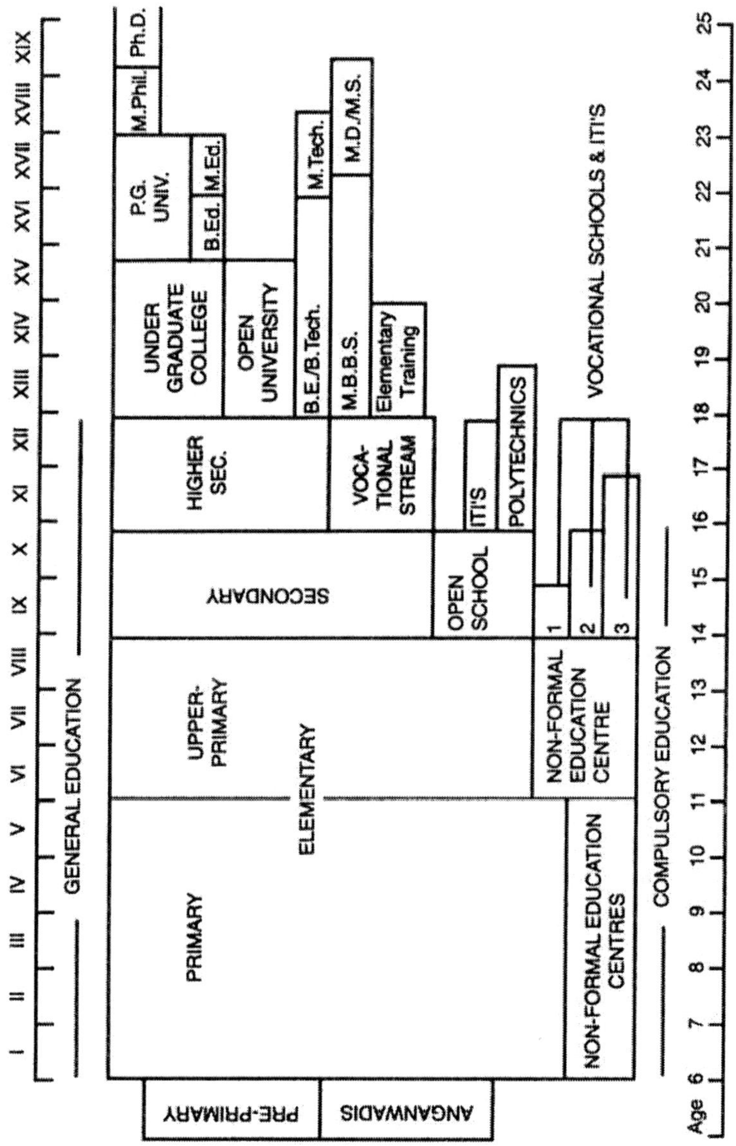

20

Survey of Education Commissions, Committees and Other Documents Since Independence

20.1 INTRODUCTION

More than one hundred Committees, Commissions and other documents on education have been published at the national level. These documents deal with the various educational issues at different levels. After examining the progress as well as limitations of the educational programmes, Committees, Commissions and Working Groups have suggested reforms in education.

The documents start with the University Education Commission (1948-1949). They reveal a number of interesting developments of the second half of the 20th century.

There has been a tendency to postpone the implementation of recommendations to better times on grounds of lack of resources, thus creating a vicious circle. Recommendations cannot be acted upon for want of resources and resources are not there because education is not suitably geared to our economic growth.

The National Policy on Education considers education as the highway to reach the goals as enshrined in our Constitution.

Here documents are categorized according to levels of education but at the same time, documents dealing with all levels are separately dealt with. Recommendations of almost all most significant documents have been given in the relevant chapters.

20.2 DOCUMENTS ON PRIMARY EDUCATION

Although Article 45 of the Constitution stipulated the provision of free and compulsory education by 1960, no separate Commission has been appointed to look into the issues of primary education. Separate Commission on secondary education as well as University education went into all aspects of education at the particular stage.

Following Committees have been appointed on primary education:

1. Committee on the Relationship Between State Governments and Local Bodies in the Administration of Primary Education (1951-54).
2. National Seminar on Orientation of Elementary Schools Towards Basic Pattern (1959).
3. Single Teacher Schools (1972).
4. Report of the Working Group on Elementary Education (1991).
5. Committee on the Relationship Between State Governments and Local Bodies on the Administration of Primary Education (1951-54).

The Committee appointed under the Chairmanship of B. G. Kher, Chief Minister, Bombay, made the following important recommendations:

(1) *Association of local bodies with the administration of primary education*: It would be an advantage to associate local bodies with the administration of primary education in some form or other.

(2) *Creation of education bodies*: (a) In all village panchayats and smaller municipalities which have been given only a limited control over primary education, the local body should be required to elect a school committee and to delegate to it the task of supervizing the local school or schools.

(b) In district local boards and in bigger municipalities which exercise wider powers over primary education, a school board be constituted and charged with the responsibility of looking after its educational powers as well as an administrative officer having adequate authority to carry on the day-to-day administration of its primary schools.

(c) The State Governments should adopt the independent system of associating education bodies with the corresponding local authorities generally.

(d) The appointment of administrative officers should be obligatory under the statute in the case of all district school boards and the larger municipalities. They should be servants of the State Government.

6. Report of the Working Group on Elementary Education (1991)

The Working Group appointed by the Central Advisory Board of Education, made the following suggestions:

(1) The strategy of Minimum Levels of Learning (MLL) should be accepted as an important component of all educational planning for universalisation of elementary education, including non-formal education.

(2) Micro-planning approach for improvement of elementary education should be adopted by all State Governments.

(3) School Calendar should match the major agricultural activities, and socio-economic factors of the region.

(4) The transferability of children between Formal and Non-Formal system should be made easy and convenient.

(5) Management system should be improved to ensure timely payment to instructors and other personnel working in the field of Non- Formal Education.

20.3 DOCUMENTS ON BASIC EDUCATION

1. *The Basic Education Standing Committee of the Central Advisory Board of Education (1956)*: A publication entitled *'The Concept of Basic Education'* prepared by the Central Advisory Board of Education made the following significant observation on Basic Education.

Basic Education is Essentially an Education for Life

(i) Basic education, as conceived and explained by Mahatma Gandhi, is essentially an education for life, and what is more, an education through life. It aims at creating eventually a social order free from exploitation and violence. That is why productive, creative and socially useful work in which all boys and girls may participate, irrespective of any distinction of caste or class, is placed at the very centre of basic education.

(ii) The effective teaching of a basic craft, thus becomes an essential part of education at this stage, as productive work, done under proper condition not only makes the acquisition of much related knowledge more concrete and realistic but also adds a powerful contribution to the development of personality and character and instills respect and love for all socially useful work. It is also to be clearly understood that the sale of products of craft work will meet some part of the expenditure incurred in running the school or that the products will be used by the school children for getting a mid-day meal or a school uniform or help to provide some of the school furniture and equipment.

2. *Assessment Committee on Basic Education (1955-56)*: The Assessment Committee appointed by the Ministry of Education under the Chairmanship of G. Ramachandran made the following recommendations for the promotion of Basic Education.

I. The Government of India: 1. The Government of India should take appropriate steps to make it clear to all those concerned that the elucidation of basic education given by the Basic Education Standing Committee of the Central Advisory Board of Education has their concurrence.

2. All India and Regional Conferences of the basic education should be arranged periodically.

II. The Government of the States: 1. State Governments should no longer delay to make a clear unambiguous declaration of policy that all elementary schools will be converted into basic schools and that all teacher training at this level will become basic teacher training within reasonable time limits.

III. The Universities: It will presently become necessary for universities to recognise post-basic education for purposes of admitting pupils passing out of post-basic schools into colleges.

IV. The Administration: 1. Inspecting staff concerned with basic education should be fully trained in basic education.

2. English should be offered as an optional subject from the 6th grade onwards, wherever knowledge of English is considered necessary for entrance into high schools and other similar institutions.

V. Basic Teachers' Training: It is urgently necessary to make teachers' training more efficient and real. Improvement is called for in craft training, in handling the technique of correlated teaching and in a new and dynamic approach to the study of psychology.

VI. Basic Schools: No school may be considered a basic school or assessed as such, unless the following requisites at least are fulfilled:

(a) It provides for an integrated course of 8 years of basic education and where there are only the junior 5 grades, such a school should necessarily be the feeder for a senior basic school.

(b) Adequate quantities of needed raw materials are supplied in time.

(c) Adequate craft equipment and repair material is provided.

(d) There is minimum land available, and in no case less than three acres for a senior basic school of 8 grades.

20.4 DOCUMENTS ON SECONDARY EDUCATION

1. Committee on Secondary Education in India (1948). The first committee on Secondary Education in free India was appointed by the Government of India, Ministry of Education, under the Chairmanship of Dr. Tara Chand. Important suggestions included:

(a) Admission to the degree course should be preceded by a course of Primary and Secondary Education for at least 12 years.

(b) English should be compulsory throughout the secondary stage, so long it remains the medium of instruction in the universities.

(c) The Federal Language should become a compulsory subject at the secondary stage when English ceases to be the medium of instructions in the universities.

(d) Secondary schools should be ordinarily of the multilateral type.

(e) There should be one public examination at the end of the secondary stage.

(f) A number of Public schools may be established to foster the growth of leadership among pupils.

The recommendations of the Committee may be regarded as the forerunner of the recommendations of the Secondary Education Commission.

2. Secondary Education Commission (1952-53). The Secondary Education Commission appointed by the Ministry of Education, under the Chairmanship of Dr. A. Lakshmanaswami Mudaliar, Vice-Chancellor, Madras University made valuable recommendations on all aspects of secondary education. (See Chapters 8 and 9)

3. Panel on Science Education in Secondary Schools (1964).

4. Committee on School Buildings (1970)

5. National Committee on 10+2+3 Educational Structure (1973). The National Committee was appointed by the Ministry of Education, under the Chairmanship of Dr. P. D. Shukla, Dr. R.P. Singhal, Secretary, Central Board of Secondary Education, New Delhi was its Member-Secretary.

The Committee's important recommendations were as under:

Curriculum Reconstruction: The new educational structure does not envisage mere addition of one year to the total period of education or taking away of one class from the collegiate stage to school education or *vice versa.* The opportunity of reconstructing should be duly utilized by completely reorganizing the curriculum and raising the standard of education at all stages so as to make it internationally comparable. The curriculum should also be in accordance with the current needs of the society, allow mobility of children from one State or Territory to another, and help national integration.

Secondary Stage Curriculum: The new classes IX and X should provide for a good course of general education. This is too early a stage for any specialization. The curriculum, therefore, should include, compulsory teaching of the following:

1. Teaching of Language(s)
2. Modern Mathematics
3. Sciences
4. Social Sciences
5. Moral Education
6. Physical Education
7. Craft or Trade.

The curriculum should in addition, provide for one optional subject out of the usual academic and practical subjects relevant to this stage of education.

Higher Secondary Stage (Classes XI and XII): The curriculum of the new classes XI and XII should be built on the latest curriculum for the new classes IX and X and should provide for two streams, *i.e.*,

(i) Academic Stream, and
(ii) Vocational Stream.

Academic Stream: The curriculum of the academic stream should provide for teaching in five subjects. One of these should be language. The other four subjects should be chosen out of a list of the available academic and practical subjects relevant to this stage of education.

Every student of the academic stream should participate on a compulsory basis, in at least two of the co-curricular activities, *viz.*, N.C.C., N.S.C., Physical education, and social and community service.

A provision at this stage should be made for teaching many of the academic subjects at two levels—advanced and ordinary.

Vocational Stream: The vocational stream at the higher secondary stage should be taken to supplement the existing facilities for vocational education provided by the ITIs, polytechnics, and vocational schools.

The report was very helpful in organising 10+2 structure at the secondary level of education.

6. *Review Committee on NPE or Ramamurti Committee Report:* The National Front/Janata Dal that came into power in December 1989 had mentioned in its election manifesto that the New Education Policy of 1986 as being implemented by the Central Government run by the Congress Party would be reviewed and revised. Accordingly when it assumed office, it appointed on May 7, 1990, a Committee headed by Acharya Ramamurti, to review the NPE. The Committee submitted its report to the Minister of State in the Ministry of Human Resource Development on December 26, 1990.

The report is entitled *'Towards an Enlightened and Humane Society'.*

The report died its natural death as the Janata Dal Government was short-lived.

20.5 DOCUMENTS ON HIGHER EDUCATION, *See Chapters 11 and 12.*

20.6 DOCUMENT ON EMOTIONAL INTEGRATION, *See Chapter 14.6.*

20.7 COMMITTEE ON RELIGIOUS AND MORAL EDUCATION (1959-60)

The Committee was appointed under the Chairmanship of Sri Prakasa, Governor of Bombay.

Following extracts from the report provide adequate guidance in planning religious and moral education.

What is Religion?

'Religion' etymologically means something that helps to bind man to man (*religare*, to bind). Broadly speaking every religion can be divided into four parts:

1. *Personality of the Founder*—Dealing with the greatness and holiness of the founder of the faith.

2. *Genesis*—Seeking to give an account of the Creator and the Universe created by Him.

3. *Ritual*—Prescribing some outward forms which the followers adopt and follow.

4. *Ethical Code*—Telling what is right and what is wrong.

India has many other faiths which must be understood by us to appreciate the spirit of India and spiritual strength. We, therefore, advocate an objective, comparative and sympathetic study of all the important religions of India.

Moral and Spiritual Values Defined

The Committee defined moral and spiritual values as follows:

'Anything that helps us to behave properly towards others is of *moral value.*' (Para 30)

'Anything that takes us out of our self, and inspires us to sacrifice for the good of others or for a great cause is of *spiritual value.*'

Need for the Teaching of Moral and Spiritual Values

We have to lay special stress on the teaching of moral and spiritual values. Moral values particularly refer to the conduct of man towards man in the various situations in which human beings come together in the home, in social and economic fields, and in the life of the outside world generally. It is essential that from the earliest childhood, moral values should be inculcated in us. We have to influence the home first. We fear that our homes are not what they ought to be. Habits, both of mind and body, formed early at home, persist, and influence our life afterwards. Good manners are a very important part of moral education. It is not unusual that when a people attain freedom suddenly after long years of bondage, they are inclined to become self-willed, arrogant and inconsiderate. In such situations good manners are easily set aside and young people tend to express the first flush of freedom in license and rowdyism.

We are in favour of a comparative and sympathetic study of religions and the teaching of their underlying philosophies and ethical codes.

20.8 COMMITTEE ON VOCATIONAL EDUCATION

National Review Committee for Plus Two Curriculum (1978)

The National Review Committee was appointed by the Ministry of Education under the Chairmanship of Dr. Malcolm S. Adiseshiah, Vice-Chancellor University of Madras. The Committee submitted its report in 1978 under the Title *'Learning to Do—Towards a Learning and Working Society'*. The report is popularly known as Adiseshiah Report after the name of its Chairman.

It is also known as National Review Committee Report for Plus Two Curriculum of School Education as its recommendations relate to the curriculum for classes XI and XII.

It is also called the Report of the National Review Committee on Higher Secondary Education with special reference to Vocationalisation of Education as it gives recommendations on vocationalisation of education.

Terms of Reference

(i) To review the NCERT Documents "Higher Secondary Education and Its Vocationalization" and to suggest modifications therein, if any.

(ii) To study the syllabi and courses of the CBSE (Central Board of Secondary Education) and a few State Boards with special reference to a few selected vocations and to recommend appropriate syllabi.

(iii) To recommend a plan of action for introduction of vocationalization at the secondary stage.

The report was very helpful in organising vocational stream at the 10 +2 stage. It provided guidelines in various dimensions of vocational education. (*For details see Chapter 10*)

20.9 COMMITTEES ON WOMEN EDUCATION, *See Chapter 16.*

20.10 EDUCATION COMMISSION (1964-66) AND NATIONAL POLICIES (1968, 1986 AND 1992)

1. Education Commission. For Education Commission (1964-66), *See Chapters 8, 9 and 10.*

2. National Policy on Education (1968). The Education Commission 1964-66 recommended that the Government of India should issue a statement on the National Policy on Education which should provide guidance to the State Governments and the local authorities in preparing and implementing educational plans. In 1967 the Government of India constituted a committee of Members of Parliament on Education to prepare the draft of a statement on the National Policy of Education. The Committee brought together, for the first time in recent history, leading members of almost all the political parties in the country and prepared a draft which was considered by the Central Advisory Board of Education. A general consensus on the national policy on education emerged in the course of the Board's deliberations. Thereafter the Government of India issued the Resolution on National Policy on Education in 1968. The Resolution remained the basis of educational reforms in India till the formation of the New Policy in 1986.

Extracts from the Policy

The Government of India is convinced that a radical reconstruction of education on the broad lines recommended by the Education Commission is essential for economic and cultural development of the country, for national integration and for realizing the ideal of a socialist pattern of society. This will involve a transformation of the system to relate it more closely to the life of the people; a continuous effort to expand educational opportunity; a sustained and intensive effort to raise the quality of education at all stages; an emphasis on the development of science and technology and the cultivation of moral and social values. The educational system must produce young men and women of character and ability committed to national service and development. Only then will education be able to play its vital role in promoting national progress, creating a sense of common citizenship and culture, and strengthening national integration. This is necessary if the country is to attain its rightful place in the comity of nations in conformity with its great cultural heritage and its unique potentialities.

3. National Policy on Education (NPE 1986 and 1992). It was the first time that a Prime Minister in independent India has shown such a deep concern for education and initiated action for the formulation of NPE to meet the present and future needs of the country. Again for the first time there was a nationwide debate on various aspects of education. But this was not considered enough. The Policy document was discussed in the Parliament and a Programme of Action was approved for the implementations of the New Policy.

The Ministry of Education, Government of India renamed itself as the Ministry of Human Resource Development.

Among the most important merits, following may be mentioned—

1. *National System of Education*: The NPE proposed a national system of education to provide access to education of a comparable quality to all students, to have a common educational structure with national curricular framework containing a common core. (10+2+3)

2. *Navodaya Schools*: Setting up Navodaya Vidyalayas was a great landmark in the history of education in India.

3. *Vocational Targets*: The policy fixed realistic targets of covering 10 per cent of higher secondary students by 1990 and 25 per cent by 1995.

4. *Delinking Degrees from Jobs*: Beginning to be made in delinking degrees from jobs in selected areas.

5. *Performance and Accountability*: Stress has been laid on performance and accountability at all levels.

6. *Decentralisation of the Management of Education*: The Policy calls for evolving a strategy of decentralisation and the creation of a spirit of autonomy for educational institutions.

7. *Indian Education Service*: It is envisaged that the constitution of the Indian Education Service is likely to bring about a national perspective in education.

8. *National Testing Service*: This is likely to be helpful in determining suitability of candidates for specified jobs and to pave the way for the emergence of norms of comparable competence across the nation.

9. *Raising Resources*: The Policy has suggested appropriate methods of financing education. These are : (i) Beneficiary Communities to maintain school buildings and supplies of some consumables; (ii) Raising fees at the higher levels of education; (iii) Levying a cess or charge on user research and development agencies; and (iv) Affecting savings by the efficient use of facilities.

Two Committees namely, Ramamurti Committee (1990) and Janardhana Reddy Committee (1992) reviewed the implementation of the NPE and made some suggestions. The Janardhana Committee led to the modification of NPE 1986 in 1992. Some minor changes were made in the 1986 NPE.

Several references to NPE are made in appropriate chapters. It has become the basis of educational reforms in India at all levels and in all dimensions.

21

Literacy in India (1951-2001): Census 2001

21.1 INTRODUCTION: IMPORTANCE OF LITERACY

Literacy and education are the two most important indicators of development of a nation. Higher levels of literacy and education act as a catalyst for cultural, economic, political and social development.

The literacy rates obtained at the census give a reflection of the government policies and programmes.

21.2 LITERACY RATES IN INDIA (1951-2001)

Table 21.1 provides comparative data on literacy since independence.

Table 21.1 : Literacy rates in India (1951-2001)

Census year	*Persons*	*Males*	*Females*	*Male-female gap in literacy rate*
1	2	3	4	5
1951	18.33	27.16	8.86	18.30
1961	28.30	40.40	15.35	25.05
1971	34.45	45.96	21.98	23.98
1981	43.57	56.38	29.76	26.62
1991	52.21	64.13	39.29	24.84
2001	65.38	75.85	54.16	21.69

Notes:

1. Literacy rates for 1951, 1961 and 1971 Censuses relate to population aged five years and above. The rates for the 1981, 1991 and 2001 Censuses relate to the population aged seven years and above.
2. The 1981 Literacy rates exclude Assam where the 1981 Census could not be conducted. The 1991 Census Literacy rates exclude Jammu & Kashmir where the 1991 Census could not be conducted due to disturbed conditions.
3. The 2001 Census, literacy rates exclude entire Kachchh district, Morvi, Maliya-Miyana and Wankaner talukas of Rajkot district, Jodiya taluka of Jamnagar district of Gujarat State and entire Kinnaur district of Himachal Pradesh where population enumeration of Census of India, 2001, could not be conducted due to natural calamities.

21.3 ANALYSIS OF LITERACY RATES

The literacy rates for the country as a whole in 2001 work out to 65.38 per cent for the population aged seven years and over. The corresponding figures for the males and females are 75.85 and 54.16 per cent respectively. Thus three-fourth of the males and more than half of the females aged seven years and above are literate in the country to-day. However, this figure is far below the several countries which have nearly 98 per cent literacy.

The literacy rates in Table 21.1 for the 1951, 1961 and 1971 Census relate to the population aged five years and above, those for the 1981, 1991 and 2001 relate to the population seven years and above.

As compared with the literacy rates of 1991, there has been a jump of 13.7 per cent points from 52.21 to 65.38 in 2001.

While male literacy rates increased by 11.72 per cent (from 64.13 to 75.85), female literacy rates increased by 14.87 (from 39.29 to 54.16 per cent) during the period 1991 to 2001. Nevertheless there is still a gap of 21.69 per cent between the literacy rates of male and females.

Table 21.2 presents the number of literates and illiterates among population aged 7 years and above and their difference between 1991 and 2001. The total number of illiterates has come down from 328,167,228 in 1991 to 296,208,952 i.e. 21.4 Literates and Illiterates (1991 and 2001)

Table 21.2: Number of literates and illiterates among population aged 7 years and above and their change-India : 1991 and 2001

Literates/Illiterates	*Persons*	*Males*	*Females*
1	2	3	4
Literates			
1991	358,402,626	228,983,134	129,419,492
2001	562,010,743	336,969,695	225,041,048
Increase in 2001 over 1991	203,608,117	107,986,561	95,621,556
Illiterates			
1991	328,167,288	128,099,211	200,068,077
2001	296,208,952	106,654,066	189,554,886
Decrease in 2001 over 1991	31,958,336	21,445,145	10,513,191

Notes :

1. To make the data comparable shown against literates for the years 1991 and 2001, the corresponding figures for Jammu and Kashmir have not been included in both the years as the data for 1991 Census for Jammu and Kashmir is not available because the 1991 Census could not be conducted in this state due to disturbed conditions.
2. To make the data comparable the figures of literates and illiterates shown against 1991 and 2001 do not include the figures for entire district of Kachchh, Morvi, Maliya-Miyana and Wankaner talukas of Rajkot district, Jodiya taluka of Jamnagar district of Gujarat State and entire Kinnaur district of Himachal Pradesh where population enumeration of Census of India, 2001, could not be conducted due to natural calamities.

21.5 STATE AND UNION LITERACY RATES (1991-2001)

Table 21.3: State and Union Territory Wise Literacy Rates and Percentage Increase during 1991-2001

S. No.	*States*	*Literacy Rates*		*% Increase*
		1991	2001	
1.	A & N. Island	73.02	81.18	8.16
2.	Andhra Pradesh	44.09	61.11	17.02
3.	Arunachal Pradesh	41.59	54.74	13.15
4.	Assam	52.89	64.28	11.39
5.	Bihar	38.48	47.53	9.05
6.	Chandigarh	75.51	81.76	6.25

S. No.	States	Literacy Rates		% Increase
		1991	2001	
7.	Chhattishgarh	–	65.18	–
8.	Dadra & N. Haveli	40.71	60.03	19.32
9.	Daman & Diu	71.20	81.09	9.89
10.	Delhi	75.29	81.82	6.53
11.	Goa	75.51	82.32	6.81
12.	Gujarat	61.29	69.97	8.68
13.	Haryana	55.85	68.59	12.64
14.	Himachal Pradesh	63.86	77.13	13.27
15.	Jammu Kashmir	–	54.46	–
16.	Jharkhand	–	54.13	–
17.	Karnataka	56.04	67.04	11.00
18.	Kerala	89.81	90.92	1.11
19.	Lakshadweep	81.78	87.52	5.74
20.	Madhya Pradesh	44.20	64.11	19.91
21.	Maharashtra	64.87	77.27	12.40
22.	Manipur	59.89	68.87	8.98
23.	Meghalaya	49.10	63.31	14.21
24.	Mizoram	82.27	88.49	6.22
25.	Nagaland	61.65	67.11	5.46
26.	Orissa	49.09	63.61	14.52
27.	Pondicherry	74.74	81.49	6.75
28.	Punjab	58.51	69.68	13.16
29.	Rajasthan	38.55	61.03	22.46
30.	Sikkim	56.94	69.68	13.16
31.	Tamil Nadu	62.66	73.47	10.81
32.	Tripura	60.44	73.66	13.22
33.	Uttar Pradesh	41.60	57.36	15.76
34.	Uttranchal	–	72.28	–
35.	West Bengal	57.70	69.22	11.52
	INDIA	**52.21**	**65.38**	**13.17**

21.6 OBSERVATION

It would be observed from the above Table that Rajasthan has made phenomenal progress in literacy. Literacy rates rose by 22.48 per cent during the period 1991-2001. However, still its rank is 29. Bihar has not made any headway in this regard. Here literacy rates rose by 9.05 per cent and it is at the bottom. Andhara Pradesh and Madhya Pradesh have made substantial progress i.e. 19.32 and 19.1 per cent respectively. India's place on the literacy map of the world figures quite low.

21.7 RANK WISE AND SEX WISE LITERACY RATES

Table 21.4: Literacy Rates in States and Union Territories by Sex and Rank

Rank	Persons		Males		Females	
	India/States/ Union Territories*	Literacy rates	India/States/ Union Territories*	Literacy rates	India/States/ Union Territories*	Literacy rates
1	2	3	4	5	6	7
1	Kerala	90.92	Kerala	94.20	Kerala	87.86
2	Mizoram	88.49	Lakshadweep*	93.15	Mizoram	86.13
3	Lakshadweep*	87.52	Mizoram	90.69	Lakshadweep*	81.56
4	Goa	82.32	Pondicherry*	88.89	Chandigarh*	76.65
5	Delhi*	81.82	Goa	88.88	Goa	75.51
6	Chandigarh*	81.76	Daman & Diu*	88.40	A & N Islands*	75.29

1	2	3	4	5	6	7
7	Pondicherry*	81.49	Delhi*	87.37	Delhi*	75.00
8	A & N Islands*	81.18	Maharashtra	86.27	Pondicherry*	74.13
9	Daman & Diu*	81.09	A & N Island*	86.07	Daman & Diu*	70.37
10	Maharashtra	77.27	Himachal Pradesh	86.02	Himachal Pradesh	68.08
11	Himachal Pradesh	77.13	Chandigarh*	85.65	Maharashtra	67.51
12	Tripura	73.66	Uttaranchal	84.01	Tripura	65.41
13	Tamil Nadu	73.47	Tamil Nadu	82.33	Tamil Nadu	64.55
14	Uttaranchal	72.28	Tripura	81.47	Punjab	63.55
15	Gujarat[3]	69.97	Gujarat	80.50	Nagaland	61.92
16	Punjab	69.95	Haryana	79.25	Sikkim	61.46
17	Sikkim	69.68	Manipur	77.87	Meghalaya	60.41
18	West Bengal	69.22	Chhatisgarh	77.86	Uttaranchal	60.26
19	Manipur	68.87	West Bengal	77.58	West Bengal	60.22
20	Haryana	68.59	Madhya Pradesh	76.80	Manipur	59.70
21	Nagaland	67.11	Sikkim	76.73	Gujarat	58.60
22	Karnataka	67.04	Rajasthan	76.46	Karnataka	57.45
	INDIA[1]	**65.38**	Karnataka	76.29	Haryana	56.31
23	Chhatisgarh	65.18	Orissa	75.95	Assam	56.03
24	Assam	64.28	**INDIA**	**75.85**	**INDIA**	**54.16**
25	Madhya Pradesh	64.11	Punjab	75.63	Chhatisgarh	52.40
26	Orissa	63.61	Dadra & Nagar Haveli*	73.32	Andhra Pradesh	51.17
27	Meghalaya	63.31	Assam	71.93	Orissa	50.97
28	Andhra Pradesh	61.11	Nagaland	71.77	Madhya Pradesh	50.28
29	Rajasthan	61.03	Andhra Pradesh	70.85	Rajasthan	44.34
30	Dadra & Nagar Haveli*	60.03	Uttar Pradesh	70.23	Arunachal Pradesh	44.24
31	Uttar Pradesh	57.36	Jharkhand	67.94	Dadra & Nagar Haveli*	42.99
32	Arunachal Pradesh	54.74	Meghalaya	66.14	Uttar Pradesh	42.98
33	Jammu & Kashmir	54.46	Jammu & Kashmir	65.75	Jammu & Kashmir	41.82
34	Jharkhand	54.13	Arunachal Pradesh	64.07	Jharkhand	39.38
35	Bihar	47.53	Bihar	60.32	Bihar	33.57

Note: The Literacy rates for India have been worked out by excluding entire Kachchh district, Morvi, Maliya-Miyana and Wankaner talukas of Rajkot district, Jodiya taluka of Jamnagar district of Gujarat State and entire Kinnaur district of Himachal Pradesh where population enumeration of Census of India, 2001, could not be conducted due to natural calamities.

21.8 RURAL-URBAN LITERACY RATES (1951-2001)

Table 21.5 Reflects the relative position of literacy in rural and urban areas.

Table 21.5 Rural-Urban Literacy Rates (1951-2001)

Year	*Male*	*Female*	*Persons*
1951			
Rural	19.02*	4.87*	12.10*
Urban	45.60*	22.33*	34.59*
Total	27.16	8.86	18.33
1961			
Rural	34.30	10.10	22.50
Urban	66.00	40.50	54.40
Total	40.40	15.35	28.30
1971			
Rural	48.60	15.50	27.90
Urban	69.80	48.80	60.20
Total	45.96	21.97	34.45

1981			
Rural	49.60	21.70	36.00
Urban	76.70	56.30	67.20
Total	56.38	29.76	43.57
1991			
Rural	57.90	30.60	44.70
Urban	81.10	64.00	73.10
Total	64.13	39.29	52.21
2001			
Rural	71.40	46.70	59.40
Urban	86.70	73.20	80.30
Total	75.85	54.16	65.38

Note:

1. For 1951, the population male, female and persons refers to effective literacy rates and the break up of Rural, Urban and male-female components are crude literacy rates.
2. Literacy rates for 1951, 1961 and 1971 Censuses relate to population aged five years and above. The rates for 1981, 1991 and 2001 Census relate to population aged seven years and above.
3. The 1981 Literacy rates exclude Assam where census could not be conducted and the 1991 literacy rates exclude Jammu & Kashmir where Census could not be conducted due to disturbed conditions.
4. The 2001 Census, literacy rates exclude entire Kachchh district, Morvi, Maliya-Miyana and Wankaner talukas of Rajkot district, Jodiya taluka of Jamnagar district of Gujarat State and entire Kinnaur district of Himachal Pradesh where population enumeration of Census of India, 2001, could not be conducted due to natural calamities.

Source: Census of India 2001

21.9 CONCLUDING OBSERVATIONS

Kerala, which has the highest literacy rate of 90.92 per cent, occupies the top slot in both male and female literacy, at 94.20 and 87.86 per cent respectively. Bihar has the lowest literacy rate of 47.53 per cent, along with the lowest literacy rate for males at 60.32 per cent and for females, at 33.57 per cent. The number of literates has more than doubled in Dadra and Nagar Haveli and Rajasthan during the decade 1991-2001. As per the 2001 Census, all States and Union Territories have now achieved a male literacy rate of over 60 per cent. State/UTs having less than 50 per cent female literacy rates are: Rajasthan, Arunachal Pradesh, Dadra and Nagar Haveli, Uttar Pradesh, Jammu and Kashmir, Jharkhand and Bihar.

The rate of growth of literacy in the decade ending 2001 has been higher in the rural areas at 14.75 per cent as compared to the 7.2 per cent increase in urban areas.

22

Curriculum Reconstruction in India

National Curriculum Framework (2005)

22.1 BRIEF HISTORY OF CURRICULUM RECONSTRUCTION SINCE THE FORMULATION OF NPE, 1986

In response to the National Policy on Education (NPE) 1986, the NCERT developed the "*National Curriculum for Elementary and Secondary Education: A Framework*" in 1988. In 2000, it prepared the '*National Curriculum Framework for School Education*'. This curriculum was prepared by the Government formed by the National Democratic Alliance (NDA) led by the B.J.P. Syllabi and Textbooks were prepared in the light of this curriculum. The curriculum came into operation with the academic session 2002-03.

In May 2004, the NDA Government was replaced by the United Progressive Alliance (UPA) led by the Indian National Congress. Immediately after taking charge of the Ministry of Human Resource Development, the Minister appointed a committee to screen History and Social Studies textbooks. The textbooks introduced earlier during the NDA Government were replaced. It was stated that these did not respond to the values of secularism. The Ministry of HRD asked the NCERT to review the National Curriculum Framework for School Education (NCFSE) 2000 in the light of the Report '*Learning without Burden*' (1993). A 35-member National Steering Committee was constituted under the chairmanship of Prof. Yash Pal, former Chairman University Grants Commission. Out of 35 members, 15 were drawn from NCERT/Colleges of Education.

A Draft National Curriculum was prepared and circulated across different sections, and then placed before the Central Advisory of Education for its approval in June 2005. Some members suggested a few changes. This DNC underwent certain changes and came up for approval of the C.A.B.E. Discussions took place on September 6 and 7, 2005.

The BJP/State Governments raised several objections to the curriculum and also staged a walkout. A few members of the CABE wanted some clarification on a number of observations contained in the NCF.

It may be recalled that the Central Advisory Board of Education is an advisory board. Its decisions may not be binding on all Boards which are autonomous. All Boards of Education in the country are expected to include contents in accordance with the changing requirements.

The Human Resource Development Minister assured the members that a monitoring committee would be set up while preparing the syllabi and textbooks and the Committee would give due consideration to the views expressed by some members. Thereupon the National Curriculum was approved by the CABE on September 7, 2005.

22.2 CHAPTERS

The National Curriculum Framework (NCF) 2005

It contains the following Chapters:

1. Perspective
2. Learning and Knowledge
3. Curricular Areas, School Stages and Assessment
4. School and Classroom Environment
5. Systemic Reforms

22.3 SUMMARY

Chapter 1

- Strengthening a national system of education in a pluralistic society
- Reducing the curriculum load based on insights provided in 'Learning Without Burden'
- Systemic changes in tune with curricular reforms
- Curricular practices based on the values enshrined in the Constitution, such as social justice, equality, and secularism
- Ensuring quality education for all children.
- Building a citizenry committed to democratic practices, values, sensitivity towards gender justice, problems faced by the Scheduled Castes and the Scheduled Tribes, needs of the disabled, and capacities to participate in economic and political processes.

Chapter 2

- Reorientation in our perception of learners and learning
- Holistic approach in the treatment of learners' development and learning
- Creating an inclusive environment in the classroom for all students.
- Learner engagement for construction of knowledge and fostering creativity
- Active learning through experiential mode
- Adequate room for voicing children's thinking, curiosity and questions in curricular practices

- Connecting knowledge across disciplinary boundaries to provide a broader frame for insightful construction of knowledge
- Forms of learner engagement — observing, exploring, discovering, analyzing, critical reflection, etc. — are as important as the content of knowledge
- Activities for developing critical perspectives on socio-cultural realities need to find space in curricular practices
- Local knowledge and children's experiences are essential components of textbooks and pedagogic practices
- Children engaged in undertaking environment-related projects may contribute to generation of knowledge that could help create a transparent public database on India's environment
- The school years are a period of rapid development, with changes and shifts in children's capabilities, attitudes and interests that have implications for choosing and organising the content and process of knowledge.

Chapter 3

Language

- Language skills — speech and listening, reading and writing — cut across school subjects and disciplines. Their foundational role in children's construction of knowledge right from elementary classes through senior secondary classes needs to be recognised
- A renewed effort should be made to implement the three-language formula, emphasizing recognition of children's mother tongue(s) as the best medium of instruction. These include tribal languages
- English needs to find its place along with other Indian languages
- The multilingual character of Indian society should be seen as a resource for enrichment of school life.

Mathematics

- Mathematization (ability to think logically, formulate and handle abstractions) rather than 'knowledge' of mathematics (formals and mechanical procedures) is the main goal of teaching mathematics
- The teaching of mathematics should enhance the child's ability to think and reason, to visualize and handle abstractions, to formulate and solve problems. Access to quality mathematics education is the right of every child.

Science

- Content, process and language of science teaching must be commensurate with learner's age-range and cognitive reach
- Science teaching should engage the learner in acquiring methods and

processes that will nurture their curiosity and creativity, particularly in relation to the environment

- Science teaching should be placed in the wider context of children's environment to equip them with the requisite knowledge and skills to enter the world of work
- Awareness of environmental concerns must permeate the entire school curriculum.

Social Sciences

- Social science content needs to focus on conceptual understanding rather than lining up facts to be memorised for examination, and should equip children with the ability to think independently and reflect critically on social issues
- Interdisciplinary approaches, promoting key national concerns such as gender, justice, human rights, and sensitivity to marginalised groups and minorities
- Civics should be recast as political science, and significance of history as a shaping influence on the children's conception of the past and civic identity should be recognized.

Work

- School curricula from the pre-primary stage to the senior secondary stage need to be reconstructed to realise the pedagogic potential of work as a pedagogic medium in knowledge acquisition, developing values and multiple-skill formulation.

Art

- Arts (folk and classical forms of music and dance, visual arts, puppetry, clay work, theatre, etc.) and heritage crafts should be recognised as integral components of the school curriculum
- Awareness of their relevance to personal, social, economic and aesthetic needs should be built among parents, school authorities and administrators
- The arts should comprise a subject at every stage of school education.

Peace

- Peace-oriented values should be promoted in all subjects throughout school years with the help of relevant activities.
- Peace education should form a component of teacher education.

Health and Physical Education

- Health and physical education are necessary for the overall development of learners. Through health and physical education programmes (including yoga), it may be possible to handle successfully the issues of enrolment, retention and completion of school.

Chapter 4

- Availability of minimum infrastructure and material facilities, and support for planning a flexible daily schedule are critical for improved teacher performance
- A school culture that nurtures children's identities as ' learners' enhances the potential and interests of each child
- Specific activities ensuring participation of all children — abled and disabled — are essential conditions for learning by all
- The value of self-discipline among learners through democratic functioning is as relevant as ever
- Participation of community members in sharing knowledge and experience in a subject area helps in forging a partnership between school and community
- Reconceptualization of learning resources in terms of:
  - textbooks focussed on elaboration of concepts, activities, problems and exercises encouraging reflective thinking and group work
  - supplementary books, workbooks, teachers' handbooks, etc. based on fresh thinking and new perspectives
  - multimedia and ICT as sources for two-way interaction rather than one-way reception
  - school library as an intellectual space for teachers, learners and members of the community to deepen their knowledge and connect with the wider world
- Decentralized planning of school calender and daily schedule and autonomy for teacher professionalism practices are basic to creating a learning environment.

Chapter 5

- Quality concern, a key feature of systemic reform, implies the system's capacity to reform itself by enhancing its ability to remedy its own weaknesses and to develop new capabilities
- It is desirable to evolve a common school system to ensure comparable quality in different regions of the country and also to ensure that when children of different backgrounds study together, it improves the overall quality of learning and enriches the school ethos
- A broad framework for planning upwards, beginning with schools for identifyıng focus areas and subsequent consolidation at the cluster and block levels, could form a decentralised planning strategy at the district level

- Meaningful academic planning has to be done in a participatory manner by headmasters and teachers
- Monitoring quality must be seen as a process of sustaining interaction with individual schools in terms of teaching-learning processes
- Teacher education programmes need to be reformulated and strengthened so that the teacher can be an:
  - encouraging, supportive and humance facilitator in teaching-learning situations to enable learners (students) to discover their talents, to realise their physical and intellectual potentialities to the fullest, to develop character and desirable social and human values to function as responsible citizens; and
  - active member of a group of persons who make conscious efforts for curricular renewal so that it is relevant to changing social needs and the personal needs of learners.
- Reformulated teacher education programmes that place thrust on the active involvement of learners in the process of knowledge construction, shared context of learning, teacher as a facilitator of knowledge construction, multidisciplinary nature of knowledge of teacher education, integration theory and practice dimensions, and engagement with issues and concerns of contemporary Indian society from a critical perspective
- Centrality of language proficiency in teacher education and in integrated model of teacher education for strengthening professionalisation of teachers assume significance
- In service education needs to become a catalyst for change in school practices
- *The Panchayati Raj* system should be strengthened by evolving a mechanism to regular the functioning of parallel bodies at the village level so that democratic participation in development can be realised
- Reducing stress and enhancing success in examinations necessitate:
  - a shift away from content-based testing to problem solving skills and understanding. The prevailing typology of questions asked needs a radical change
  - a shift toward shorter examinations
  - setting up of a single nodal agency for coordinating the design and conduct of entrance examinations
- Institutionalisation of work-centred education as an integrated part of the school curriculum from the pre-primary to the +2 stage is expected to lay the necessary foundation for reconceptualising and restructuring vocational education to meet the challenges of a globalised economy
- Vocational Education and Training (VET) need to be conceived and implemented in a mission mode, involving the establishment of

separate VET centres and institutions from the level of village clusters and blocks to sub-divisional/district towns and metropolitan areas in collaboration with the nation wide spectrum of facilities already existing in this sector

- Availability of multiple textbooks to widen teachers' choices and provide for the diversity in children's needs and interests
- Sharing of teaching experiences and diverse classroom practices to generate new ideas and facilitate innovation and experimentation
- Development of syllabi, textbooks and teaching-learning resources could be carried out in a decentralized and participatory manner involving teachers, experts from universities, NGOs and teachers' organisations.

(*Source*: National Curriculum Framework, 2005).

22.4 OBSERVATIONS

The title of the document 'National Curriculum Framework 2005' appears to be misleading for it does not indicate whether it pertains to school education or higher education.

Of late, Curriculum Reforms in India seem to have been influenced more by political considerations and less by educational considerations. The NDA Government led by the BJP (1998-2004) and the UPA Government led by the Congress (2004) moved in the opposition direction in the field of education.

It is ironical that both the National Curriculum Framework (2004) and the National Curriculum Framework 2005 for school education prepared by and large, by the same organisation i.e. NCERT-supposed to be an organisation of experts, were quite the opposite. This tends to create an impression that experts do not have their own views or they do not apply their minds independently.

A persual of the curriculum shows that for its implementation, huge infrastructure is needed in educational institutions for which huge resources are needed.

There is too much emphasis on soft pedagogy in the approach of curriculum reconstruction and its implementation. Constant criticism of the existing system of education hardly serves any purpose and it creates confusion.

23

Review of Important Initiatives in Education

23.1 INTRODUCTION

In this chapter, an attempt is made to have a quick review of important initiatives/schemes taken as a follow up — of the revised National Policy on Education (NPE) 1992.

23.2 UNIVERSALISATION OF ELEMENTARY EDUCATION

Since the formulation of the NPE (1992), following major programmes have been initiated for achieving the objectives of Universalisation of Elementary Education.

1. District Primary Education Programme (DPEP).
2. Sarva Shiksha Abhiyan
3. National Programme of Nutritional Support to Primary Education (NPNSPE) or Mid-day Meals.
4. Education Guarantee Scheme and Alternative and Innovative Education.
5. National Programme of Education of Girls at Elementary Stage (NPEGL) Scheme
6. Kasturba Gahdhi Balika Vidyalaya Scheme.
7. Prathmik Shiksha Kosh.

District Primary Education Programme (DPEP)

The District Primary Education Programme (DPEP) launched in 1993 is a Centrally Sponsored Scheme for holistic development of primary education covering Classes I to V. The three major objectives of the DPEP are to (i) reduce drop-out rates to less than 10 per cent, (ii) reduce disparities among gender and social groups in the areas of enrolment, learning achievement, etc. to less than 5 per cent and (iii) improve the level of learning achievement compared to the baseline surveys.

The Programme components include construction of classrooms and new schools, opening of Alternative Schooling Centres, appointment of new teachers, setting up early childhood education centres, strengthening of State Councils of Educational Research and Training (SCERTs)/District Institutes of Educational Training (DIETs), setting up of Block Resource Centres/ Cluster Resource Centres, teacher training development of teaching-learning material, special interventions for education of girls, SC/ST, working children, etc. Initiatives for providing integrated education to disabled children and distance education for teacher training have also been incorporated in the DPEP Scheme.

Additionality Factor of DPEP—DPEP is based on the principle of 'additionality' and is structured to fill in the existing gaps by providing inputs over and above the provisions made under Central and State Sector Schemes for primary education.

District Selection Criteria—(a) Educationally backward districts with female literacy below the national average, and (b) Districts where Total Literacy Campaigns (TLCs) have been successful leading to enhanced demand for elementary education.

Funding of the Project—DPEP is an externally aided project. 85 per cent of the project cost is met by the Government of India and the remaining 15 per cent is shared by the concerned State Government. The Government of India share is resourced through external assistance. External assistance of about Rs. 6938.00 crore, comprising Rs. 5137.00 crore as credit from IDA and Rs. 1801.00 crore as grant from BC/DFID/UNICEF/Netherlands has been tied up for DPEP till date.

Coverage of DPEP—At present, DPEP is in operation in 9 states covering 129 districts. DPEP at its peak, was operational in 273 districts in 18 states. However, with the progressive closure of different phases of the programme, it now exists in 129 districts only.

Monitoring and Evaluation of DPEP—The programme is periodically reviewed through the mechanism of Joint Review Missions, Project Management Information System (PMIS), Educational Management System (EMIS), programme impact studies, etc. A mid-term in-depth review of DPEP Phase-I, II and III states have also been carried out by the Joint Review Missions in 1997-98, 1999-2000 and 2003-04. The reviews and evaluation studies of the programme have brought out that the programme has resulted in significant increase in enrolment, improvement in learning achievement, reduction in repetition rates/drop-outs with increased community involvement and improvements in classroom processes.

Allocation of Funds under DPEP—Position of Budget Estimates, Revised Estimates and Actual Expenditure for last three years is given as under:

(Rs. in crore)

Year	*BE*	*RE*	*Actual*
2000-01	969.00	820.00	856.39
2001-02	1098.00	1198.00	1198.00
2002-03	1380.00	1380.00	1285.03
2003-04	1200.00	800.00	791.19

Expenditure on DPEP—The cumulative expenditure on DPEP up to February 2004, works out to Rs. 6076.75 crore and the cumulative reimbursement to Rs. 4807.51 crore. Expenditure incurred during the financial year 2003-04 is Rs. 847.68 crore and reimbursement Rs. 609.57 crore.

Sarva Shiksha Abhiyan

The Scheme of Sarva Shiksha Abhiyan (SSA) evolved from the recommendations of the State Education Ministers' Conference held in October 1998 to pursue universal elementary education in a mission mode. The scheme of Sarva Shiksha Abhiyan was approved by the Cabinet in its meeting held on 16 November 2000. It was started in 2001.

The assistance under the programme of Sarva Shiksha Abhiyan was on a 85:15 sharing arrangement during the Ninth Plan, 75:25 sharing arrangement during the Tenth Plan, and 50:50 sharing thereafter, between the Central Government and the State Government.

The programme covers the entire country and addresses the needs of 192 million children in 11 lakh habitations. 8.5 lakh existing primary and upper primary schools and 33 lakh existing teachers would be covered under the scheme. The programme seeks to open new schools in habitations which do not have schooling facilities and strengthen existing school infrastructure through provision of additional class rooms, toilets, drinking water, maintenance grant and school improvement grant. Existing schools with inadequate teacher strength would be provided additional teachers under the programme. The capacity of existing teachers would be built by extensive training, provision of grant for developing teaching-learning material and development of academic support structure. SSA has a special focus on girls and children of weaker sections A number of initiatives, including free textbooks, target these children under the programme. SSA also seeks to provide computer education even in rural areas, to bridge the digital divide.

The approach is community-owned, and the village education plans prepared in consultation with Panchayati Raj Institutions, will form the basis of district elementary education plans. The Sarva Shiksha Abhiyan covers the entire country with a special focus on educational needs of girls, Scheduled Castes and Scheduled Tribes and other children in difficult circumstances.

Goals of Sarva Shiksha Abhiyan

- All 6-14 age children in school/EGS centre/bridge course by 2003.
- All 6-14 age children complete five year primary education by 2007.
- All 6-14 age children complete eight years of schooling by 2010.
- Focus on elementary education of satisfactory quality with emphasis on education for life;
- Bridge all gender and social category gaps at primary stage by 2007 and at elementary education level by 2010;
- Universal retention by 2010.

National Level Mission

The Ministry has also set up national-level mission under the chairmanship of Prime Minister vide Resolution dated 2-1-2001.

During Tenth Plan, an allocation of Rs. 17,000 crore has been made for SSA. For 2003-04, BE is Rs. 1951.25 crore, RE is Rs. 2732.32 crore and the final grant is Rs. 2732.32 crore. The total expenditure under SSA for the year 2003-04 was Rs. 3,650 crore.

Monitoring Under SSA

Monitoring under SSA is a three-tiered monitoring at the local community level, at the state level and the national level. The community, through its representative institutions like village education committees, has been entrusted with the primary level of ensuring that the schools are functioning effectively. Being local stakeholders, they are best placed to ensure quality education in the schools.

For assisting the various levels of management in the task of monitoring, two kinds of information systems have been developed. One is the Educational Management Information System (EMIS), also known as District Information System on Education (DISE), under which school-level data is collected every year with 30 September as the record date. This was first developed in DPEP in 1995 for capturing school-level information from primary sections. Starting from 42 districts, it grew to 273 districts during the peak of DPEP programme. With the advent of SSA, the system was expanded to the upper primary sections also and to all districts in the country. The data, as on 30 September 2002, was received from 459 districts in the 18 DPEP states. It is expected that the data from 30 September 2003 would become available for all the 600 districts in the country.

Table 23.1: Approved Annual Plans under SSA During 2002-03 and 2003-04

	2002-2003	*2003-04*
No. of Districts	592	596
Amount Approved under SSA (Rs. in crore)	3411 crore	8547 crore
Amount Approved under DPEP (Rs. in crore)	2291 crore	1253 crore
Total Amount Approved (Rs. in crore)	5702 crore	9600 crore

The second information system developed is the Project Management Information System (PMIS), in which the emphasis is on recording the progress made, towards the implementation of the annual plans, as well as to capture the quality of the education process. The system has been developed with the assistance of NIEPA and NCERT, and is a complete monitoring framework for every tier of management. Several formats have been prescribed at various levels to assist in monitoring the implementation of the programme at those levels. Only the abstract useful at the national level is received nationally under the system.

Seeing the enormity of this task of monitoring, assistance has been taken from professional institutions, such as IIMs, departments of education of different universities and the ICSSR. These institutions have been allocated individual states, the number of institutions allocated to the states depending on the size of the State and the extent of monitoring required. They not only carry out the task of supervision and monitoring but also act as partners of the states in the implementation of the programme. The selected institutions make field visits and send their reports every quarter. Their quarterly visits to select districts help in assessing the ground-level realities.

Table 23.2: Physical Items Approved in 2002-2003 and 2003-2004

	2002-2003			*2003-2004*		
	SSA	*DPEP*	*Total*	*SSA*	*DPEP*	*Total*
No. of schools approved	18.159	1,640	19,699	67,190	57	67,247
No. of teachers sanctioned	25,782	17,108	42,890	2,98,189	5,201	4,03,390
No. of school buildings	8,095	8,849	16,944	40,960	1,586	42,546
Additional classrooms	32,028	7,485	39,523	68,779	3,950	72,729
Toilets	39,699	11,130	50,829	46,272	5,488	51,760
Drinking water	26,805	6,590	33,395	33,161	6,053	41,214
Teacher grant (No. of teachers)	21,61,514	8,52,445	30,13,959	29,67,053	3,70,798	33,37,851
School grant (No. of schools)	5,61,558	3,07,414	8,68,972	6,33,303	1,46,143	8,29,446
Repair grants (No. of schools)	5,15,700	0	5,15,700	7,33,000	42,133	7,75,133
Free text books (No. of children)	31139754	14086909	45226663	4,60 crore	1.21 crore	5.81 crore

Apart from the above, an independent agency has also been engaged to monitor the programme from the financial management aspect. The agency selected is the Institute of Public Auditors of India (IPAI) whose patron is CAG, and which consists of personnel formerly working with the Audit and Accounts Department. They take up six states every year for monitoring the financial aspects of the programme, such as fund flow, utilisation of funds, propriety of procurement, etc. This monitoring is apart from the statutory audit of the State Societies as per law and the audit by CAG of India.

Impact of SSA

Implementation of SSA in the first two years of the Tenth Plan has seen significant developments in the field of education sector. There has been a particular emphasis in these two years to ensure that all out-of-school children are brought to school through multi-pronged strategies. The focus has been on improving the existing infrastructure of regular schools as well as on alternate strategies for mainstreaming children who are left out of the schooling process due to a number of reasons.

Towards the objective of improving the infrastructure, arrangements have been made to open more than 80,000 new schools and appointing around 4.5 lakh teachers in the last two years. Further, physical infrastructure has been sought to be improved through provision of more than 1 lakh additional classrooms, around 60,000 school buildings, 1 lakh toilets and 75,000 drinking water facilities. With the objective of improving the quality of teaching and classroom atmosphere, grants are given to all teachers for developing teaching-learning materials, 20-day training is expected to be given to all teachers and free textbooks distributed to all girls and children belonging to Scheduled Castes and Scheduled Tribes. In addition, maintenance grant for civil repairs and a school grant for replacement of equipment is given to all schools.

For children who are difficult to bring to school, SSA has relied on the Education Guarantee Scheme and Alternative and Innovative Education to bring these children to school. In the last two years approvals have been given for getting 1.42 crore children to school.

As a result of all these interventions, the number of out-of-school children has come down from 3.5 crore in 2001 to 2.3 crore in the beginning of 2003-04.

Education Guarantee Scheme and Alternative and Innovative Education

The Education Guarantee Scheme (EGS) and Alternative and Innovative Education (AIE) component of Sarva Shiksha Abhiyan (SSA) is operationally proactive and provides avenues to children in the age group of 6-14 years. This component was designed to cover those children who are habitants of remotely located inaccessible habitations, never been to school, dropouts or could not continue/complete their elementary education because of one or the other reason.

EGS & AIE is, therefore, a vital component of SSA for achieving Universalisation of Elementary Education (UEE). It has the following broad strategies:

- Setting up of EGS schools in school-less habitations.
- Interventions for mainstreaming of 'out-of-school' children through bridge courses (residential as well as non-residential), back to school camps, etc.
- Strategies for specific groups of children, who need flexible and

innovative interventions to meet their requirements of elementary education.

FGS & AIE programme also envisages centres for street and slum children, remedial coaching for children enrolled in formal schools, short duration summer camps, etc.

The ratio of sharing of expenditure between the Centre and states on this component is 75:25 respectively. In case of support to voluntary agencies (VAs), Central Government bears 100 per cent cost (within the overall cost ceilings). The EGS & AIE, being a part of SSA, has no separate budget provision and expenditure on the scheme is incurred from overall budget provision of SSA.

The scheme is largely implemented and monitored by state-level societies set up for SSA by the State/UT Governments, which have powers to appraise and approve proposals running either through state agencies or voluntary sector.

The Department of Elementary Education and Literacy persuaded the State Governments to constitute state-level GIACs as per the framework of SSA and a Hand Book for EGS/AIE, in order to encourage the participation of NGOs. The GIACs have already been constituted in 22 states. The States of Bihar, Uttaranchal and Uttar Pradesh have processed 289, 272 and 425 proposals respectively from NGOs.

In order to enhance state capacities for implementation of the EGS/AIE scheme in SSA, one national and three regional-level workshops to strengthen the capacity of implementers at state as well as district-level were organised. A three-day national-level workshop was organised in Kolkata in April 2003 and 2004 and three regional workshops were organised in Pune, Allahabad and Kolkata.

The Department of Elementary Education and Literacy regularly monitors the implementation of EGS/AIE component in the States through convening quarterly meetings of Alternative Schooling Coordinators of the State SSA programmes regularly, wherein state-wise progress is reviewed, interstate experiences and good practices are shared and the issues concerning the programme are deliberated upon for better execution.

National Programme of Nutritional Support to Primary Education

A nation-wide programme of Nutritional Support to Primary Education (popularly called Mid-day Meals Scheme or MDM) was launched on 15 August 1995, with the objectives to give a boost to UPE and simultaneously impacting on the nutritional status of students in primary classes studying in government, local body and government-aided schools. During the current year, the programme has also been expanded to children of EGS centres which are being opened in the school-less habitations.

The programme aims to provide wholesome cooked/processed food through local bodies/authorities such as Panchayats and Nagar Palikas who are expected to develop institutional arrangement has not taken place, foodgrains (wheat/rice) at the rate of 3kg per student per month are distributed to the targeted children, subject to a minimum attendance of 80 per cent.

The programme was expanded in a phased manner and has seen all-India coverage during 1997-98 except for Lakshadweep, which runs its own programme. The Central support under this programme is to provide foodgrains free of cost to children through the Food Corporation of India. The cost is being reimbursed at BPL rate. The year-wise details of children targeted for coverage and quantity of foodgrains allocated and lifted by state agencies and expenditure incurred is given below.

Supreme Court in its order dated 29 November 2001 directed that under the Scheme, cooked meals be provided in a time bound manner by those States/UTs that do not have such a programme. As a result, cooked meals are now being served in a number of States.

Table 23.3 : NPNSPE

Year	*No. of Children*	*Quantity of Foodgrains*		*Expenditure incurred*
		Allocated	*Lifted*	
1995-96	3.34	713223	536016	441.21
1996-97	5.57	1585388	1112489	800.00
1997-98	9.10	2567372	1810164	1017.38
1998-99	9.79	2706274	1147917	1600.15
1999-2000	9.90	2767251	1401765	1500.00
2000-01	10.54	2480692	1517816	1300.00
2001-02	10.35	2862475	2076764	1030.27
2002-03	10.26	2826248	901756 (upto Sept. 2002)	952.44

National Programme for Education of Girls at Elementary Level (NPEGEL) Scheme

In July, 2003, Government of India approved a new programme called 'National Programme for Education of Girls at Elementary Level' (NPEGEL) as an amendment to the existing scheme of Sarva Shiksha Abhiyan (SSA) for providing additional support for education of underprivileged/disadvantaged girls at the elementary level. The scheme is implemented in Educationally Backward Blocks (EBBs) where the level of female literacy is below, and the gender gap is above the national average in blocks of districts which are not covered under EBBs but have at least 5 per cent SC/ST population and where SC/St female literacy is below 10 per cent, and also in select urban slums.

Kasturba Gandhi Balika Vidyalaya Scheme

An estimated provision of Rs. 1064.80 crore has been kept for the Tenth Plan. Apart from NPEGEL, a new scheme called *Kasturba Gandhi Balika Vidyalaya (KGBV)* was approved for launching during 2004-05 for setting up 750 residential schools with boarding facilities at elementary level for girls belonging predominantly to the SC, ST, other backward castes (OBC) and minorities in difficult areas. A provision of Rs. 489 crore has been made for the Tenth Plan; and Annual Plan allocation for the year 2004-05 is Rs. 100 crore. 525 KGBVs have been approved by the Department of Elementary Education, involving an amount of Rs. 123.03 crore for 2004-05.

Prathmik Shiksha Kosh

An education cess of 2 per cent on all direct and indirect Central taxes has been imposed through the Finance (No. 2) Act, 2004. Soon after the relevant Bill was introduced in Parliament on July 8, 2004, action was initiated for the creation of a separate, dedicated, non-lapsable Fund to be named as *Prathmik Shiksha Kosh* and maintained by the Ministry of HRD, Department of Elementary Education and Literacy. The proceeds would be available on a rollover basis for the schemes of Basic Education and the Mid-Day Meal Scheme. Budget provision for the Mid-day Meal Scheme during 2004-05 was Rs. 1,675 crore. In addition Rs. 1,232 crore has been provided to the States/UTs as Additional Central Assistance (ACA) under State Sector as earmarked outlay for meeting cooking cost.

23.3 FREE AND UNIVERSAL COMPULSORY ELEMENTARY EDUCATION RIGHT TO EDUCATION

After independence, the Government of India realised the significance of elementary education as it is the base of progress and accordingly incorporated Article 45 in the Constitution. Since the progress in the field was not in accordance with the provisions of this Article, it was considered necessary to amend it to give more impetus.

Following amendments in the Constitution were made in 2002.

1. *Article 21A: "Right to Education"*—The State shall provide free and compulsory education to all children of the age six to fourteen years in such manner as State, may, by law determine".

2. *Article 45: "Provision for early childhood care and education to children below the age of 6 years*—The State shall endeavour to provide early childhood care and education for all children under the age of six years".

(Substituted by the Constitution (Eighty-sixth Amendment) Act, 2002.

3. *Article 51A (K) : "Fundamental Duties"*—It shall be the duty of every citizen of India who is a parent or guardian to provide opportunities for education to his child or, as the case may be, ward the age of six and fourteen years.

[Inserted by the Constitution (Eighty-sixth Amendment) Act, 2002)

Compulsory Education Acts already exist in 19 states but these have not been enforced on account of several constraints, primarily on account of lack of political will.

More than two years have passed in making amendments in the constitution regarding 'Right to Education'. However, nothing substantial has been done to fulfil this obligation. The original target for providing compulsory primary education was the year 1960.

23.4 DROP-OUT RATES

Of the estimated population of 205 million in the age group of 6-14 years on March 1, 2002, nearly 82.5 per cent was enrolled in schools, compared to 82.4 per cent in 2001-02. The retention rate of students at the primary school stage was about 59 per cent (1992-97).

The rates of drop out decreased from 64.5 per cent in 1960-61 to 39.0 per cent in 2001-2002 in primary classes. The rate of dropouts which was 78.3 per cent in 1960-61 came down to 54.6 per cent in 2001-2002 in the Classes I-VIII. Similarly the rate of dropouts which was 82.5 per cent in 1980-81, decreased to 66.0 per cent in 2001-2002 in the secondary classes, implying an improvement in retention rates as would be evident from Table.

23.5 RESTRUCTURING TEACHER EDUCATION

The National Council for Teacher Education (NCTE) which had been in existence for the last more than two decades was given a statuary recognition by a gazette notification issued on August 17, 1995 by the Ministry of Human Resource Development (Department of Education). This was done in pursuance of the National Council for Teacher Education Act, 1973. This Act has been enacted with a view to achieving planned and coordinated development of the Teacher Education System throughout the country. However, the NCTE has not been able to check the mushroom growth of substandard hundreds of teacher education collages.

498 DIETs, 86 CTEs and 38 IASTs have been established under the 'Centrally-Sponsored Scheme of Reconstruction and Reorganisation of Teacher Education' since 1987.

23.6 SECONDARY EDUCATION

A Centrally Sponsored Scheme of Pre-vocational Education at lower Secondary School was introduced in 1993-94, primarily to impart training in simple marketing skills to the students of classes IX and X.

From above, it is clear that there is a long way to reach the goal.

The Central Institute of Vocational Education was set up at Bhopal in July 1993, to provide technical and academic support to vocational education in the country.

The progress of vocationalisation of senior secondary education has not made much head way.

23.7 CURRICULUM REFORMS IN SCHOOL EDUCATION

Curriculum reforms in school education have been taken up separately.

23.8 EXPENDITURE ON EDUCATION

The NPE 1986 and as modified in 1992 set a goal of expenditure on education at 6 percent of the GDP. As against the target, the combined total expenditure on education by Central and State Governments was 3.49 percent of GDP in 2004 (B.E.)

24

Expansion of Educational Facilities and Expenditure on Education in India Since 1950-51

OVERVIEW OF EXPANSION AT ALL LEVELS OF EDUCATION

There has been a phenomenal expansion of educational facilities and correspondingly expenditure on education in India since 1950-51. While primary schools increased by nearly 2.8 times, upper primary schools and secondary schools by 18 times.

Colleges for general and professional education increased by 26 times and the Universities (Including deemed Universities and Institutions of National Importance by 10 times.

The total enrolment at the primary stage increased by nearly 6 times and that of the girls by 9 times.

At the upper stage, there was 15 times increase in overall enrolment while in the case of girls it was more than 32 times.

At secondary and senior secondary stage, the total increase was about 20 times and in the case of girls it was nearly 49 times.

Whereas enrolment at the higher education stage in 1950-51 was of the order of about 3.6 lakhs, in 2003-2004 it was 99 lakhs. Thus the increase was about 27 times. The enrolment of girls was 37 lakhs. In 1950-51 enrolment of girls per hundred men was 14 and in 2003-2004, it went upto 68 per hundred men.

Literacy rates increased from 18.33 per cent to 64.86 per cent in 2001.

The expenditure on education also increased on a mammoth scale.

The following tables illustrate the growth.

At present in our country we have nearly 55 lakh teachers spread over around 10 lakh schools to educate about 2042 lakh children. While 82% of habitations have a primary school within a radius of one kilometre, there is an upper primary school within 3 kilometres for 75% of habitations. At least 50% of our children who appear at the school leaving examinations passout of the secondary school system. Despite these trends, 37% people of India lack literacy skills, about 53% children drop out at elementary stage and over 75% of our rural schools are multigrade.

The following tables illustrate the growth in education.

Table 24.1: Expansion of Educational Facilities at the Elementary Stage (Class I to VIII) (1950-51 and 2003-2004)

S.No.	*Indicators*	*1950-51*	*2002-03*
1.	**Schools**		
	Primary	210,000	770,471
	Upper Primary	13,000	262,469
2.	**Teachers**		
	Primary	538,000	1.92 m
	Upper Primary	86,000	1.58 m
3.	**Enrolment**		
	Primary	19.2 m	122.4 m
	Upper Primary	3.1 m	46.8 m
4.	**GER (Gross Enrolment Ratio)**		
	Primary	42.6%	98.3%
	Upper Primary	12.7%	62.49%
5.	**Drop out Rate**		
	Primary	65% (1960-61)	31.4%
	Upper Primary	78% (1960-61)	52.8%
6.	**Female Teachers**		
	Primary	15.2%	39.02%
	Upper Primary	15.0%	40.80%
7.	**PTR**		
	Primary	1:24	1:42
	Upper Primary	1:20	1:34
8.	**Access in habitations**		
	Primary	83.3% (1986)	87% (2002)
	Upper Primary	76.0% (1986)	78% (2002)
9.	**% Girls**		
	Primary	28.1%	46.8%
	Upper Primary	16%	43.8%
10.	**Population 6-14 years**	72.3 m	201.0 m
11.	**Enrolment 6-14 years**	22.3 m	169.2 m
12.	**Out of school children 6-14 years**	50.0 m	95 lakhs

Table 24.2: Enrolment at the Elementary Stage (1950-51 to 2002-03)

(*in Million*)

Year	*Primary*			*Upper Primary*		
	Boys	*Girls*	*Total*	*Boys*	*Girls*	*Total*
1950-51	13.8	5.4	19.2	2.6	0.5	3.1
1960-61	23.6	11.4	35.0	5.1	1.6	6.7
1970-71	35.7	21.3	57.0	9.4	3.9	13.3
1980-81	45.3	28.3	73.8	13.9	6.8	20.7
1990-91	57.0	40.4	97.4	21.5	12.5	34.0
1999-00	64.1	49.5	113.6	25.1	17.0	42.1
2002-03	64.9	57.2	122.1	26.3	20.6	47.0

Table 24.3: Gross Enrolment Ratios (GER) (in per cent) Since 1950-51

Year	*Primary (I-V)*			*Upper Primary (VI-VIII)*			*Elementary (I-VIII)*		
	Boys	*Girls*	*Total*	*Boys*	*Girls*	*Total*	*Boys*	*Girls*	*Total*
1950-51	60.6	24.8	42.6	20.6	4.6	12.7	46.4	17.7	32.1
1960-61	82.6	41.4	62.4	33.2	11.3	22.5	65.2	30.9	48.7
1970-71	95.5	60.5	78.6	46.5	20.8	33.4	75.5	44.4	61.9
1980-81	95.8	64.1	80.5	54.3	20.6	41.9	82.2	52.1	67.5
1990-91	114.0	85.5	100.1	76.6	47.0	62.1	100.0	70.8	86.0
1991-92	112.8	86.9	100.2	75.1	49.6	61.4	101.2	73.2	87.7
1992-93	95.0	73.5	84.6	72.5	48.9	67.5	87.7	65.7	77.2
1993-94	90.0	73.1	81.9	62.1	54.4	54.2	80.2	63.7	72.3
1994-95	96.6	78.2	87.7	68.9	50.0	60.0	87.5	68.8	78.4
1995-96	97.1	79.4	88.6	67.8	49.8	59.3	86.9	69.4	78.5
1996-97	97.0	80.1	88.8	65.8	49.2	58.0	85.9	69.4	78.0
1997-98	99.3	82.2	91.1	66.3	49.7	58.5	87.4	70.7	79.4
1998-99	100.9	82.9	92.1	65.3	49.1	57.6	87.6	70.6	79.4
1999-00	104.1	85.2	94.9	67.2	49.7	58.8	90.1	72.0	81.3
2000-01	104.9	85.9	95.7	66.7	49.9	58.6	90.3	72.4	81.6
2001-02	105.3	86.9	96.3	67.8	52.1	60.2	90.7	73.6	82.4
2002-03	97.5	93.1	95.4	65.3	56.2	60.9	85.4	79.3	82.5
2003-04	100.75	95.67	98.37	68.37	57.69	62.48	88.02	81.57	84.91

* Provisional.

Source: *Selected Educational Statistics 2002-2004*, Ministry of Human Resource Development.

Table 24.4: Percentage of Girls Enrolment to Total Enrolment a the Elementage Stage (1950-51 to 2002-03)

Years	*Primary Schools (Grades I-V)*	*Upper Primary Schools (Grades VI-VIII)*
1950-51	28.1	16.1
1960-61	32.6	23.9
1970-71	37.4	29.3
1980-81	38.6	32.9
1990-91	41.5	36.7
1993-94	42.7	39.1
1994-95	42.8	38.9
1999-00	43.6	40.4
2000-01	43.7	40.9
2001-02	44.1	41.8

Table 24.5: Growth in Elementary Schools (1950-51 to 2001-2004)

Years	*Primary Schools*	*Upper Primary Shools*
1950-51	209671	13596
1960-61	330399	49663
1970-71	408378	90621
1980-81	494503	118555
1990-91	560935	151456
1999-00	641695	198004
2002-03	651375	245271
2003-04	710471	262649

Table 24.6: Drop-out Rates at the Elementary Stage (1960-61 to 2002-03)

(*in Percent*)

	1960-61	*1970-71*	*1980-81*	*1990-91*	*1999-2000*	*2003-04*
Class I-V						
Boys	61.7	64.5	56.2	40.1	38.67	33.7
Girls	70.9	70.9	62.5	46.0	42.28	28.6
Total	64.9	67.0	58.7	42.6	40.25	31.5
Classes I-VIII						
Boys	75.0	74.6	68.0	59.1	51.96	51.8
Girls	85.0	83.4	79.4	65.1	58.00	52.9
Total	78.3	77.9	72.7	60.9	54.53	52.3

Table 24.7: Teachers in Elementary Schools (1950-51 to 2003-04)

(*in Thousand*)

Year	*Primary*			*Upper Primary*		
	Male	*Female*	*Total*	*Male*	*Female*	*Total*
1950-51	456	82	538	73	13	86
1960-61	615	127	742	262	83	645
1970-71	835	225	1060	463	175	638
1980-81	1021	342	1363	598	253	851
1990-91	1143	473	1616	717	356	1073
1999-00	1236	683	1919	829	469	1298
2002-03	1166	746	1912	936	645	1581
2003-04	1259	837	2096	943	649	1592

Table 24.8: Enrolment Rate of Scheduled Castes (2003-04) (Classes I to VIII)

Class	*Boys*	*Girls*	*Total*
I to V	93.1	83.0	88.3
VI to VIII	79.4	63.3	71.9

Table 24.9: Expansion of Secondary Education Since 1950-51

Year	*No. of High/Hr. Sec./Inter/Junior Colleges/Pre-degree*	*No. of Students (In Lakhs)*
1950-51	7416	15.0
1960-61	17257	28.9
1968-69	33487	61.5
1978-79	46874	84.1
1988-89	72635	185.2
1990-91	79796	249.0
1998-99	112438	277.6
1999-00	116820	282.1
2002-03	137207	332.0
2003-04	145899	350.1

Table 24.11: Number of Schools, Sections, and Enrolment Capacity in States/UTs under the Scheme of Vocationalisation of Secondary Education (2001-2002)

Sl. No.	*States/UTs*	*No. of Schools*	*No. of Sections*	*Enrolment Capacity*
1.	Andhra Pradesh	668	1880	94000
2.	Arunachal Pradesh	4	4	200
3.	Assam	225	510	25500
4.	Bihar	251	752	37600
5.	Chhattisgarh	—	—	—
6.	Delhi	38	93	4650
7.	Goa	43	106	5300
8.	Gujarat	364	1032	51600
9.	Haryana	170	876	43350
10.	Himachal Pradesh	40	82	410
11.	Jammu & Kashmir	38	38	1900
12.	Jharkhand	—	—	—
13.	Karnataka	564	1427	71350
14.	Kerala	363	1008	50400
15.	Madhya Pradesh	465	1307	65350
16.	Maharashtra	1141	3480	17400
17.	Manipur	19	57	2850

(Contd.)

(*Contd.*)

Sl. No.	States/UTs	No. of Schools	No. of Sections	Enrolment Capacity
18.	Meghalaya	10	20	1000
19.	Mizoram	17	51	2550
20.	Nagaland	8	16	800
21.	Orissa	231	924	46200
22.	Punjab	282	846	42300
23.	Rajasthan	155	465	23250
24.	Sikkim	7	9	450
25.	Tamil Nadu	700	2140	107000
26.	Tripura	12	12	600
27.	Uttar Pradesh	910	2350	117500
28.	Uttaranchal	—	—	—
29.	West Bengal	39	39	1950
30.	Andaman and Nicobar	3	3	150
31.	Chandigarh	17	58	2900
32.	Dadra & Nagara Haveli	2	2	100
33.	Daman & Diu	2	5	250
34.	Lakshadweep	—	—	—
35.	Pondicherry	12	16	800
	Total	6800	16599	979950

Table 24.12: Number of Teachers in High/Hr. Secondary/Intermediate Stages (1950-51 to 2003-2004) (in thousand)

Year	High/Hr. Secondary/Intermediate		
	Male	Female	Total
1950-51	107	20	127
1955-56	155	35	190
1960-61	234	62	296
1965-66	368	111	479
1970-71	474	155	629
1975-76	559	200	759
1980-81	669	257	926
1985-86	793	339	1132
1990-91	917	417	1334
1991-92	931	450	1381
1992-93	941	454	1395
1993-94	953	492	1445
1994-95	986	495	1481
1995-96	1030	519	1549
1996-97	1069	544	1613
1997-98	1086	558	1644
1998-99	1168	579	1747
1999-00	1142	578	1720
2000-01	1184	577	1761
2001-02	1157	620	1777
2003-04	1250	774	2024

Table 24.13: Percentage of Trained Teachers at the School Stage (1990-91 to 2003-2004)

Stage	*1990-91*	*2003-2004*
Primary School	89.81	86.00
Middle School	91.04	87.00
Secondary School	90.10	89.00
Sr. Secondary School	92.39	90.00

Table 24.14: Teachers Training Schools and Colleges

Year	*Teacher Training Schools*	*Teacher Training Colleges*
1990-91	1167	506
2000-01	1283	834
2003-04	1300	940

Table 24.15: Teacher Training Colleges and Enrolment

Year	*No. of Colleges*	*Total Enrolment*
1950-51	36	4100
1960-61	125	19000
1965-66	193	33600
1970-71	258	56900
1975-76	315	76600
1980-81	331	71200
1985-86	403	82700
1990-91	506	99600
1995-96	565	147700
2001-02	834	150000

Table 24.16: Enrolment in Higher Education Since 1950-51

Year	*Enrolment (in Lakhs)*	*App. Percentage to Total Population in the Age Group 17/18-23/24*
1950-51	3.6	0.8
1960-61	8.9	1.8
1970-71	17.2	3.4
1980-81	26.5	4.2
1990-91	49.2	4.9
2000-01	84.0	6.0
2001-02	88.2	6.0
2002-03	92.3	6.0
2003-04	99.5	6.0

Table 24.17: Number of Colleges and Universities Since 1950-51

Year	*No. of Colleges*	*Universities/Deemed Univerties/Institutes of National Importance*
1950-51	578	27
1960-61	1819	45
1970-71	2384	82
1980-81	6963 (Includes institutions	111
1990-91	5748 of Post-matric cources)	184
2000-01	10149	272
2001-02	14832	280
2002-03	15343	287
2003-04	16885 (Provisional)	315

Notes: 1. There is slight difference in data as mentioned in different documents.
2. The University Grants Commission's Annual Report 2002-2003 gives the details of Institutes of Higher Education as:
(a) No. of colleges = 15343
(b) Universities = 206
(c) Institutes Deemed to be Universities = 81
(d) Institutes of National Importance = 13

Table 24.18: Percentage of Girls Enrolment to Total Enrolments by Stages (1950-51 to 2001-2002)

Year	*Primary I-V*	*Middle VI-VIII*	*Sec./Hr. Sec/ Intermediate (IX-XII)*	*Hr. Education (Degree & Above Level)*
1950-51	28.1	16.1	13.3	10.0
1955-56	30.5	20.8	15.4	14.6
1960-61	32.6	23.9	20.5	16.0
1965-66	36.2	26.7	22.0	20.4
1970-71	37.4	29.3	25.0	20.0
1975-76	38.1	31.3	26.9	23.2
1980-81	38.6	32.9	29.6	26.7
1985-86	40.3	35.6	30.3	33.0
1990-91	41.5	36.7	32.9	33.3
1991-92	41.9	38.2	33.8	32.3
1992-93	42.6	38.8	33.9	33.2
1993-94	42.7	39.1	34.3	33.5
1994-95	42.9	39.3	35.9	34.0
1995-96	43.1	39.5	36.1	36.0
1996-97	43.2	39.9	36.4	36.7
1997-98	43.5	40.3	36.6	37.5
1998-99*	43.5	40.5	37.8	38.1
1999-2000*	43.6	40.4	38.9	38.7
2000-2001*	43.7	40.9	38.6	39.4
2001-2002*	44.1	41.8	39.5	39.9

* Provisional.

Table 24.19: No. of Women Colleges Since 1986-87 to 2003-2004

Year	*No. of Women's Colleges*
1986-87	780
1996-97	1195
1998-99	1359
1999-2000	1503
2000-2001	1578
2001-2002	1625
2002-2003	1650
2003-2004	1798 (Provisional)

Table 24.20: Women Students Per Hundred Men Students

Year	*Total Women Enrolment (000s)*	*Enrolment Per Hundred Men*
1950-51	40	14
2002-2003	3696	67
2003-2004	4003	67

Table 24.21: Literacy Rate: 1951-2001

Census Year	*Persons*	*Males*	*Females*
1951	18.33	27.16	8.86
1961	28.3	40.40	15.35
1971	34.45	45.96	21.97
1981	43.57	56.38	29.76
1991	52.21	64.13	39.29
2001	64.84	75.26	53.67

Notes: 1. Literacy rates for 1951, 1961 and 1971 Census relate to population aged five years and above, the rates for the 1981, 1991 and 2001 Censuses relate to the population aged seven years and above.

2. The 1981 Literacy rates exclude Assam where the 1981 Census could not be conducted.

3. The 1991 Literacy rates exclude Jammu and Kashmir where the 1991 Census could not be concluded due to disturbed conditions.

Table 24.22: Statewise and Sexwise Gross Enrolment Ratios in Classes I to V, VI to VIII and I to VIII (2003-2004)

Sl. No.	*States/UTs*	*Classes I-V (6-11 years)*			*Classes VI-VIII (11-14 years)*			*Classes I-VIII (6-14 years)*		
		Boys	*Girls*	*Total*	*Boys*	*Girls*	*Total*	*Boys*	*Girls*	*Total*
(1)	(2)	(3)	(4)	(5)	(6)	(7)	(8)	(9)	(10)	(11)
1.	Andhra Pradesh	87.42	88.03	87.72	67.10	62.49	64.86	79.80	78.58	79.20
2.	Arunachal Pradesh	115.35	103.47	109.56	67.99	59.06	63.60	98.68	87.64	93.29
3.	Assam	88.22	88.09	88.16	66.02	61.15	63.65	80.10	78.32	79.23

(*Contd.*)

(*Contd.*)

(1)	(2)	(3)	(4)	(5)	(6)	(7)	(8)	(9)	(10)	(11)
4.	Bihar	80.20	64.20	72.57	30.64	19.21	25.33	62.37	48.50	55.82
5.	Chattisgarh	123.69	122.86	123.29	78.51	62.21	70.52	106.99	99.97	103.58
6.	Goa	100.30	95.50	97.96	104.77	97.55	101.23	102.07	96.31	99.26
7.	Gujarat	117.67	108.62	113.41	81.88	57.40	70.40	104.19	89.38	97.23
8.	Haryana	73.53	77.31	75.25	68.24	62.40	65.51	71.53	71.49	71.51
9.	Himachal Pradesh	106.10	106.88	106.47	99.91	96.49	98.24	103.62	102.61	103.13
10.	Jammu & Kashmir	87.47	76.42	82.10	65.20	52.95	59.28	78.77	67.31	73.21
11.	Jharkhand	86.70	71.10	79.09	42.47	32.19	37.54	70.51	57.15	64.04
12.	Karnataka	110.53	107.23	108.91	78.95	73.32	76.20	97.95	93.76	95.89
13.	Kerala	97.25	96.59	96.92	95.69	91.49	93.64	96.61	94.51	95.58
14.	Madhya Pradesh	112.11	100.68	106.59	71.78	53.88	63.30	96.89	83.43	90.44
15.	Maharashtra	108.32	106.84	107.60	89.41	85.52	87.55	100.71	98.31	99.56
16.	Manipur	139.30	135.64	137.51	86.95	81.57	84.33	118.85	114.60	116.77
17.	Meghalaya	104.19	106.88	105.51	60.27	62.02	61.14	88.01	90.34	89.16
18.	Mizoram	122.54	117.71	120.17	77.25	76.70	76.98	105.10	101.86	103.51
19.	Nagaland	80.95	79.97	80.48	43.56	45.85	44.66	66.11	66.50	66.30
20.	Orissa	114.23	107.44	110.91	58.13	49.69	54.01	93.28	85.86	89.65
21.	Punjab	71.04	76.38	73.45	59.31	60.93	60.6	66.52	70.25	68.22
22.	Rajasthan	120.18	109.41	115.07	74.30	47.22	61.54	103.65	87.19	95.87
23.	Sikkim	116.54	116.48	116.51	52.02	61.63	56.75	90.63	94.77	92.68
24.	Tamil Nadu	117.47	115.49	116.51	102.28	98.44	100.41	111.57	108.88	110.26
25.	Tripura	125.73	119.68	122.76	75.34	70.23	72.84	105.01	99.41	102.27
26.	Uttar Pradesh	96.69	92.58	94.75	53.61	42.97	48.64	81.09	74.86	78.16
27.	Uttaranchal	106.10	107.66	106.85	81.08	79.59	80.36	96.57	96.88	96.72
28.	West Bengal	107.45	107.21	107.33	65.90	62.57	64.28	91.57	90.20	90.90
29.	A&N Islands	118.78	113.23	116.05	100.13	91.41	95.85	111.27	104.47	107.92
30.	Chandigarh	72.00	70.77	71.44	69.19	69.85	69.50	70.95	70.42	70.71
31.	Dadar & Nagar Haveli	133.92	117.88	126.06	95.75	66.08	81.64	120.14	99.86	110.30
32.	Daman & Diu	111.66	111.01	111.35	100.85	94.11	97.62	107.76	104.81	106.36
33.	Delhi	90.34	89.81	90.10	84.83	85.91	85.34	88.26	88.33	88.30
34.	Lakshadweep	111.65	100.93	106.37	104.04	89.77	97.09	108.51	96.38	102.56
35.	Pondicherry	121.94	118.72	120.37	121.89	117.37	119.68	121.92	118.18	120.09
	India	**100.75**	**95.67**	**98.31**	**66.87**	**57.69**	**62.49**	**88.02**	**81.51**	**84.91**

Source: *Selected Educational Statistics, 2003-04*, Ministry of Human Resource Development, Government of India.

Table 24.23: Total Number of Recognised Educational Institutions in India (2003-2004) (Provisional)

Sl. No.	*State/UTs*	*Primary/ Junior Basic School*	*Middle/ Senior Basic Schools*	*High Sch./ Hr. Sec./ Intermediate/ Jr. College*	*Colleges for General Education*	*Pro-fessional Education*	*Universities/Deemed Univ./Instt. of National Importance Research Instt.*
(1)	(2)	(3)	(4)	(5)	(6)	(7)	(8)
1.	Andhra Pradesh	63897	15215	3267	1330	238	28
2.	Arunachal Pradesh	1364	449	74	10	1	4
3.	Assam	30068	8143	731	317	3	7
4.	Bihar	40337	9922	685	743	7	23
5.	Chattisgarh	32556	9350	1439	213	2	9
6.	Goa	1009	79	80	24	4	1
7.	Gujarat	7233	30646	2427	422	32	28
8.	Haryana	11500	2171	1776	163	41	7
9.	Himachal Pradesh	11013	2076	820	69	2	7
10.	Jammu & Kashmir	10488	3976	380	73	4	5
11.	Jharkhand	16417	4324	122	146	5	7
12.	Karnataka	26163	25612	2237	930	120	20
13.	Kerala	6717	2975	1286	186	66	10
14.	Madhya Pradesh	66648	30592	4211	513	56	17
15.	Maharashtra	41258	26033	4212	1208	177	54
16.	Manipur	2552	832	112	58	1	2
17.	Meghalaya	5851	1559	80	48	0	1
18.	Mizoram	1504	908	71	26	0	1
19.	Nagaland	1495	480	52	36	0	1
20.	Orissa	42104	11510	744	567	19	9
21.	Punjab	13265	2493	1695	209	16	8
22.	Rajasthan	55757	23942	3159	456	39	15
23.	Sikkim	497	126	41	2	1	2
24.	Tamil Nadu	32242	6825	4136	441	96	28
25.	Tripura	2075	453	242	14	1	1
26.	Uttar Pradesh	119404	35427	7369	733	69	40
27.	Uttaranchal	14304	3557	1071	47	2	7
28.	West Bengal	49865	1984	2868	354	43	28
29.	A&N Islands	209	56	49	2	0	0
30.	Chandigarh	24	9	52	12	2	2
31.	Dadar & Nagar Haveli	127	91	9	0	0	0
32.	Daman & Diu	53	24	6	1	0	0
33.	Delhi	2126	681	1212	63	16	16
34.	Lakshadweep	20	4	4	0	0	0
35.	Pondicherry	329	125	77	11	5	1
	India	**710471**	**262649**	**46796**	**9427**	**1068**	**389**

Note: Professional Education includes Engineering, Technology and Architecture, Medical and Teacher Training Colleges.

Source: *Selected Educational Statistics, 2003-04*, Ministry of Human Resource Development, Government of India.

Table 24.24: Percentage of Expenditure on Education to GDP (1951 to 2004)

Year	Percentage of Expenditure on Education to GDP
1951	0.64
1961	1.58
1971	2.26
1981	3.16
1991	4.29
2001	3.99
2004	3.49

Table 24.25: Expenditure on Education in India (1951-52 to 2001-2002) (In Crore)

Years	Total Exp. on Education & Trg. (Rev.)	Total Exp. on All Sectors (Rev.)	GDP at Current Prices (at Factor Cost) Base Year 1993-94	% of Education Exp. to All Sectors Exp.	% of Edu. Exp. to GDP
1951-51	64.46	814.13	10080	7.92	0.64
1952-53	72.26	857.67	9941	8.43	0.73
1953-54	80.06	908.20	10824	8.82	0.74
1954-55	95.82	973.74	10168	9.84	0.94
1955-56	118.39	1111.26	10332	10.65	1.15
1956-57	132.88	1158.01	12334	11.47	1.08
1957-58	150.26	1614.62	12610	10.61	1.19
1958-59	173.78	1594.36	14106	10.90	1.23
1959-60	207.59	1770.06	14816	11.73	1.40
1960-61	239.56	1997.93	16220	11.99	1.48
1961-62	260.30	2225.40	17116	11.70	1.52
1962-63	278.76	2942.67	18302	9.47	1.52
1963-64	313.93	3488.97	20916	9.00	1.50
1964-65	369.29	3844.91	24436	9.60	1.51
1965-66	432.61	4404.82	25586	9.82	1.69
1966-67	487.83	5100.24	29123	9.56	1.68
1967-68	593.14	5619.77	34225	10.55	1.73
1968-69	649.13	6922.07	36092	9.38	1.80
1969-70	960.23	7908.07	39691	9.61	1.92
1970-71	892.36	8787.12	42222	10.16	2.11
1971-72	1011.07	10610.89	44923	9.53	2.25
1972-73	1150.43	11863.56	49415	9.70	2.33
1973-74	1300.72	12884.48	60560	10.10	2.15
1974-75	1570.67	14625.03	71283	10.74	2.20
1975-76	1849.47	17958.99	75709	10.30	2.44
1976-77	2039.09	20482.83	81381	9.96	2.51
1977-78	2630.60	22666.31	92881	11.61	2.83
1978-79	2994.69	26134.84	99823	11.46	3.00
1979-80	3347.57	30915.39	108927	10.83	3.07

(Contd.)

(*Contd.*)

Years	*Total Exp. on Education & Trg. (Rev.)*	*Total Exp. on All Sectors (Rev.)*	*GDP at Current Prices (at Factor Cost) Base Year 1993-94*	*% of Education Exp. to All Sectors Exp.*	*% of Edu. Exp. to GDP*
1980-81	3884.20	36398.39	130178	10.67	2.98
1981-82	4435.29	33667.31	152056	13.17	2.92
1982-83	5509.17	43996.18	169525	12.52	3.25
1983-84	6229.53	61889.25	198630	10.07	3.14
1984-85	7455.88	69025.45	222705	10.80	3.35
1985-86	8713.02	67091.41	249547	12.99	3.49
1986-87	9497.13	80454.66	278258	11.78	3.41
1987-88	11798.35	92518.38	315993	12.75	3.73
1988-89	14069.82	107543.75	378491	13.08	3.72
1989-90	17192.50	126045.97	438020	13.64	3.93
1990-91	19615.85	146711.53	510954	13.37	3.84
1991-92	22393.69	170370.38	589086	13.14	3.80
1992-93	25030.30	190327.45	673221	13.15	3.72
1993-94	28279.22	218535.15	781345	12.94	3.62
1994-95	32606.22	251691.92	917058	12.95	3.56
1995-96	38178.09	286194.55	1073271	13.34	3.56
1996-97	43896.48	329389.92	1243546	13.33	3.53
1997-98	48552.14	380728.45	1390148	12.75	3.49
1998-99	61578.91	439768.11	1598127	14.00	3.85
1999-2000	74816.09	512519.33	1761932	14.60	4.25
2000-2001	82486.43	572160.14	191772P	14.42	4.30
2001-2002	84179.46 (R.E.)	639048.06	2094013Q	13.17	4.02

P – Provisional estimates, Q – Quick estimates, RE – Revised estimates

Source: 1. *National Accounts Statistics* published by C.S.O.

2. Expenditure on Education. Figure is taken from the publication titled '*Analysis of Budgeted Expenditure on Education*' published by D/o Secondary and Higher Education.

3. *Selected Educational Statistics* (2002-2003).

Adult Education was 0.05% during 1990-91 showing a gradual decrease of 0.01% in 2000-2001. It improved slightly to 0.02% during 2001-2002. The percentage expenditure on University and Higher Education to GDP, which was 0.77% in 1990-91 shows a gradual decrease to 0.62% during 1997-98 and rise to 0.88% in 2000-2001.

The share of expenditure on Elementary Education to total expenditure on all sectors was 6.19% during 1990-91 and which shows irregular rise and fall and finally settled at 6.61% during 2001-2002. The share of Secondary and Higher Secondary Education to total expenditure on all sectors was highest in 1999-2000 i.e. 4.97% and the lowest (4.09%) during 2001-2002. The share of adult expenditure in total expenditure on all sectors was the highest in 1990-91 (0.19%) and shows a gradual decreasing trend to 0.05% in 2001-02. The percentage share of higher education to total expenditure remained between 2.32% to 2.96% in the last decade.

Table 24.26: Expenditure by Level on Education in India

(in Crore)

Total Expenditure on Education & trg. (Rev.) by Education and other Departments

Year	Elementary			Secondary/Higher secondary			Adult Education			University & Higher Education*			Total		
	Expenditure	% age to GDP	% age to Total expt. on all sector	Expenditure	% age to GDP	% age to Total expt. on all sector	Expenditure	% age to GDP	% age to Total expt. on all sector	Expenditure	% age to GDP	% age to Total expt. on all sector	Expenditure	% age to GDP	% age to Total expt. on all sector
1990-1991	9076.28	1.78	6.19	6310.33	1.24	4.30	273.15	0.05	0.19	3956.09	0.77	2.70	19615.85	3.84	13.37
1991-1992	10367.8	1.76	6.09	7400.56	1.26	4.34	228.52	0.04	0.13	4396.78	0.75	2.58	22393.69	3.80	13.14
1992-1993	11321.5	1.68	5.95	8574.97	1.27	4.51	210.97	0.03	0.11	4922.90	0.73	2.59	25030.30	3.72	13.15
1993-1994	13071.14	1.67	2.54	9371.34	1.20	4.29	280.01	0.04	0.13	5557.20	0.71	2.54	28279.69	3.62	12.94
1994-1995	15133.1	1.65	6.01	10835.33	1.18	4.30	338.31	0.04	0.13	6299.53	0.69	2.50	32606.69	3.62	12.94
1995-1996	18433.9	1.72	6.44	12530.38	1.17	4.38	259.71	0.02	0.09	6954.07	0.65	2.43	38178.09	3.56	13.33
1996-1997	21543.6	1.73	6.54	14164.00	1.14	4.30	205.74	0.02	0.06	7983.11	0.64	2.42	43894.48	3.53	13.33
1997-1998	24083.2	1.73	6.49	15663.5	1.13	4.22	209.80	0.02	0.06	8595.67	0.62	2.32	48552.14	3.49	13.09
1998-1999	30191.1	1.89	6.87	20100.97	1.26	4.57	189.45	0.01	0.04	11097.42	0.69	2.52	61578.91	3.85	14.00
1999-2000	34068.8	1.93	6.65	25447.89	1.44	4.97	186.53	0.01	0.04	15112.89	0.86	2.95	74816.09	4.25	14.60
2000-2001	39274.60	2.05	6.86	26057.50	1.36	4.55	226.12	0.01	0.04	16928.21	0.88	2.96	82486.43	4.30	14.42
2001-2002 (RE)	42209.81	2.02	6.61	26155.21	1.25	4.09	337.87	0.02	0.05	15476.57	0.74	2.42	84179.46	4.02	13 17

* Including expenditure on Physical education. Technical education, Language development etc.

Note: Expenditures on education by other Departments has been distributed by level on the basis of expenditure (%) by education departments.

Source: Selected Educational Statistics 2001-2002.

Table 24.27: Plan Expenditure/Outlays on Education During Plans

Sector	*First Plan Expdt. 1951-56*	*Second Plan Expdt. 1956-61*	*Third Plan Expdt. 1961-66*	*Plan Holiday Expdt. 1966-69*	*Fourth Plan Expdt. 1969-74*	*Fifth Plan Expdt. 1974-79*	*Sixth Plan Expdt. 1980-85*	*Seventh Plan Expdt. 1985-90*	*1990-92 Expdt.*	*Eighth Plan Outlay 1992-97*	*Ninth Plan Outlay (1997-2002) (Central Sector)*	*Ninth Plan Expdt. (1997-2002) (Central Sector)*	*Tenth Plan Outlay (2002-2007) (Central Sector)*
(1)	(2)	(3)	(4)	(5)	(6)	(7)	(8)	(9)	(10)	(11)	(12)	(13)	(14)
Elementary Education	58 (870)	35 (950)	34 (2010)	24 (750)	50 (3743)	52 (5913)	32 (8414)	37 (28494)	37 (17290)	48 (103940)	66 (163696)	65.7 (145233)	65.6 (287500)
Secondary Education	5 (83)	19 (510)	18 (1030)	16 (530)	@	@	20 (5344)	24 (18315)	22 (10530)	24 (52311)	10 (26035)	10.5 (23227)	9.9 (43250)
Adult Education					2 (126)	2 (248)	6 (1533)	6 (4690)	9 (4160)	5 (11421)	3 (6304)	2.4 (5204)	2.9 (12500)
Higher Education	8 (117)	18 (480)	15 (870)	24 (770)	25 (1883)	28 (3188)	21 (5604)	16 (12011)	12 (5880)	10 (20944)	10 (25000)	10.3 (22709)	9.5 (41765)
Others	15 (227)	10 (300)	12 (730)	11 (370)	13 (936)	9 (1071)	11 (2729)	3 (1980)	2 (1180)	3 (7398)	2 (4314)	1.6 (3492)	1.4 (6235)
Technical Education	15 (215)	18 (490)	21 (1250)	25 (810)	10 (786)	9 (1015)	10 (2563)	14 (10833)	17 (8230)	10 (21987)	9 (23735)	9.5 (21095)	10.7 (47000)
Total	100 (1512)	100 (2730)	100 (5890)	100 (3230)	100 (7474)	100 (11435)	100 (26187)	100 (76329)	100 (47270)	100 (218001)	100 (249084)	100 (220960)	100 (438250)

Source: *India 2005*. Publication Division, Ministry of Information and Broadcasting, Government of India, 2006.

Note: 1. Figures in parenthesis in millions of rupees.

2. Figures in col. 2 to col. 11 includes the share of States/UTs

@ Included under Elementary Education

GRAPHS AND FIGURES

Fig. 1: Growth of Schools in India Since 1950

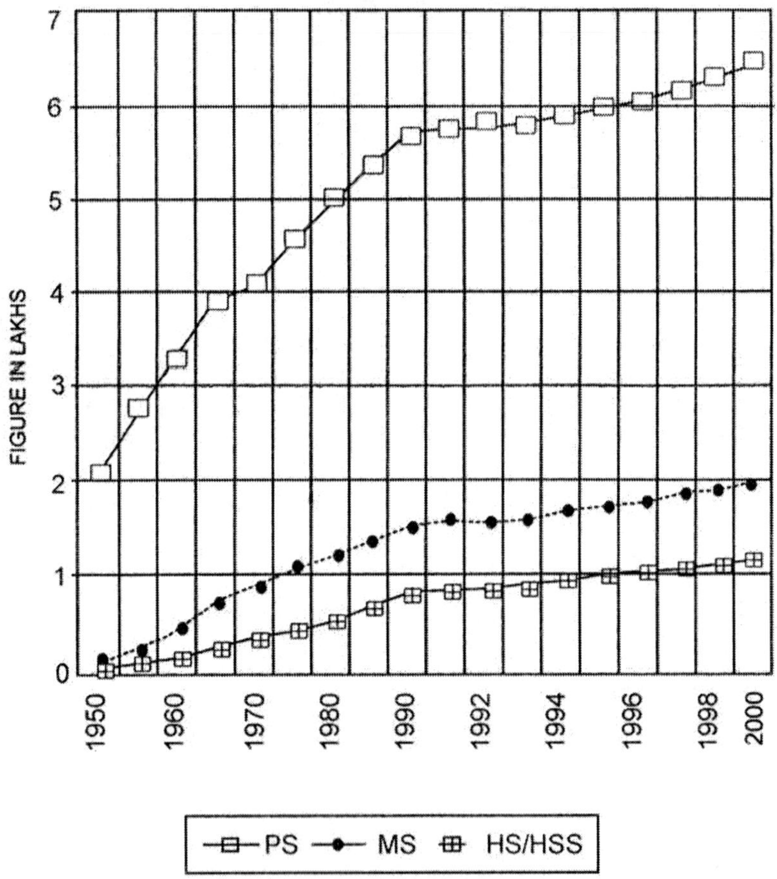

PS	:	Primary School
HS	:	Middle School
HS/HSS	:	High School/Higher Secondary School

Fig. 2: Growth of School Enrolment in India 1950-2003

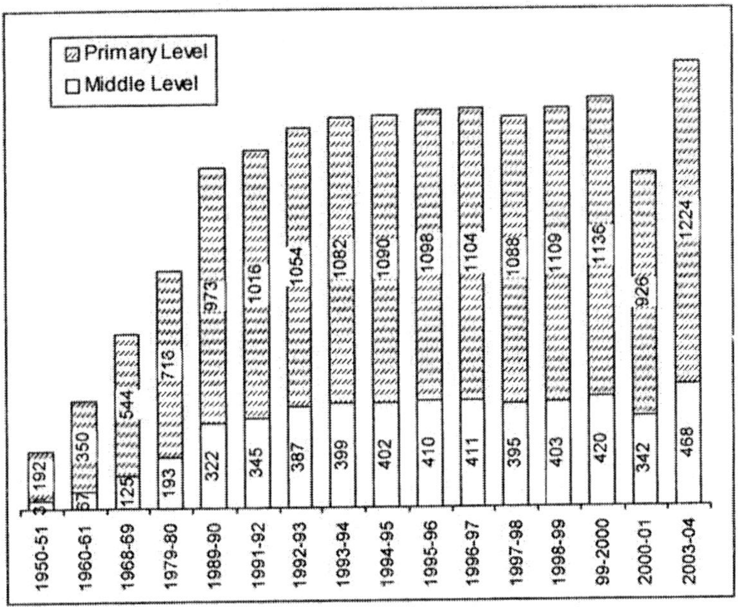

Fig. 3: Gross Enrolment Ratio at Elementary Stage 1950-2000

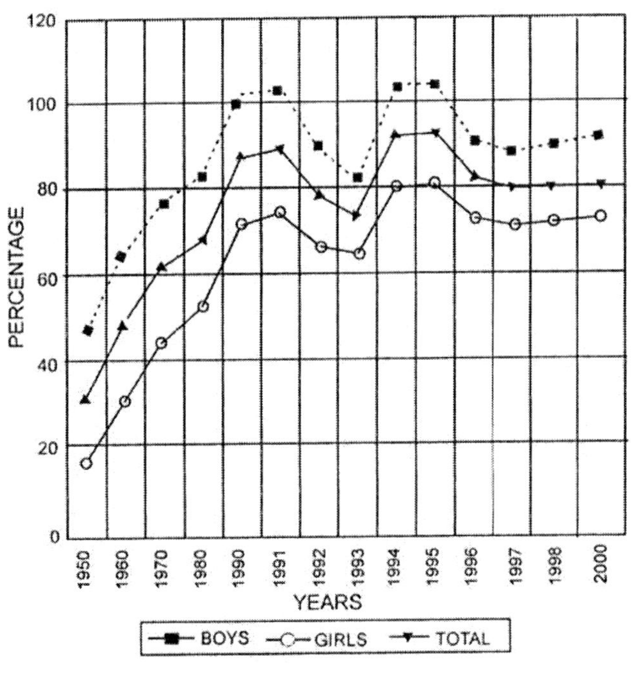

Fig. 4: Growth of School Teachers 1950-2000

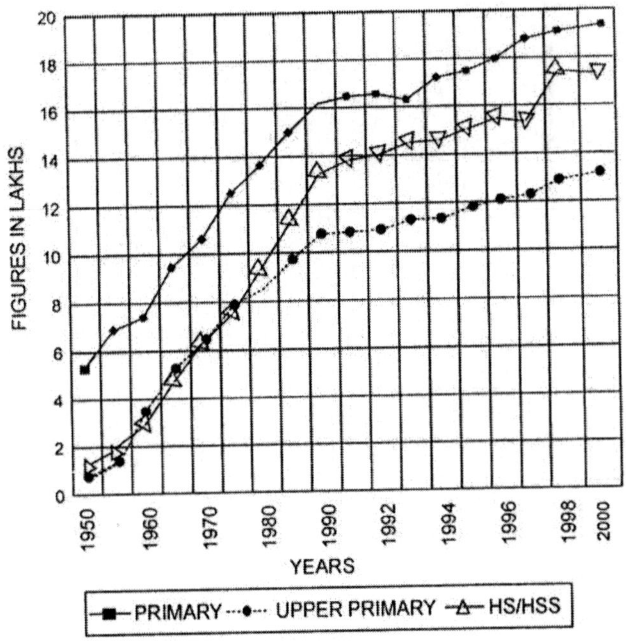

Fig. 5: Drop-out Rates at Primary and Upper Primary Stages (1991-2000)

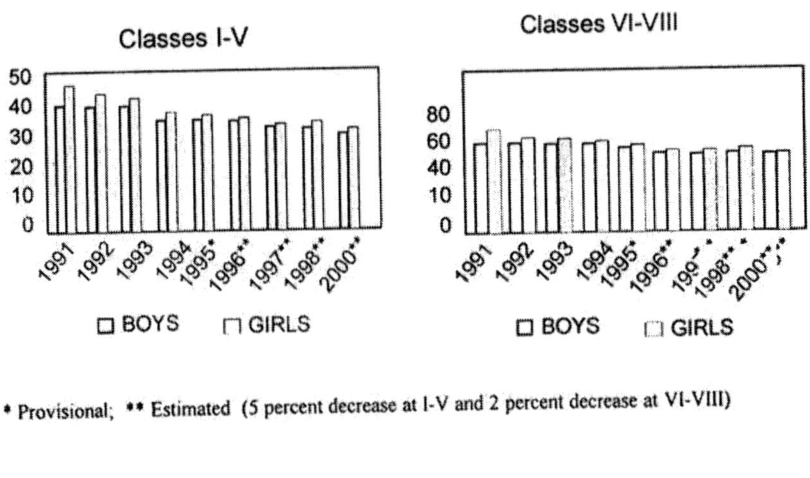

* Provisional; ** Estimated (5 percent decrease at I-V and 2 percent decrease at VI-VIII)

Fig. 6: Pupil-Teacher Ratio in Schools by Type (1990-2000)

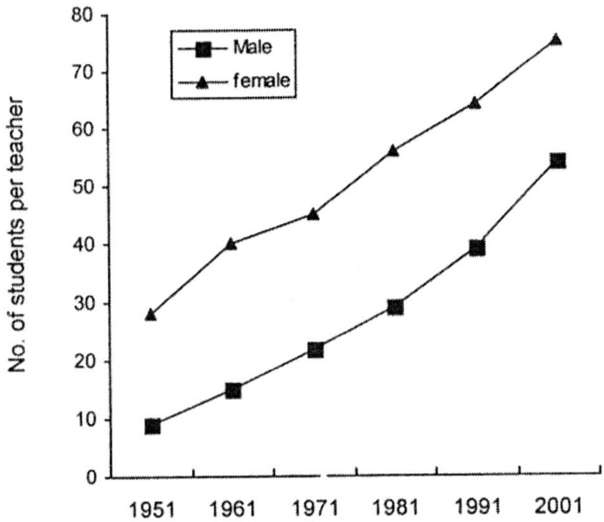

Fig. 7: Literacy Rate of India (1951-2001)

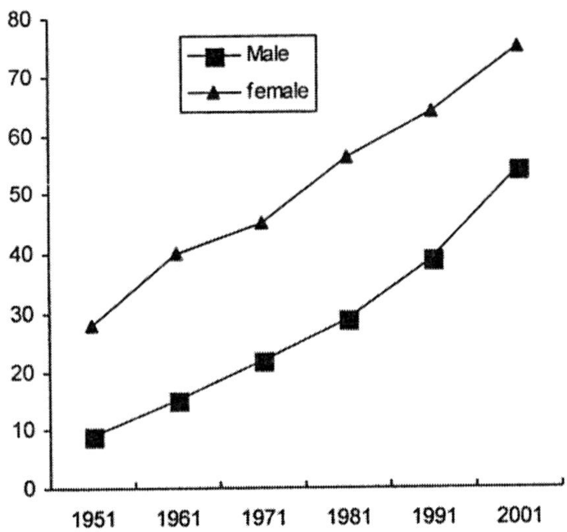

Fig. 8: Rural-Urban Literacy Rates (1951 to 2001)

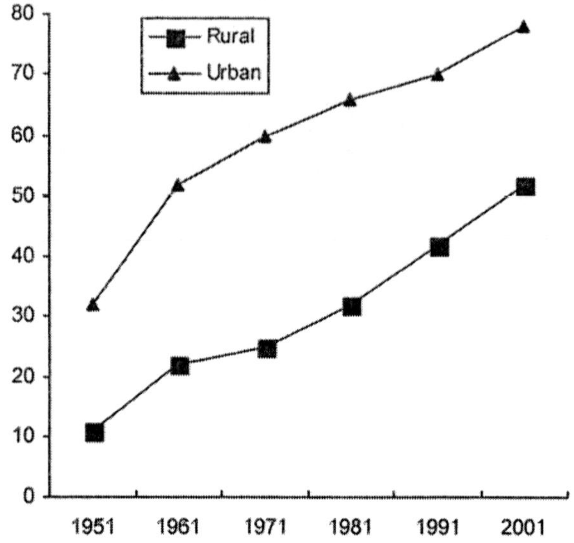

Fig. 9: Male-Female Literacy Rates (1951-2001)

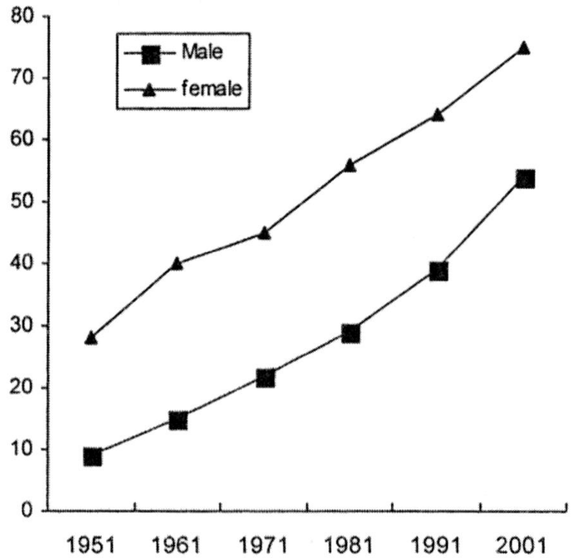

Fig. 10: Literacy of Indian States and Union Territories (2001)

Growth of Schools in India

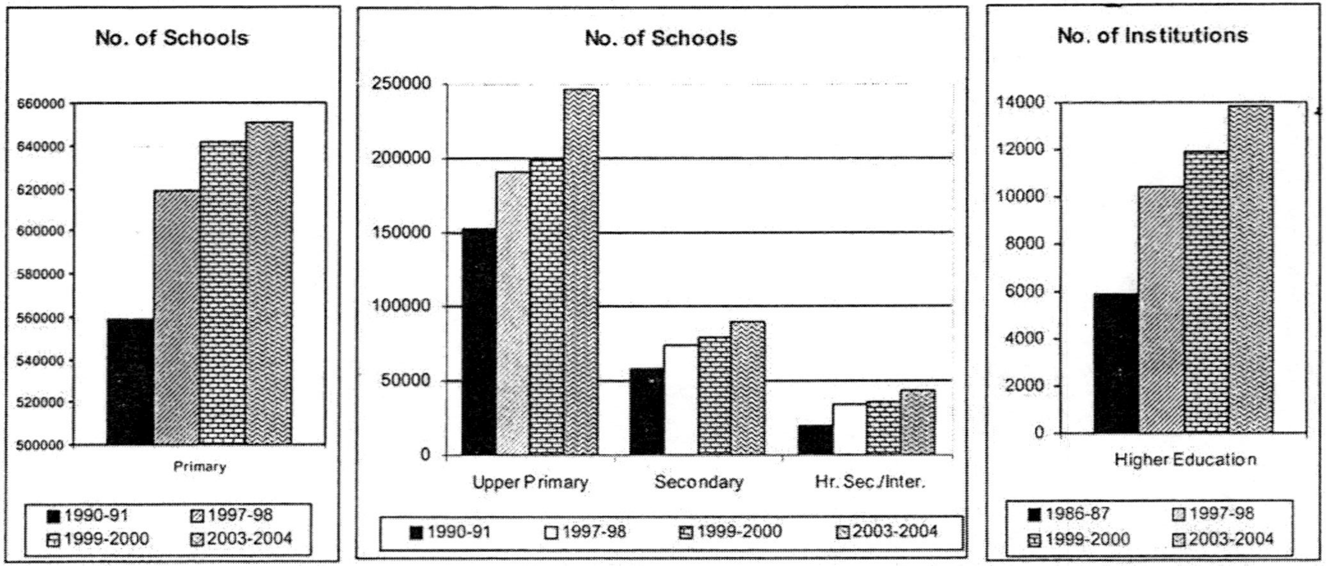

Fig. 11: Growth of Schools in India (1990-2004)

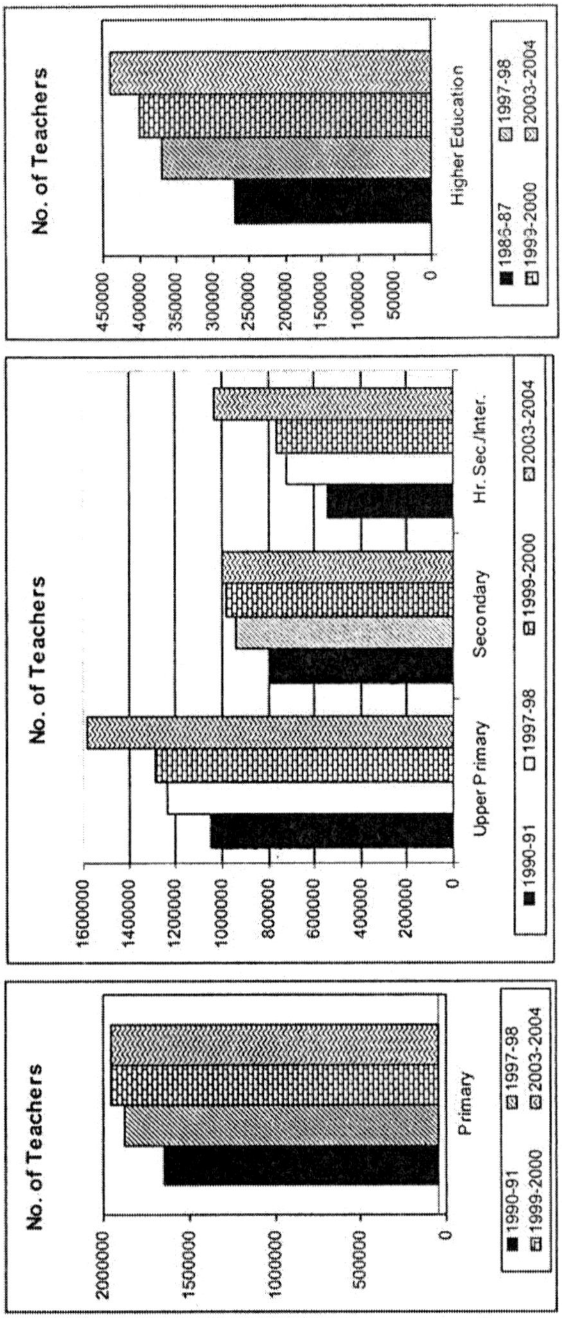

Fig. 12: Growth of School Tachers in India (1990-2004)

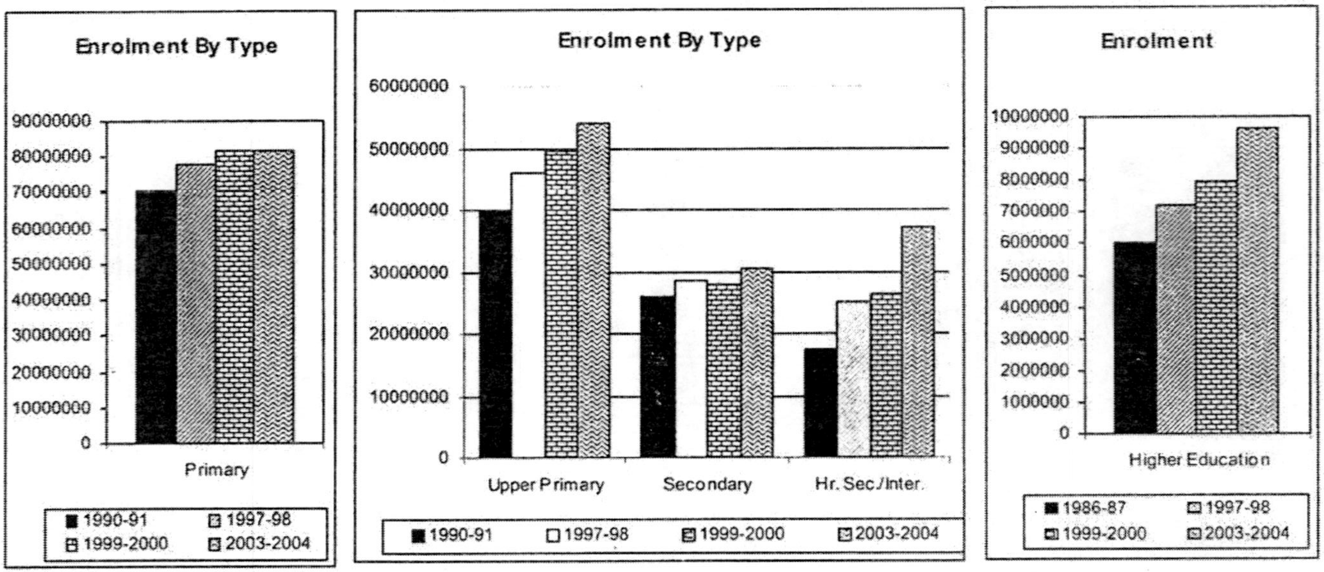

Fig. 13: Growth of Enrolment by Type (1990-2004)

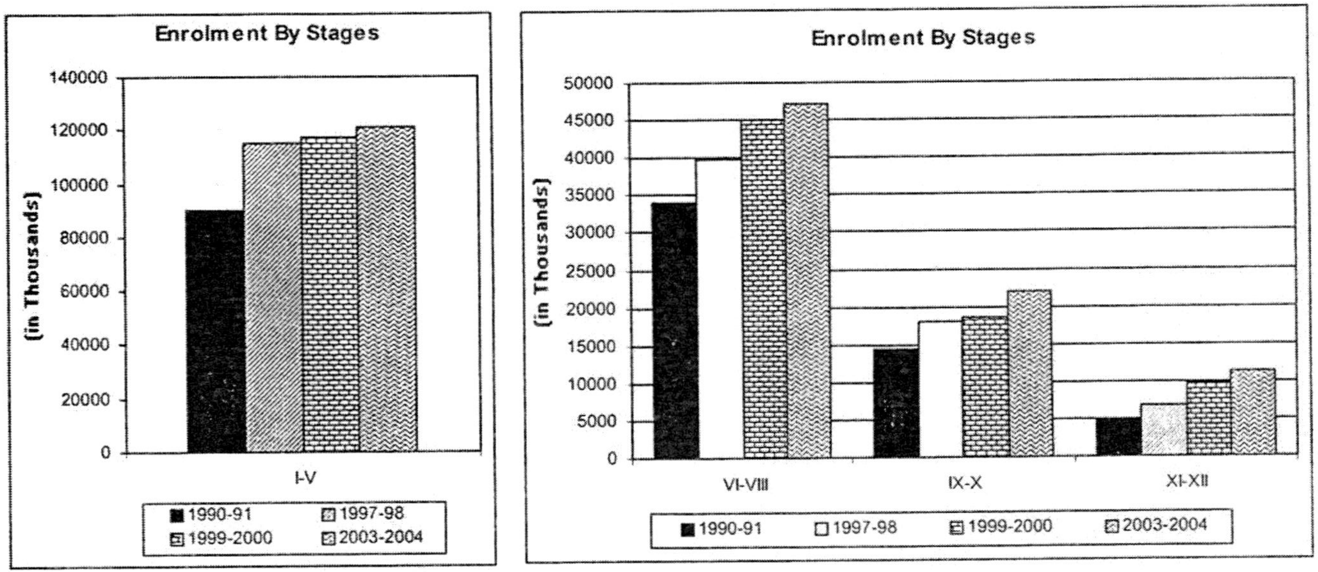

Fig. 14: Growth of Enrolment by Stages (1990-2004)

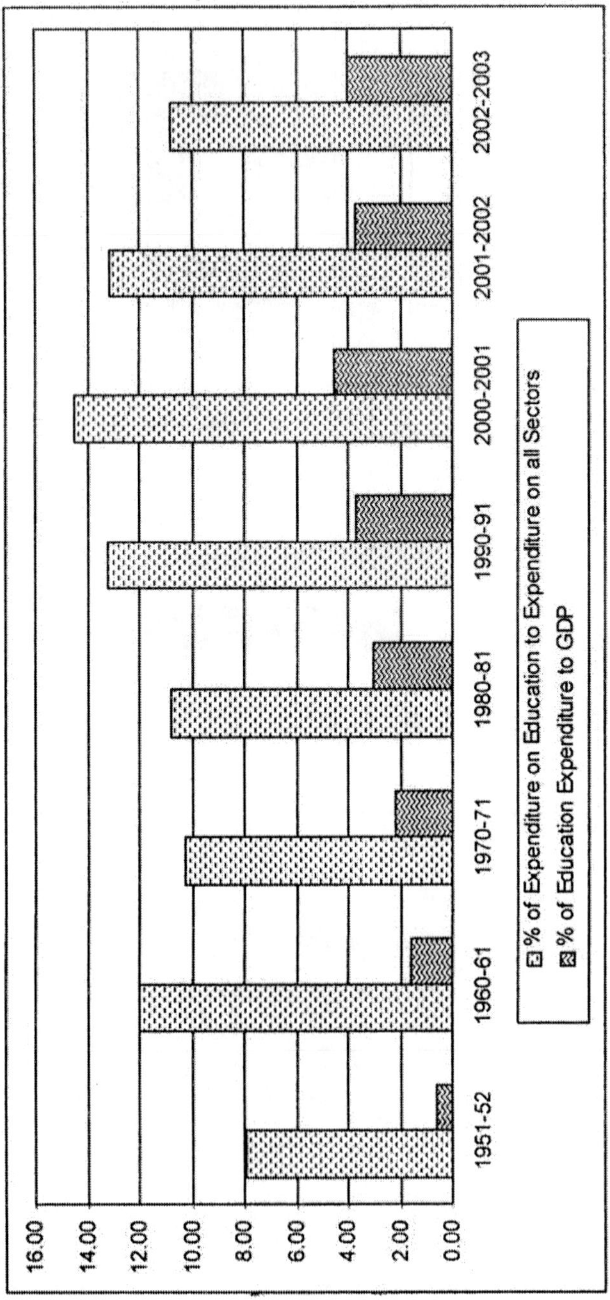

Fig. 15: Percentage of Education Expenditure to Total Expenditure and GDP for Year 1951-52 to 2002-2003

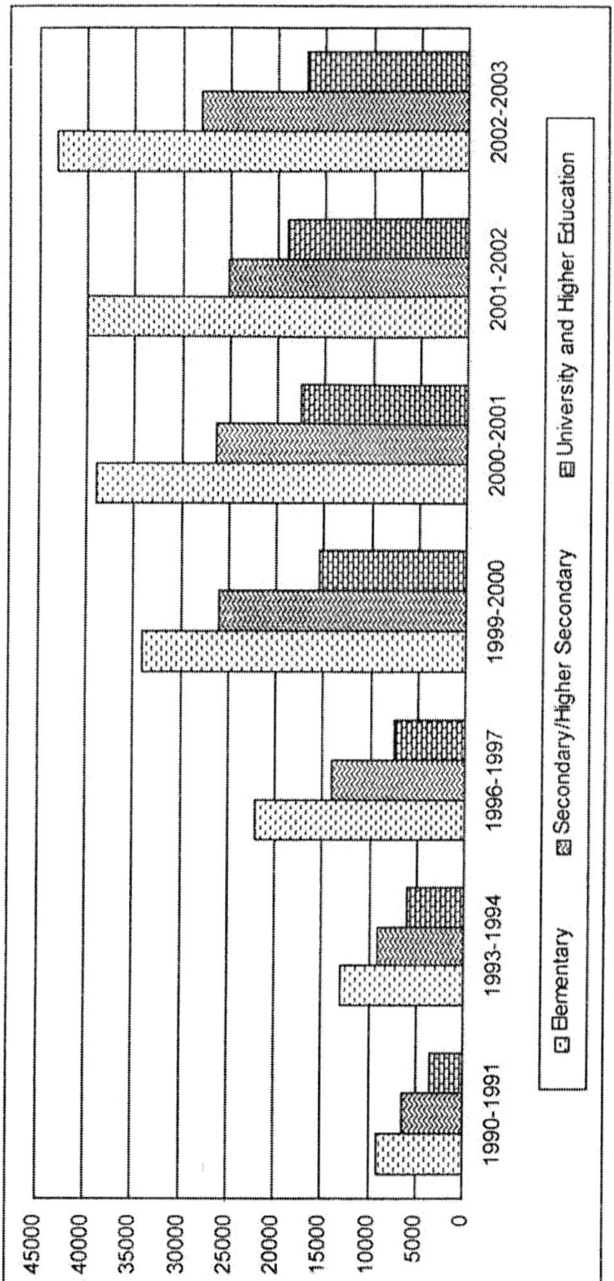

Fig. 16: Government Expenditure by Level of Education in India (1990-2003)

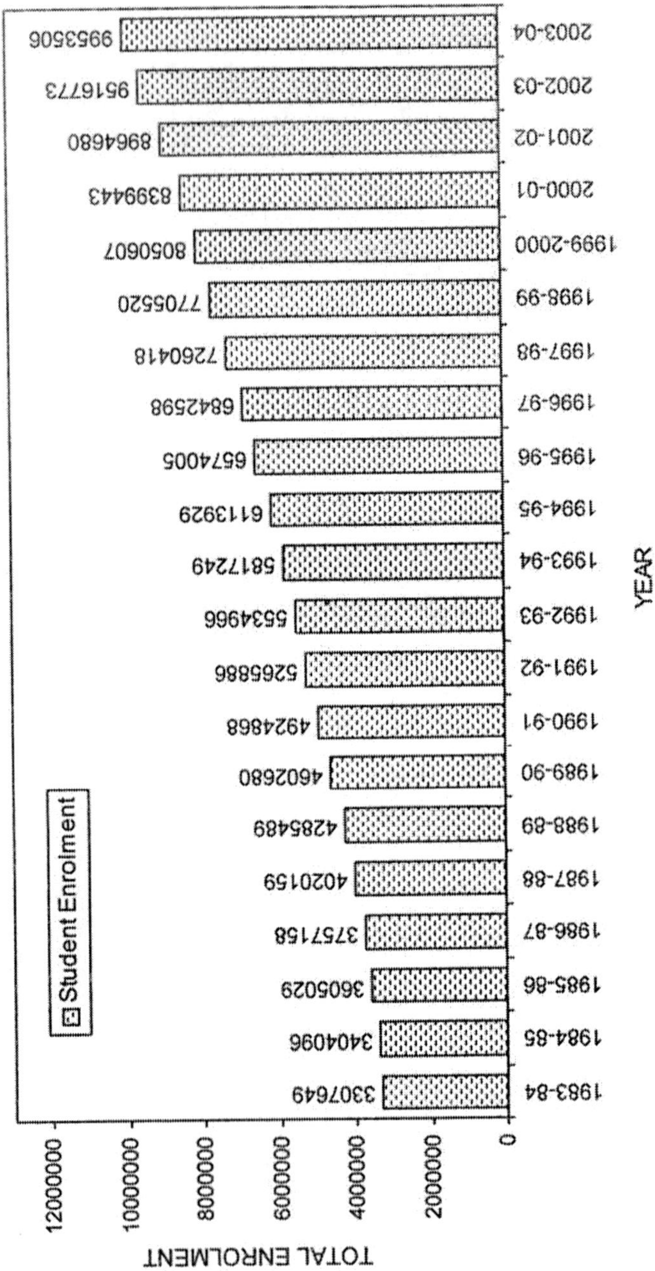

Fig. 17: All India Growth of Students Enrolment: 1983-84 to 2003-2004

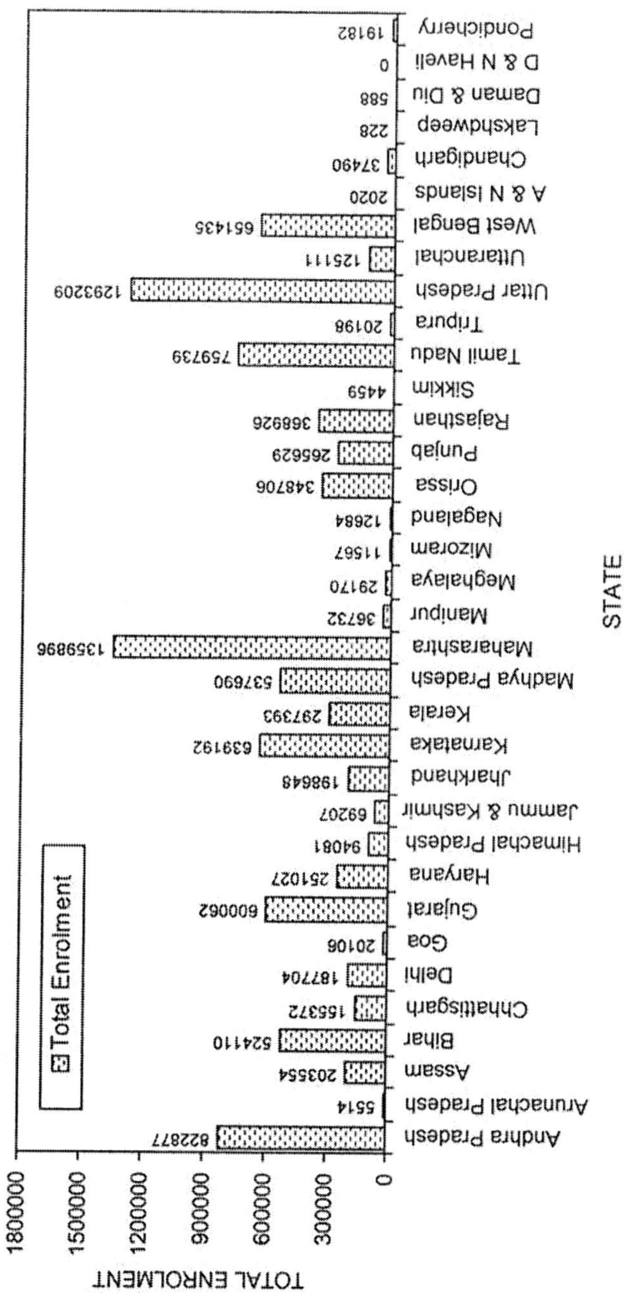

Fig. 18: State-wise Students Enrolment in Universities and Colleges 2003-2004

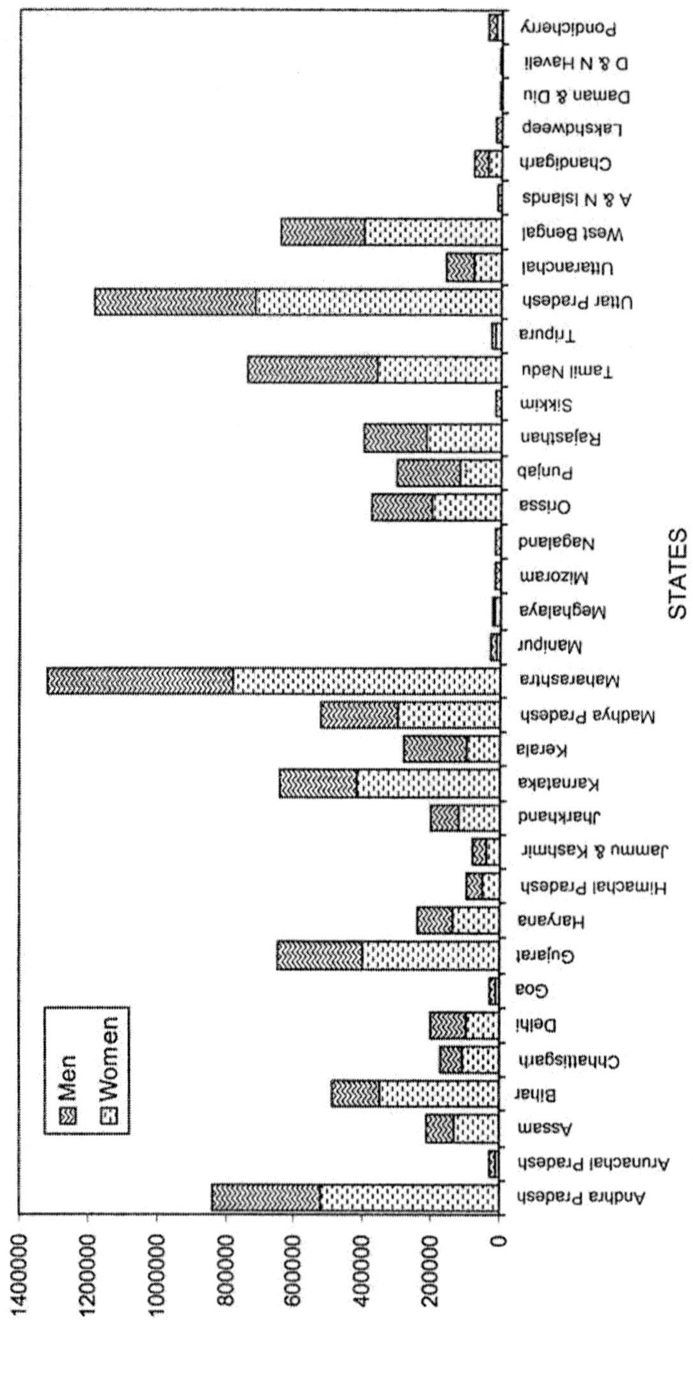

Fig. 19: State-wise Students Enrolment Gender-wise in Universities and Colleges 2003-2004

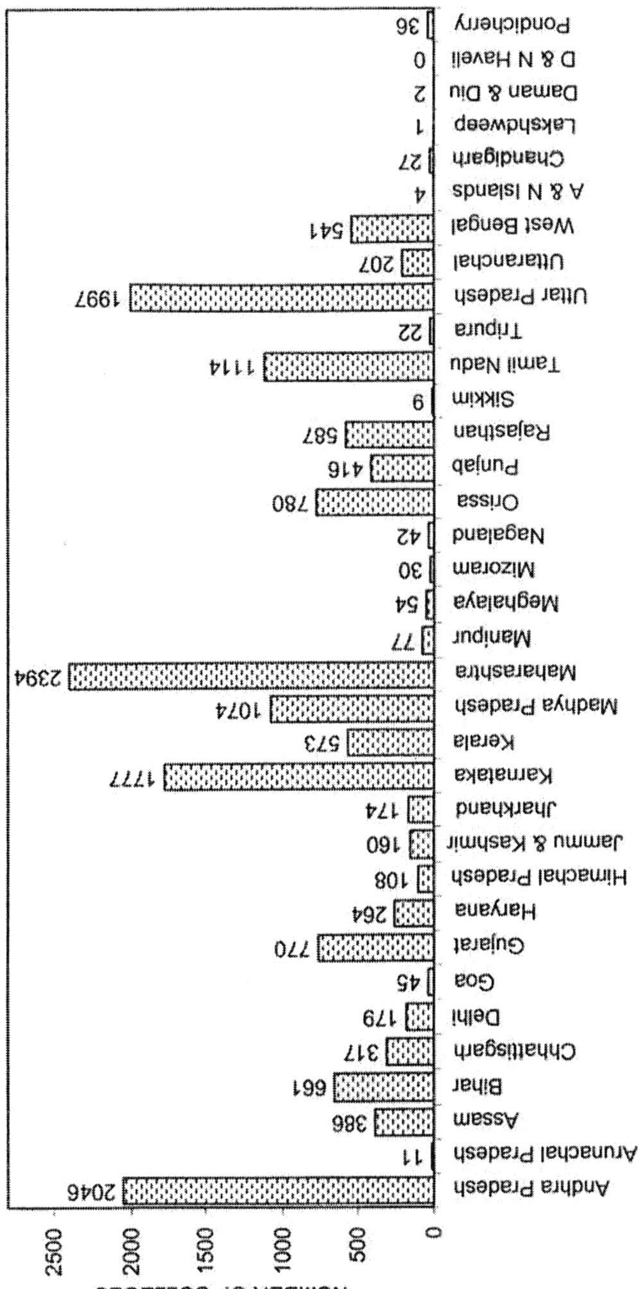

Fig. 20: State-wise Number of Colleges during the Year 2003-2004

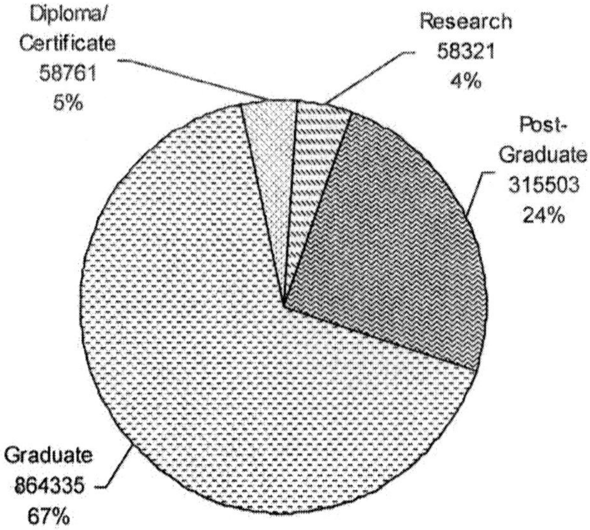

Fig. 21: Level-wise Students Enrolment in University-Teaching Department and University Colleges 2003-2004

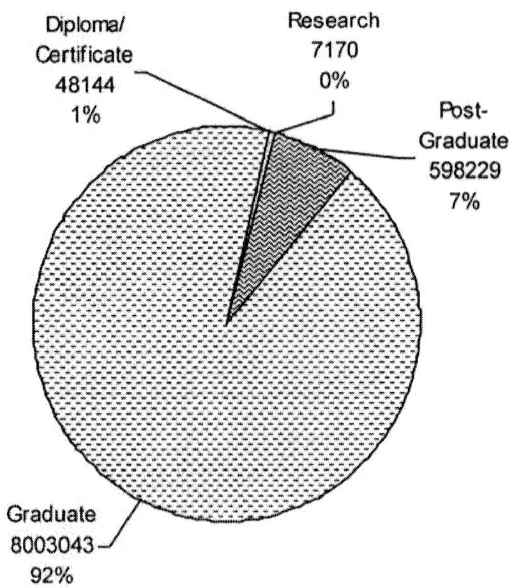

Fig. 22: Level-wise Students Enrolment in Affiliated Colleges 2003-2004